Let Horses Be Horses

Let Horses Be Horses

The Horse Owner's Guide to Ethical Training and Management

LESLEY SKIPPER

J.A. ALLEN • LONDON

First published in Great Britain 2005

ISBN 0 85131 902 5

J. A. Allen
Clerkenwell House
Clerkenwell Green
London EC1R 0HT

J. A. Allen is an imprint of Robert Hale Limited

A catalogue record for this book is available from the British Library

Edited by Martin Diggle
Design and typesetting by Paul Saunders
Photographs by the author, except for those reproduced with permission
as detailed in the Acknowledgements
Diagrams by Rodney Paull
Charts on pages 108 and 139 by Dick Vine

Colour separation by Tenon & Polert Colour Scanning Limited, Hong Kong
Printed by New Era Printing Co. Limited, Hong Kong

For Racheal

With thanks for all your help and support

Contents

Acknowledgements

In writing a book of this nature, it has been necessary to draw on the knowledge of a number of experts, who have all been most generous with their advice. I must stress that any anomalies in the interpretation of data are mine, not theirs. In the field of equine behaviour and ethology I give particular thanks to the following: Andy Beck of the White Horse Equine Ethology Project, New Zealand; Dr Francis Burton of Glasgow University; Dr Sharon Cregier; Telané Greyling in South Africa and Dr Hayley Randle, Senior Lecturer in Animal Behaviour, University of Plymouth.

For thought-provoking discussion of various aspects of training and the principles of learning, I thank Catherine Brocksopp, Emma Kurrels, Sylvia Loch, Kelly Marks, Charles Wilson and fellow Classical Riding Club members Jord-Ann Ramoudt and Anne Wilson.

Mention must also be made of those who kindly provided me with, or assisted me to obtain, illustrations. These include Professor W.R. 'Twink' Allen, Elizabeth Furth, Telané Greyling, Dr Colin P. Groves, Elaine Herbert, Racheal Jones, Sylvia Loch, Kelly Marks and Vicki Rowe.

Thanks also to Andy Beck, Dr Sharon Cregier and Emma Kurrels for permission to quote from Internet-published articles and personal e-mails.

Thanks for permission to reproduce photographs must go to the following: Professor W.R. Allen, University of Cambridge, Department of Clinical Veterinary Medicine Equine Fertility Unit (p.13), George Chadfield (for permission to use his late wife's photograph on p.39), Sr Arsenio Raposo Cordeiro (p.119), Eventer Equestrian Photographer (p.215), Elizabeth Furth (p.165), Telané Greyling (pp.9, 10, 40 and 54), Colin P. Groves (p.8), Racheal Jones (p.152), Harry McMillan, Peak Photography (p.166) and Kelly Marks (p.129).

Author's Note

The text assumes at least a moderate level of competence, knowledge and experience among its readers: it is not intended for complete novices. Every care has been taken to alert readers to safety concerns but, ultimately, the responsibility for safety lies with the rider and/or handler. The author and publishers cannot accept any responsibility for any injury or damages which may arise as a result of following procedures mentioned in this book.

I must apologize to female horses for using the pronoun 'he' when referring to equines in general. This is not intended to slight or devalue mares; I used 'he' because the unisex pronoun 'they', acceptable when referring to humans, somehow did not seem quite right when talking about horses. To me, horses are 'he' or 'she', not an 'it' (the latter term treats the horse as if he were an object, instead of an individual), but it would have been too cumbersome to keep saying 'he or she' or 'him or her'. So I hope owners of mares will forgive me!

Please note that, throughout the book, footnotes are indicated by Arabic numerals (e.g. 'Company of Horses'[1] refers to a footnote at the bottom of the page), while endnotes, to be found on the last page of each chapter, are indicated with lower case Roman numerals (e.g. 'contradicted with actions'[iii] refers to a note at the end of the chapter.

The majority of the photographs which appear in the book are of our own horses. They are:

Count Kruger	Arabian x Belgian Warmblood gelding.
Guisburn Nivalis	Pure-bred Arabian stallion, son of Roxzella.
Imzadi	Arabian x (Cleveland Bay x Thoroughbred) mare, daughter of Nivalis and Kiri.
Kiri	Cleveland Bay x Thoroughbred mare, mother of Toska.
Mikenah (Tiff)	Pure-bred Arabian mare.
Roxzella	Pure-bred Arabian mare, mother of Nivalis.
Tariel	Pure-bred Arabian colt, son of Nivalis and Mikenah.
Toska	Belgian Warmblood x (Cleveland Bay x TB) gelding, son of Kiri.
Zareeba	Pure-bred Arabian gelding, half-brother to Kruger.

Introduction

> It is the customary fate of new truths to begin as heresies and to end as superstitions.
>
> THOMAS HENRY HUXLEY, *The Coming of Age of the Origin of Species*

The last two decades of the twentieth century, and the first few years of the twenty-first century, have seen something of a revolution in attitudes towards horses kept for pleasure. More and more people are questioning established methods of keeping horses and looking at ways in which we can make domestic life more 'natural' for them. The emphasis has increasingly been on attempting to deal with horses on their terms instead of solely on ours, and on the elimination of coercive methods of training. Great importance is attached to understanding what matters to horses in their natural state, and trying to ensure that we meet the needs arising from their concerns and priorities.

At the same time there has been an immense growth of interest in what is often called 'natural horsemanship': training methods based on the idea that, in order to train horses without the use of force, we must learn to understand their social organization, their body language and how they communicate with each other. The implication is that not only will this help us to predict how horses will behave; it will also help us to influence their behaviour and their responses.

One might think that this can only be a good thing, not only for horses but for the people who handle, train and ride them. However, in our desire to do what is best for our horses, are we too readily abandoning one type of dogma for another, based on assumptions which may not always be correct? And how does this affect our relationships with our horses?

Part of the problem is that many of the training methods mentioned above are based on perceptions of natural equine behaviour – especially social organization

– that are inadequate and in many respects inaccurate. They are usually derived from popular misconceptions about social behaviour in mammals and, while stressing the importance of understanding equine social structure, they have usually over-emphasized the role of aggression in that social structure. Too often the truly important aspects, such as family ties and bonds of friendship and affection, are given insufficient attention. Some trainers focus almost exclusively on stallion behaviour, often observed in highly artificial situations, largely ignoring the fact that mares and (to some extent) geldings have different priorities from stallions. There is a heavy reliance on 'dominance', so-called 'pecking orders', and similar ideas, in particular the inaccurate and outdated concept of the 'alpha animal'. There is also a widespread failure to understand that equine behaviour, especially with regard to social organization, is far more flexible than is generally realized.

In other words, many current ideas about the natural lives of horses are muddled or quite simply wrong, yet they have been repeated so often that they are now widely accepted as fact. This leads to confusion regarding what is important to horses.

The result of all this is that, despite the apparent success of so-called 'natural horsemanship' and related methods of training, an increasing number of people are starting to criticize such methods. Much of this criticism has come from trained behavioural scientists, many of whom feel that some proponents of 'natural' training methods fail to understand the fundamental principles underlying learning processes. The result is often a contradiction between a trainer's stated philosophy and their actual training methods, and confusion in the minds of their students regarding the principles they are being asked to apply. As Emma Kurrels of the Company of Horses[1] points out:

> Lack of a balanced education creates and compounds problems for equines. By constantly speaking on their behalf the tendency is to stop listening to them. In such cases, words such as 'partnership' and 'respect' rapidly lose all meaning. However good they make everyone feel, words such as 'choice' and 'bonding' are pointless when contradicted with actions.[i]

I should stress that it is not my intention to denigrate or devalue the work of people using the natural behaviour of horses as a basis for their training. On the contrary, I recognize that much excellent work has been done, by some exceptional trainers, to change attitudes regarding training and managing horses. However, I also recognize that changing people's attitudes is not enough; if we truly wish to understand our horses and establish mutual trust and respect, we

1 See 'Useful Organizations'.

must base our understanding on facts and reasoned arguments, not simply on theories which, in some cases, may reflect nothing more than an individual trainer's world-view.

I have often been critical of scientists in the behavioural sciences, because too many of them have been arrogant and narrow-minded, especially with regard to animal cognition and sentience, and also because some of them seek to explain every aspect of animal behaviour in terms of evolutionary adaptation, often presenting as fact what is actually nothing more than speculation based on unexamined assumptions. However, when it comes to observation of animal behaviour, there is no real substitute for systematic scientific methods. There are techniques for recording and analysing data which are aimed at producing results which are as objective as is realistically possible (for no scientist, whatever they may believe to the contrary, is ever totally objective; none of us lives in a vacuum, and we are all subject to cultural and personal influences and prejudices). I believe that the best approach is to combine what has been learned through such systematic observation with knowledge gained from everyday experience of what horses do, and how they respond to us.

This is the approach I have adopted in writing this book. It draws on my systematic observations of my own and other people's horses, the observations of other horse owners (most particularly the work of Dr Marthe Kiley-Worthington with her own domestic group), scientific studies (especially the recent field work of Telané Greyling among the feral horses of Namibia and that of Joel Berger on the feral horses of the Granite Range of North West Nevada) and other works, published and unpublished.

We do not by any means know all that there is to know about the natural lives of horses. However, as long as we do not fall into the trap of thinking that we now know all that can be known, we can use the information we do have to build better relationships with our horses, based not on coercion or concepts of dominance, but on mutual trust, liking and respect.

i Emma Kurrels, 'Mind over Methods', Articles, www.companyofhorses.com

Chapter 1

What is Natural?

> Colon drew himself up to attention again. 'Not natural, in my view, sah. Not in favour of unnatural things.'
>
> Vetinari looked perplexed. 'You mean, you eat your meat raw and sleep in a tree?'
>
> Terry Pratchett, *The Fifth Elephant*

When we talk about 'natural' behaviour, or a 'natural' lifestyle, what exactly do we have in mind? In its strictest sense 'natural' simply means anything that exists in nature, which does not really help us very much. I think that what most of us have in mind when we talk about a 'natural' lifestyle for our horses is the kind of lifestyle which allows them to live in a manner closest to what they would choose for themselves, and to perform those behaviours appropriate to their species. In this way of thinking, the horse's welfare is more important than the owner's convenience, although the latter has to be taken into account to some extent, or most of us would not be able to keep horses at all!

The five freedoms

So what living conditions are necessary for the welfare of our horses? The Farm Animal Welfare Council has identified a number of conditions which it deems essential for the welfare of farm animals. These are known as the Five Freedoms and have been adopted by a number of other organizations, notably the RSPCA, and extended to non-agricultural animals such as horses. They are:

- Freedom from hunger and thirst by ready access to fresh water and a diet to maintain full health and vigour.

- Freedom from discomfort by providing an appropriate environment, including shelter and a comfortable resting area.
- Freedom from pain, injury and disease by prevention or rapid diagnosis and treatment.
- Freedom to express normal behaviour by providing sufficient space, proper facilities and company of the animal's own kind.
- Freedom from fear and distress by ensuring conditions and treatment which avoid mental suffering.[i]

Many – perhaps most – responsible horse owners manage to fulfil the first three welfare requirements listed above. However, the last two are more problematical because they require an understanding of what is meant by 'normal behaviour', the ability to recognize when a horse is suffering fear and distress, and – perhaps most difficult of all – an understanding of what constitutes 'mental suffering'.

In the chapters which follow, we will be seeking ways in which we can recognize abnormal behaviour when it arises, and also identify situations in which that abnormal behaviour *might* arise, and hopefully prevent it from occurring by avoiding those situations, or at least reducing their impact. We will also be considering how we can prevent situations occurring which create mental distress. For now, though, I want to focus on some of the ideas which often create confusion when people think about what is natural for horses.

Natural horsemanship?

In the not too distant past, traditional methods of training and management were followed simply because they appeared to work sufficiently well for people not to question them. Sometimes their faith was justified: classical riding,[1] for example, is based on principles that have been tested by time and, for the most part, have been vindicated by modern scientific appraisal. In other cases a different way of doing things might have been beneficial, but the people using such methods carried on with them because that was the way things had always been done. If something did not work, it was usually deemed to be because the horse was dull, stupid, vicious or whatever; it seldom occurred to people that it might be the method itself that was wrong.

Nowadays there is no shortage of people ready to question conventional ways of doing things. There are so many different training methods, some of them heavily overlaid with philosophical and spiritual ideas, that it is almost impossible to keep track of them. Some of these methods are very good, although many

1 See Chapter 8.

can be very confusing as they use a lot of convoluted jargon. In order to assess the worth of all these methods it is necessary to understand what lies behind them. Most – even those obscured by jargon and what often sounds like mystical mumbo-jumbo – are based on the solid principles of training outlined in Chapters 7 and 8.

'Natural horsemanship' is a phenomenon that emerged in the last two decades of the twentieth century. Practitioners of natural horsemanship had, of course, been around for much longer than that, but it was only in the 1980s and 1990s that they became widely known in the equestrian world. In the middle of the first decade of the twenty-first century we now have a huge number of trainers professing to use natural horsemanship and they have proved immensely popular with horse owners desperate to 'do the right thing' by their horses. However, some of the methods used, and the philosophy behind some of these methods, have increasingly been criticized, not only by more traditionally minded trainers and ordinary horse owners, but also by animal behaviour scientists concerned by what they perceive as a lack of real understanding, on the part of some of these trainers, of equine behaviour. 'Natural' methods have become the new dogma – and with that comes the danger that people will stop questioning and simply accept what they are told, regardless of whether it is correct, or even logical.

What do we mean by 'wild'?

Most trainers who espouse the idea of natural horsemanship – as well as some more traditionally minded trainers – will tell you that they base their ideas on the behaviour of horses 'in the wild'. The problem with this is that 'wild' is a very vague expression. There are no truly wild horses now living: DNA analysis has shown that the domestic horse, *Equus caballus*, is not (as was once believed) descended from the Mongolian 'wild horse', *Equus przewalskii*, although both descend from a common ancestor. All so-called 'wild' horses are actually either free-ranging horses (that is, horses who belong to someone but are allowed to roam freely) or feral horses, *feral* being a term used to describe domestic animals who have either escaped domesticity, or are the descendants of animals who have so escaped. The horses in many feral populations may be periodically subjected to various types of human interference; for example they may be rounded up and culled, with a resulting disturbance of population balance and group stability. This can have a knock-on effect on their behaviour; certain aspects of equine behaviour, especially social behaviour, vary considerably depending on local conditions. So when people talk about basing their training methods on the behaviour of horses 'in the wild', for such statements to have any meaning we need to know exactly how they define 'wild'.

Early attempts to discover how truly wild horses might have behaved concentrated mainly on the different species of zebra. This seemed to make sense, because at the time the only representatives of *Equus przewalskii* were kept in captivity, so there were no opportunities to observe them in their natural setting. Zebras were therefore the closest living relatives of *Equus caballus* then living in the truly wild state.

The trouble with studying zebras and then generalizing what is learned about them to *Equus caballus* is that, while zebras are indeed very closely related to domestic horses, there are still considerable differences. Some of the behaviours observed in feral horses have not been observed in zebras – or at least only in one species, Grevy's zebra, which is not necessarily directly comparable to *Equus caballus*. The ecology of zebra habitat, especially that of plains zebras, differs considerably from that of feral horses living in, for example, various parts of North America, which in turn affects behaviour, especially social organization. So although the behaviour of zebras can certainly help us to understand that of other species of *Equus*, it should not be taken on its own as a model for all equine behaviour.

A number of Mongolian 'wild horses' (*Equus przewalskii*) have now been released into the steppe-land of the Askaniya Nova nature reserve in Southern Ukraine and into the Khomin Tal region of western Mongolia. As these are undoubtedly the closest living relatives of the domestic horse, can we use their behaviour as a guide to how the original wild horses would have behaved? The

Zebras and feral horses are not necessarily identical in behaviour, especially as their habitat may differ widely.

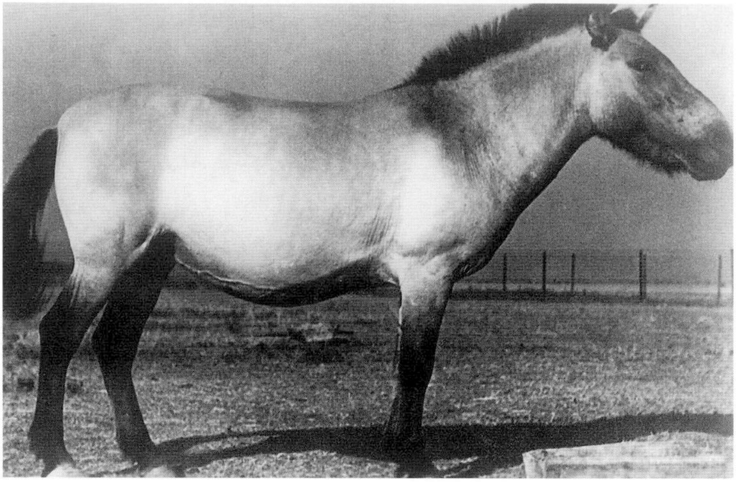

Przewalskii mare Orlitsa, Askaniya Nova, 1947. Captured in 1947 in the Takhin-Shara-Nuru mountains of the Mongolian Altai, she is the last specimen definitely recorded in the wild. (Colin P. Groves)

problem here is that the original populations were bred in captivity and the current Askaniya Nova population[2] is, if anything, even more intensively 'managed' than many feral populations of *Equus caballus*; there is also some evidence that these horses have interbred with free-ranging local domestic horse populations. And, as wildlife ecologist Joel Berger points out in his book on the horses of the Granite Range (see below), we will never know whether the behaviour patterns observed among Przewalski's horses are similar to those exhibited by their ancestors. So there is really no reason to think that we can gain any better understanding of equine behaviour by studying zebras and Przewalski's horses than from observing feral populations of domestic horses.

Since the early 1970s a number of studies have been carried out on such populations, one of the most comprehensive of these being Joel Berger's five-year observation of the horses of the Granite Range of North West Nevada. Berger selected this area precisely because the horses hardly ever came into contact with humans, and because the area was not grazed by cattle, being populated mainly by mule deer, pronghorn mountain goats, elk and bighorn sheep, none of whom interfered with the horses' grazing activities. This study resulted in Berger's 1986 publication, *Wild Horses of the Great Basin* (University of Chicago Press), one of the most valuable sources of information about how horses organize their society when not interfered with by humans, and how they behave towards each other.

Do horses form herds?

The dictionary definition of 'herd' is 'a large group of mammals living and feeding together'.[ii] With occasional exceptions, feral horses left to their own devices do not usually come together in large groups. Instead they tend to form close-knit family groups usually referred to in the scientific literature as 'bands'; these seldom contain more than around ten members and usually fewer than that. In the extremely harsh environment of the Namib Desert a band may sometimes consist of as few as two members. All-male groups form bands of their own: these so-called 'bachelor bands' consist, on average, of around four

2 The Khomin Tal horses were only released into the wild in summer 2004.

A band of horses in the Namib Desert. (Telané Greyling)

sexually mature males who have left their family groups, although larger or smaller bands are occasionally seen; these bachelor groups do not usually have the stability of a normal family group.

We can see a similar social structure in Przewalski's horses, as well as in plains and mountain zebras, who also live in small family groups. However in populations of Grevy's zebra the mares and stallions may form separate groups; in contrast to feral horses and other zebra species, they do not live together all the year round. Mountain zebra family groups do not generally join together to form large herds. There are times when small groups of plains zebras may come together into large herds; however, the smaller family groups still remain discrete entities within the larger herd. Among feral horses, family bands have home ranges within which they move about; these ranges overlap with those of other bands and several family groups may often come quite close to each other, sometimes grazing as little as 100 metres apart. However, there is little interaction between such groups, which tend to remain separate, with little if any contact between bands even when their ranges overlap. Occasionally bachelors have been seen to 'tag along' with a family band, possibly with the hope of supplanting the band stallion, but these bachelors do not form part of the stable family group.

The Namib Desert is one of the harshest environments in which horses can survive. The environment affects their behaviour, especially with regard to social organization. (Telané Greyling)

Another major difference between most feral populations and zebra populations is that the latter often graze with other species such as wildebeest and impala. In such mixed herds the different species benefit from each others' skills at detecting predators and, in some cases, from the confusion that results in the minds of predators on seeing a mixture of different shapes and sizes. Again, this kind of arrangement is not generally seen in feral horse populations, most of which inhabit areas in which large predators are either uncommon or completely absent.

So 'herd' is a term generally used by ethologists to describe an equine population in a defined area, consisting of discrete family bands which may or may not interact. It may thus be a useful term to describe a group of horses but we need to understand that it does not describe equine social organization all that accurately. The behaviour of horses kept in, say, a large, single-sex group will differ in many ways from that of horses forming a natural family group, especially if the former consists of horses who are for the most part comparative strangers to each other.

Both nature and nurture

An assumption made by many trainers appears to be that equine behaviour – indeed animal behaviour in general – is genetically determined and therefore we can predict how horses will behave in any situation.

However, the reality is that animal behaviour is shaped by a very complex interaction of genetic inheritance and the environment. 'Environment' includes even the womb in which the embryo forms and grows; this environment can influence such things as the chemical 'switches' which determine whether the effects of various genes are turned on or off, and the timing of such genetic effects. This is one reason why even identical twins are never really identical. Lifetime experiences affect and modify behaviour, as does the environment in which an animal lives and grows; all of these can vary enormously. We cannot say, for example, that such-and-such behaviour is X-per cent genetically determined, and X-per cent environmentally determined; much depends on the strength of the environmental influence and an individual organism's susceptibility to that influence. All this explains why ethologists are increasingly reluctant to use terms such as 'innate' and 'instinctive' when referring to behaviour; they know that although such terms may be useful in everyday speech, in scientific terms they are both misleading and inaccurate.

What kind of 'natural'?

So, when trainers refer to 'natural' horse behaviour and social organization, do they mean 'natural' as in a domestic situation (and if so, *whose*? – domestic situations can vary enormously), 'natural' as in large groups of free-ranging horses, or 'natural' as in the comparatively small family groups generally found among feral horses?

A comparison of a number of studies of groups of feral and free-ranging horses, as well as groups kept in a variety of domestic settings, shows that, while there are certain behaviour patterns common to all groups of horses, there are also many variations. These variations seem largely to depend on environmental factors such as climate, terrain, availability of food, group size (itself largely dependent on the foregoing factors) and – in the case of domestic horses – the culture in which they are kept.

Many trainers appear to have based their methods on horse behaviour observed in situations which would seldom if ever occur in a truly wild environment. In some cases these situations involve large single-sex groups; as we have already seen, the concept of the horse as a herd animal seems to have implanted in many people's minds the idea that horses naturally live in large herds, and that this is the best environment in which to observe their behaviour.

However, if the smaller family unit is the kind of social organization that horses prefer, does it make sense to base one's understanding of what matters to horses on observations of their behaviour in an unnatural setting, usually in single-sex groups of unrelated horses?

Every one unique

Another factor often overlooked is the fact that horses will inevitably differ in the ways in which they respond to training and management, no matter what methods are used. In sexually reproducing species such as humans and horses every individual is *unique*. This means literally that there is only *one* of each individual. We must always keep this in mind, for one of the greatest barriers to developing horses' potential is a failure to recognize that they are all – no matter how similar their breeding or upbringing – unique beings, with unique personalities.

This uniqueness of each individual is what shapes temperament and personality, both of which affect the behaviour and trainability of our horses. Even monozygotic[3] twins, who are genetically identical, are still individually unique because, as we have seen, the environment affects us even in the womb. Look at the photograph of 'identical' equine twins Romulus and Remus on page 13. At first sight they look identical but closer observation reveals that the white markings on their foreheads are actually slightly different. Although white markings are to a large extent genetically determined, there appears to be an environmental influence at work, too – in this case, the environment being that of the womb. So even though they are genetically identical, these foals still have visible differences. In temperament and personality, having been reared by different dams, they are likely to differ even more!

Traditional and modern

Nature is not obligingly tidy, as humans would like her to be, but messy and complicated. Attempts are often made to cram equine behaviour into a few over-simplified concepts, for example the idea that horses have only one or two very basic needs, when in fact their needs are many and their social lives rich and varied. These over-simplifications may appear to work superficially but in the end they only create more confusion. The situation is not helped by the fact that nowadays numerous books and articles in the equestrian press encourage the polarization of ideas about horse training and management. Authors write about the 'naturals' (i.e. the devotees of 'natural horsemanship') versus the 'traditionals', or

3 Twins derived from the splitting of a single fertilized egg.

Identical equine twins Romulus and Remus. Horses normally only produce fraternal twins, not identical twins, so in order to study differences, scientists have had to split six-day-old embryos and implant the two halves in different mares. (Professor W.R. Allen, Equine Fertility Unit, Newmarket)

those who train and manage their horses in accordance with methods laid down generations ago, which often have more relevance to the convenience of the horse-keeper rather than that of the horse. The two viewpoints are often presented as mutually exclusive, the implication being that if you are a devotee of 'natural horsemanship' you cannot follow traditional methods, and vice versa. In this way readers are pressurized into identifying themselves with either the 'naturals' or the 'traditionals'.

I believe that the polarization referred to above is damaging, because it tends to make people feel obliged to range themselves with one side or another and, having done so, to defend their position. This may then lead to bitter arguments, with neither side able to see the merits of the other. Ultimately the losers here are the horses, because people who have committed themselves to one way of doing things are less likely to see when their practices are at best ineffective and at worst actually harmful.

However, this need not be the case. One may accept and put into practice the best ideas from both approaches; indeed many of us do so without even thinking about it too much. What we need to do – as will be discussed in the chapters which follow – is develop a fuller understanding of just what it is we are putting into practice.

Unfortunately terms such as 'natural' and 'traditional' encompass a wide range of concepts and the people who use them seldom define the sense in which they are using them at specific times.

We have already considered questions connected with what is meant by 'natural', but what about the term 'traditional'? As defined in my *Collins*

Dictionary of the English Language it simply means 'of, or relating to, or being a tradition'.[iii] *Tradition* can mean 'the handing down from generation to generation of the same customs, beliefs, etc.',[iv] 'the body of customs, thought, practices, etc. belonging to a particular country, people, family, or institution over a relatively long period'[v] or 'a specific custom or practice of long standing'.[vi] None of these definitions implies any kind of value-judgement.

Some traditions are retained for excellent reasons, because they have a beneficial effect on the community that practises them. Some others may persist for less than excellent reasons, for example because they favour a privileged minority at the expense of the rest of the community. In the case of horse training and management, some traditions, for example those underpinning the training philosophy known as *classical* (see Chapter 8) are rightly revered because they benefit both the horses and the humans involved. Some, such as certain practices that are designed for human convenience rather than equine welfare, are questionable and in many cases could well be changed or dispensed with. Yet others, such as some of the harsh 'breaking' practices used in some parts of the world, are bad traditions which persist only because of ignorance and a reluctance to change.

So when people lump together 'traditional' methods of horse training and management, as so many do, and suggest that this alone is sufficient to cast doubt on their validity, they make a grave error. For a start, whose tradition are they talking about? As we have seen, there are different types of tradition, some good, some not so good, and some bad. Traditional methods vary enormously from culture to culture, and sometimes even within the same culture. To ignore all this, and to discard traditional methods without adequate discussion, does not help anyone, least of all the horse.

Where do we start?

How then can we provide our horses with as natural a lifestyle as possible, within the limits of the options available to most of us? It will be clear from this and the following chapters that the needs and priorities of horses are far more varied and complex than is generally supposed, and that there is no single set of rules that will enable us to fulfil those needs. Moreover, we must never forget that every horse is an individual and may not respond to specific conditions exactly as another horse might. All we can really do is try to identify the kind of living conditions and training methods which make horses happy and willing to respond, and those which make them miserable and create problems. We can then compare these conditions with those in which we keep our own horses, and by recognizing where we need to make changes and adjustments, we can hopefully create a lifestyle for our horses in which they can flourish.

To make this task easier, you will need to take a long, hard look at every aspect of your horse's lifestyle. Using Appendix I (which contains a profile of my own Arabian gelding Zareeba) as a guide, start by building a profile of your horse, listing his characteristics and individual quirks and peculiarities and giving details of his current management and training regime. Bear in mind that any assessment of his personality is bound to be subjective, because as yet no universally acceptable way of measuring equine personality objectively has been found. So try to put aside any prejudices you may have and make your assessment as if you were an outsider with no emotional attachment to your horse.

Then, as you read through the rest of this book, you will be able to see where any of your current practices may need adjusting or, in some cases, changing altogether. You can then make further notes next to your original ones, as a guide to what action you may need to take. Keeping horses in a domestic situation necessitates compromise, with many trade-offs; we can very rarely keep our horses in conditions that are absolutely ideal either for them or for us. But if we first of all understand the basic requirements of the Five Freedoms, we will have gone a considerable part of the way to fulfilling those requirements.

i Farm Animal Welfare Council, *Report on the welfare of dairy cattle* 1996.
ii *Collins Dictionary of the English Language*, 2nd ed. 1986, p.716, entry under *herd* (sense 1).
iii *Collins Dictionary of the English Language*, 2nd ed. 1986, p.1612, entry under *tradition* (sense 1).
iv *Collins Dictionary of the English Language*, 2nd ed. 1986, p.1612, entry under *tradition* (sense 1).
v *Collins Dictionary of the English Language*, 2nd ed. 1986, p.1612, entry under *tradition* (sense 2).
vi *Collins Dictionary of the English Language*, 2nd ed. 1986, p.1612, entry under *tradition* (sense 3).

Chapter 2

Different Strokes

> 'Look out of the winder, James, and see wot'un a night it is'... James staggered up, and after a momentary grope about the room ...exclaimed, 'Hellish dark, and smells of cheese!' 'Smells o' cheese!' repeated Mr Jorrocks, looking round in astonishment; 'smells o' cheese! – vy, man, you've got your nob i' the cupboard – this be the vinder.'
>
> R.S. Surtees, *Handley Cross*

What kind of relationship do we want with our horses? Indeed, what kind of relationship *can* we have with our horses? The answer to this question depends not only on how different horses and humans actually are from each other, but also on our perceptions of those differences. Regrettably, in their desire to promote a better understanding of why horses behave as they do, some trainers and behavioural scientists have actually overstated their case. By presenting horses and humans as behavioural opposites, they have created an artificial gulf between the two species, which can hinder understanding rather than aid it.

Predators and prey

We are constantly being reminded that horses are different from humans and a number of assumptions are routinely made about the nature of the differences. One of the most basic of these is that humans are predators by nature, while horses are prey animals. I imagine that no one would quibble about the second half of this statement, since horses, as grazing herbivores, are obviously not predators. But how accurate is the assumption that humans are naturally predators?

Many people seem to take this assumption for granted. I did so myself, until

I learned more about human origins; in the horse world it has now become widely accepted. Humans are often described as the horse's biological enemy and we are told that horses and humans think differently because horses are prey animals and people are predators.

Now it is true that, for part of our history, humans have relied on hunting as a means of subsistence, and in some parts of the world they still do so. But does this represent some deep, basic aspect of our nature, or might it be simply a cultural phenomenon?

Unlike most real predators, humans are not true carnivores (meat-eaters), but omnivores (we eat both animal and vegetable matter). Some predatory animals are also omnivores, for example foxes, who may scavenge as much food as they find by predation. This may also have been the case with the earliest meat-eating humans; there is evidence which suggests that they scavenged at the kill sites of real predators, picking shreds of meat from bones and sucking the marrow from those that had been broken.

True carnivores have long, pointed canine teeth used for killing and may have specialized cheek teeth called *carnassials*. The latter have sharp cutting edges and the carnassials in the upper and lower jaws act like shears to bite through flesh. By contrast, humans have poorly developed canine teeth and no carnassials; our cheek teeth are blunt rather than sharp, and are more suited to grinding than to

Figure 1: The teeth reveal an animal's diet: the lion's teeth are those of a carnivore, the human's those of an omnivore and the horse's those of a herbivore.

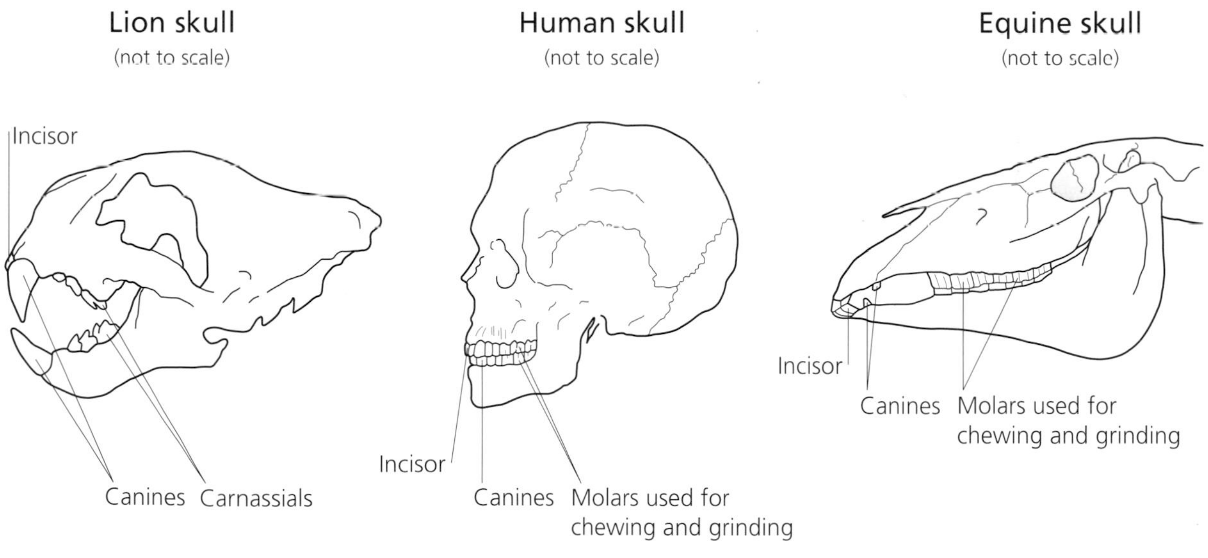

The lion has large canine teeth for inflicting lethal bites on his prey, and shear-like carnassial teeth for slicing through hide and flesh. By comparison, the human has small canine teeth resembling the incisors, and has no carnassials. The molars are relatively flat and used for chewing and grinding food. The human teeth are not those of a predator. The equine teeth are purely those of a herbivore.

cutting into flesh (humans may have developed the habit of cooking meat in order to make it easier to chew).

Besides teeth, many predators have other weapons with which to bring down, kill, and tear at their prey: think of the beak and talons of a bird of prey, or the formidable claws of the lion or tiger. Humans have no such weapons, and we are puny in comparison with predators such as wolves and big cats, with their powerful jaws and musculature. Serious hunting really became an option only once early humans had learned how to make primitive weapons for killing at a distance. 'Man the Hunter' is an outdated idea; basing their views on the available evidence, anthropologists now believe that, even when armed with such weapons as they had been able to fashion from flints, it is unlikely that the earliest hunters would have been terribly efficient.[1]

So the idea that predatory behaviour is somehow genetically 'programmed' into humans simply will not do. Hunting behaviour is more of a cultural than a genetic matter, although in certain societies people who possessed the qualities of a successful hunter would no doubt be more likely, because of their success, to raise families and pass on those qualities to further generations. In some other societies, however, the idea of humans as predators would be simply incomprehensible.

Do horses really see us as predators?

Argument	**Reality**
Humans smell like predators because we eat meat.	Not all humans eat meat and those who do generally cook it. So even those humans who do eat meat are unlikely to smell the same as a predator. In any case, only horses know how we smell to them.
We look like predators because our ears are pinned back all the time (which a horse would interpret as an expression of aggression).	Horses are perfectly capable of interpreting our body language correctly (see Chapter 6). In any case, predators are not necessarily showing aggression, they are simply doing what they have to do in order to eat; their body language may not be aggressive at all.

1 See, for example, Roger Lewin, *Human Evolution*, 4th ed. Blackwell Science 1999, p.153.

Argument	Reality
We approach horses directly, like a stalking predator.	Not all predators behave in the same way. Felids (cats, from lions and leopards down to the domestic moggy) and canids (dogs, from wolves and coyotes to Rover next door) approach their prey in different ways, and seldom directly!
Humans, like most predators, have their eyes placed at the front of their heads.	Not all mammals with forward-facing eyes are predators; for example our close cousin the gorilla is a peaceful vegetarian.

Our attitudes to horses are largely a result of cultural conditioning. In our modern Western civilization many – perhaps most – people will have no opportunity to study animals in their natural state; many urban children may never even have seen cows and sheep close up. Domestic animals have been largely taken for granted, and various cultures have (often for religious reasons) decreed that animals were put on earth for our use. So it is hardly surprising that humans have tended to adopt a rather arrogant attitude towards the animals with whom they share their lives, believing that we have the right to compel them to obey our commands. This culturally induced arrogance (and ignorance), rather than some supposed predatory instinct, is why so many humans have no idea how to act in ways that are not only comprehensible to horses, but actually make them want to co-operate with us.

So do horses run away when they see humans coming towards them because they perceive us as predators coming to catch them? Or is the answer much simpler: that horses who run away when a human goes into the field to catch them are simply avoiding what has become for them an unpleasant or unrewarding experience? I would suggest that it is the horse's previous experience of what being caught means, rather than fear of being caught by a predator, which dictates his response.

Are wild equids really difficult to tame?

Some ethologists and trainers cite the awkward temperament of Przewalski's horses and the difficulty of training zebras as evidence that wild horses would have been equally difficult in the early days of horse-keeping. The experiences of some trainers with zebras suggests that earlier difficulties may have related more to the methods employed than to the inherent nature of zebras. Some years ago Dr Marthe Kiley-Worthington, who has worked with all kinds of animals, both wild and domestic, from elephants to guinea-pigs, tried an interesting experiment. She and her partner, Chris Rendle, captured a young zebra stallion in the Imire Wildlife Ranch in Zimbabwe, where the zebras bred freely and had never been handled. Using what Dr Kiley-Worthington calls 'co-operative handling and teaching' – basically positive reinforcement techniques (see Chapters 7 and 8) – she and her team taught the zebra, whom they named Zanitaye, to stand still for them to handle his legs and lift up his feet; to stand quietly when tethered; to lead without fuss; to lunge, be bridled and long-reined. As Dr Kiley-Worthington observes:

> This experience indicates that provided the handlers do not have preconceived notions concerning the difficulty or unpredictability of this wild equine, and behaved quietly, fearlessly and with relaxed postures, used their voices much and quietly, and make every effort to ensure that fearful situations do not arise (such as sudden noises, movements, noisy, excited or cautious people around etc.), this zebra learnt extremely quickly to behave appropriately and quietly… It certainly indicates, even with this one sample that ease to be handled by humans, to learn and to work is not different between wild and domestic equines.[i]

Observations of feral horses suggest that, even if they have never seen humans before, if they are approached in the right way, i.e. in a slow, calm and relaxed manner, they will often allow people to approach quite close – far closer than they would allow any animal they believed to be a predator. It could be that this is because these horses have descended from animals bred selectively for a tractable temperament, but it is equally possible that the wild ancestors of the modern horse were never as difficult to approach – or to tame – as has generally been assumed.

Are horses intelligent?

What about the quality which, in the minds of many people, really divides humans from other animals? This is that elusive attribute, 'intelligence'. Are horses intelligent? And if so, how can we measure that intelligence? To me, both these questions are meaningless, because we have not yet managed to find a universally acceptable definition of what intelligence *is*, let alone found a satisfactory system of measuring it. While comparisons within a group may be valid, comparisons between differing groups are vacuous, because there are far too many variables to take into account, so one is not comparing like with like. Is a Shetland more or less intelligent than a Chihuahua? If so, in what way?

All we can really say is that horses are intelligent at being horses, that they have an immense capacity to learn as well as to relate to other species, and that some of them are undoubtedly brighter than others. Intelligence can take many different forms, not least of which is the ability to adapt to novel and demanding situations. By this criterion, many horses are very intelligent indeed!

In spite of this, many animal behaviour scientists and trainers have simply assumed, often working from theories about what levels of brain activity they believe would be appropriate to grazing animals such as horses, that they are not capable of reasoning or of experiencing any emotions other than the most basic primary emotions such as fear. Animal behaviour scientist Andrew McLean, writing in the online horse magazine *Today's Horse*, says, 'In the equine brain, there is no room for either extreme of the emotional spectrum like euphoric love and malevolent hatred.'[2] McLean goes on to say that 'the horse's world is, in the opinion of most scientists, not perceived by reasoning.'[ii] But as Dr Marthe Kiley-Worthington observes in her excellent book *Horse Watch – What it is to be Equine* (J.A. Allen 2005), 'Teaching people to underestimate equine mentality is not helpful if they are to understand how to relate well to equines.'[iii] Indeed, to take McLean's last point first, experiments conducted independently by a number of more open-minded scientists, such as Dr Evelyn Hanggi of the

2 Having seen horses express what can only be described as malevolent hatred, I would strongly challenge this statement!

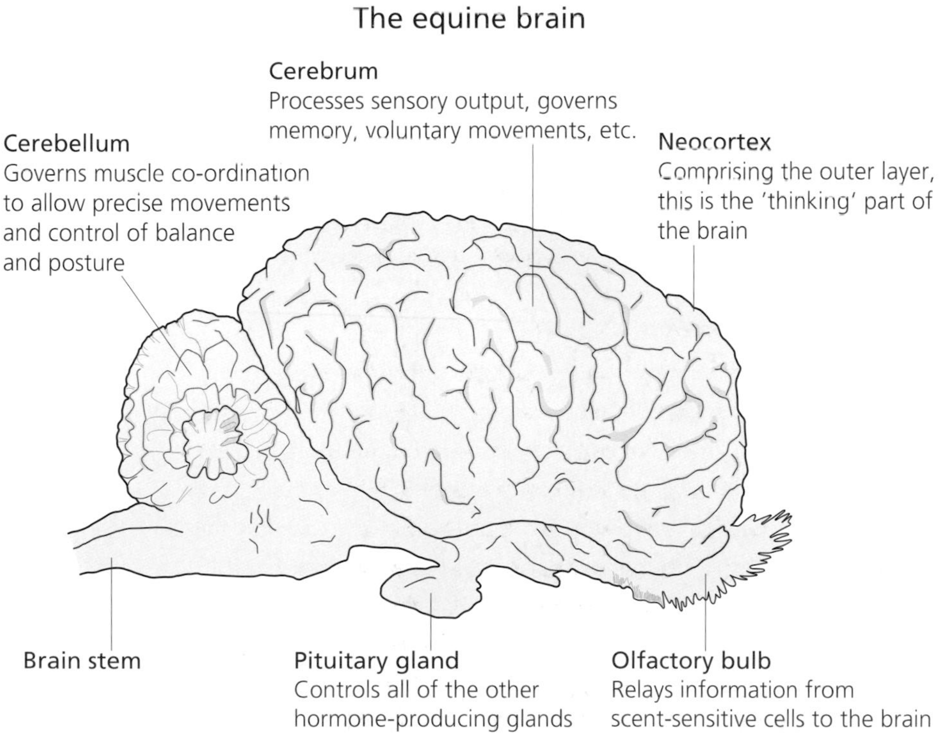

Figure 2: The equine brain is not the simple structure many people assume it to be but a complex structure with a very well-developed cortex (the 'thinking' part of the brain).

Equine Research Foundation in California, are increasingly confirming what countless horse owners have always thought: horses are indeed capable of reasoning, although the extent of this capability remains to be discovered.

Unfeeling machines or creatures of emotion?

What about emotions? Are horses like us in experiencing emotions, or is this another area in which the differences are apparent, as some scientists such as Andrew McLean suggest? Some trainers appear to adopt the old-fashioned notion that animals are little more than machines, reacting to external stimuli with pre-programmed responses. If we really believed this, it would make any kind of meaningful relationship with our horses impossible, as one cannot have such a relationship with an unfeeling machine. Nevertheless, it is a convenient viewpoint, because believing that animals do not have emotions makes it much easier to ignore their individual needs, and to use them without regard to any emotional suffering we might be inflicting.

Ironically, much of the research that has led to greater understanding of how the brain's centres of emotion interact with the neocortex (thinking part of the brain), and how this affects emotional responses, has been carried out on mammals such as rats, so we can scarcely say that emotion is a purely human quality! In any case, given the evolutionary continuity between humans and other mammals, this would not make biological sense. Indeed, as Marc Bekoff, ethologist and Professor of Biology at the University of Colorado, says in his very readable book *Minding Animals*, 'Surely it would be narrow-minded to think that humans are the only animals who have evolved deep emotional feelings. Indeed, evolutionary biology warns us that this cannot be the case.'[iv]

In fact, there is an overwhelming body of evidence from the fields of ethology, neurobiology, endocrinology, psychology, and philosophy that animals do feel a very wide range of emotions. The big question, therefore, is not whether other animals experience emotions, but *what* emotions they feel, and in what degree. It seems to be true that, because of the larger number of connections in the human brain, we do have an ability to feel the widest range of reactions to our emotions, as well as a greater number of nuances and subtleties. But let us not forget that other animals (including horses) also have complex 'wiring', as well as an enlarged neocortex. The fact that we have an advantage in this respect does not entitle us to dismiss the emotional lives of other animals, or to claim that we cannot know anything about what they might feel. Of course we can never know exactly what another creature feels, but this is as true of other humans as it is of animals – if you say you feel sad, I can never know *for certain* whether you feel the same way as I do if I feel sad. What we can do is study their behaviour, to see what emotions reveal themselves, either in actions or in physiological reactions. What we must not do is dismiss them as irrelevant. As Marc Bekoff says, 'To deny animals' emotions is to deny a large part of who these beings are.'[v]

Not aliens, but still different

After all this, it begins to appear that the differences between ourselves and our horses are by no means as great as some people would have us believe. Nevertheless the differences do exist. Some of them arise from biological differences, and some from human cultural assumptions. Dr Marthe Kiley-Worthington has described the biological differences in detail in *Horse Watch – What it is to be Equine*, so I will simply take a brief look at some of the differences in senses, abilities and lifestyle which tend to make humans and horses see life from somewhat different perspectives.

As we have seen, the perceived predator/prey relationship is really something of a non-starter. What does make a big difference is the contrast in origins and habitat. Humans evolved from tree-dwellers to bush-dwellers; it was not until well after the first true humans emerged and spread into cooler climates that we started living in caves. So cave-dwelling (which of course later developed into house-dwelling) was more of a localized phenomenon than an absolute biological necessity; in some parts of the world there are still bush-dwelling peoples who spend almost their entire lives under the open sky. Even so, most of us are so accustomed to living in warm shelters that we find it difficult to imagine living any other way. So we tend to think that horses, too, should be grateful for warm, sheltered accommodation, and often we do not ask ourselves whether our horses might not rather be outside in an open space, even if it is not so warm as their cosy stables.

Horses, for their part, are creatures of movement. They evolved from small, dog-like forest dwellers into large, swift-moving creatures of the open plains, relying on their speed for their ability to escape from predators. Although equids can defend themselves very effectively with their teeth and hooves, the kind of large predators capable of bringing a zebra or a horse down will try to do so before their prey can make use of his natural weapons. So, for the horse, flight is the best kind of defence: escaping before the enemy can get close enough to make contact is always the best policy. Hence the horse's extremely fast reflexes: the horse who reacted most quickly to real or perceived danger was the one most likely to live to reproduce (and pass on these swift reactions).

This reactivity can be inconvenient to us, as anyone who has ridden a spooky horse knows only too well. However, the reactive horse is simply being a good horse; he is the one who would probably have survived longest in the wild. The phlegmatic animal who appears virtually bomb-proof may be safer to ride, but might not have done so well if threatened by predators. He might also be less likely to give the rider warning of possible danger! Even though wild horses may not have been as difficult to approach, catch and tame as has generally been supposed, the modern horse's flight reflexes remain those of a prey animal. It is important that we understand this side of a horse's nature, because if we fail to do so we essentially fail to appreciate what a horse *is*.

Perhaps one of the biggest differences between horses and humans lies in our ability to manipulate objects. Humans generally have four fingers and an opposable thumb on each hand; horses' limbs end in a single digit, covered with hard horn composed largely of keratin. We can grasp objects in our flexible fingers and hands; horses cannot. So they lack most of our ability to manipulate objects, which severely limits their capabilities in solving the kind of practical problems which humans take in their stride. This can often lead to humans assuming that horses are stupid, when in fact the problem lies not in their mental abilities but in their anatomy. Horses can, however, manipulate some objects with their very mobile lips and muzzles, and some of them are very clever at this; even so we should not expect too much of them in this respect.

Horses differ from us, too, in that their senses are generally much more highly developed. Human vision, hearing, and sense of smell were probably once much more acute than they are now.

Equine hearing

Horses can detect a wider range of sound waves than humans. The frequency with which a sound wave vibrates is what determines its pitch, and is measured in Hertz (Hz). At its very best, human hearing can detect frequencies ranging from around 20 Hz to 20,000 Hz (20 kilohertz or kHz). Horses, on the other hand, can hear sound waves in the range of about 60 Hz to 33.5 kHz. This means that they cannot hear the low frequencies that we do but may detect them as something other than sound, e.g. as vibrations. They can however detect much higher-pitched sounds than the human ear.

We can all see how mobile equine ears are, as they rotate either together or independently in response to sound. The ears indicate where the horse's attention lies; the ridden horse whose ears are pricked forward in an alert manner may look attractive but he may not be paying attention to his rider! When horses lay their ears right back it is usually taken as a sign of aggression. This is very often the case, but it might just be that the horse is flattening his ears to protect himself from loud noises. Most horses dislike loud, raucous music and find it stressful. If you habitually play loud music in the stable yard, try turning it off and see what effect the resulting quiet has on the horses.

Equine vision

The prominence and location of his eyes give the horse an enormous range of vision, with a total field of vision of almost 350 degrees. For a grazing prey animal who needs to be aware of possible danger from any angle, this type of vision gives a clear advantage. However, there is a blind zone (see Figure 3) immediately behind the horse, which is why horses suddenly approached from the rear tend to be startled. They may move away or, if they cannot move, they may kick out in defence. There is another blind zone in front of the horse. This is why horses tend to back away from something – such as a human hand raised to touch the head – which suddenly appears in front of them; they need to step back in order to see it properly. It is a sign of trust if a horse allows you to put your hand on his nose or forehead without making a gradual approach, as he cannot see what you intend to do!

Humans have what is known as binocular vision, in which the retinas of both eyes simultaneously receive a focused image of the same object, giving it three-dimensional depth. Although most of the horse's range of vision is what is called monocular, (i.e. what is viewed is seen with one eye at a time), the wide field of vision resulting from the prominence of the equine eye means that there is an area in front of the horse where he does have binocular vision (see Figure 3). This is because the visual field of each eye overlaps slightly with that of the other. It is this limited degree of binocular vision which enables horses to judge distances when jumping.

Horses may not be able to focus on close objects as well as humans can, but they could be long-sighted, i.e. distant objects may appear clearer to them. Peripheral vision in horses is much less acute than in humans but the equine eye is exceptionally good at detecting movement, no matter where it may be in the

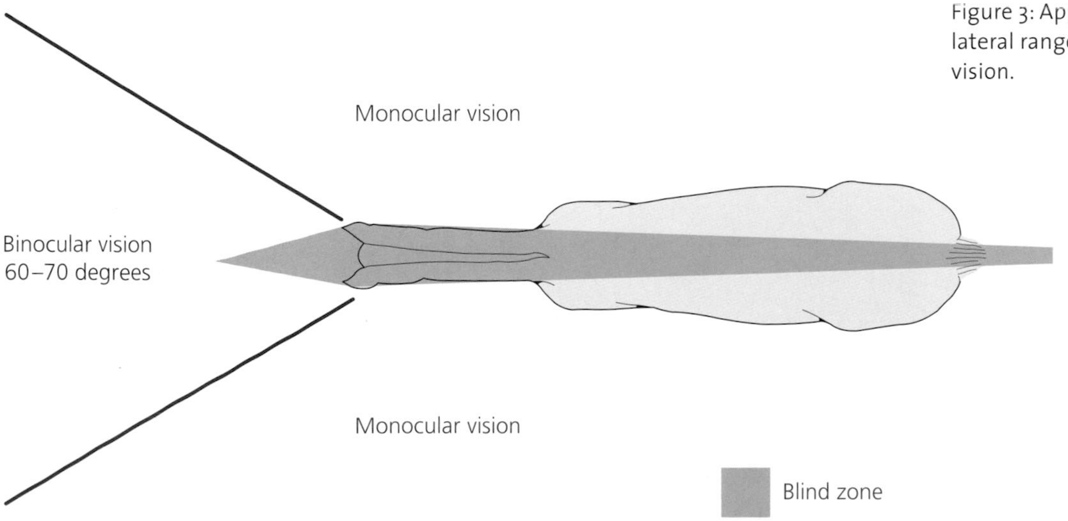

Figure 3: Approximate lateral range of equine vision.

visual field. This helps to explain why some horses shy for no reason that is apparent to humans. They may have caught sight of some movement outside their range of acute vision; survival behaviour kicks in, and they try to put some distance between themselves and a possible threat.

Taste and smell

We have comparatively little information on how horses perceive taste, but in general it seems as though they probably share similar perceptions of taste to humans. Most horses appear to like sweet flavoured foods and will readily learn to accept treats such as mints. All of our horses like Extra-Strong mints and some have a definite taste for the very strong cough sweets known as Fisherman's Friends!

Horses appear to have a very much more highly developed sense of smell than humans. This is hardly surprising, since the horse's long nose is lined with many layers of scent-sensitive cells. When two horses meet, or when regular companions are reunited after a separation, they may spend some time sniffing each other's nostrils (they may also seek to 'inspect' humans in this way). This may be a means of gathering information about what the returning horse has been doing and, possibly, what his companions have been up to in his absence. Pheromones – chemical 'messages' carried in the breath and on the skin – may tell a whole story about the horse's emotional and mental state, as well as giving indications of where he has been, what he has been doing and who he has been with. Horses

Tiff (left) and Nivalis sniff at each other's nostrils. Chemical 'messages' in the breath and on the skin reveal a great deal about a horse's physical and mental state. (L. Skipper)

will often investigate dung piles with great enthusiasm; these, too, may tell them a great deal about the emotional and physiological state of whoever deposited the dung. Stallions in particular like to spend a lot of time sniffing at dung piles.

When investigating an interesting smell, horses are often seen to raise the head and curl the upper lip, almost as if they were laughing. This is the gesture known as *flehmen* and it involves a structure in the nose called the *vomeronasal* or Jacobson's organ. The horse curls his lip to close off the nasal chambers, trapping the scent in the nostrils and allowing the Jacobson's organ to analyse the smell. All horses do this but stallions in particular will often spend a great deal of time scrutinizing smells in this way, particularly if there are mares about. By sampling the scent of a mare's urine in this way a stallion can detect whether she is in season, or about to come into season.

The facial gesture known as flehmen enables a horse to trap smells for analysis by the Jacobson's organ. (L. Skipper)

By understanding the ways in which horses' senses differ from ours we can build a flexibility into our training and management that takes account of these differences. Table 1 (at the end of this chapter) gives some examples of the kind of things we need to look out for.

Personal space

One thing that humans and horses have in common is the need for *personal space*, the distance which separates members of the same species. Ethologists sometimes describe certain species as *contact* species, lacking individual distance, and *distance* species, maintaining a certain distance from others of the same species and avoiding bodily contact. Most mammals, including humans and horses, come somewhere between these two extremes, avoiding bodily contact with certain conspecifics (creatures of the same species) and inviting or allowing it with others. With horses, as with many other social animals including humans, personal space depends on relationships. If strangers enter a horse's personal space the horse will feel uncomfortable and possibly threatened; a close friend or relative would be allowed to get much closer. Based on my own observations I would suggest the following distances within which others are tolerated:

- Family and close friends: 0 to 2 m.
- Individuals who do not know each other well: 2 to 4 m.
- Strangers: 4 m and over.

These are approximate distances only and they may vary from individual to individual. Some horses may need much more space, other will need less and individuals who dislike each other, even though they know each other well, will need more space than those who get on well. In general, horses enjoy physical

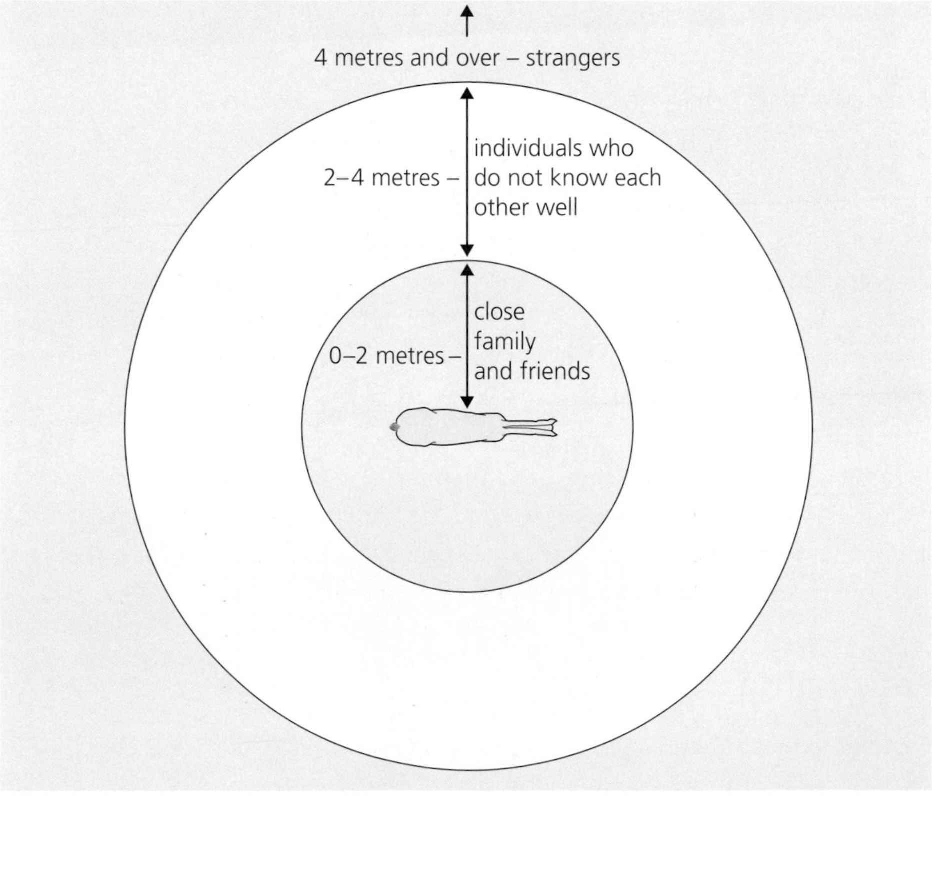

Figure 4: Distances required to maintain personal space among horses (based on the author's observations; these distances are approximate only and may vary considerably from group to group and individual to individual).

Only friends and close relatives are normally allowed into the most intimate zone of a horse's personal space. (L. Skipper)

contact with individuals (including humans) whom they like, but invasion of their personal space by strangers is very stressful for them – just as it is for humans.

The great divide

The one attribute which divides humans from the rest of the animal world is that which enables us to have this discussion in the first place: this is spoken (and, by extension, written) language. Animals, including horses, have a variety of ways in which they communicate with each other, some of them very sophisticated. Even so, they cannot (unless they employ some form of as-yet-undetected ESP) convey the kind of detailed information that is possible with the spoken word. Humans, on the other hand, rely on words so much that we tend to forget that there are other ways of communicating, some of them very subtle indeed (Chapter 6 will show us just how subtle this can be). This can lead to misunderstandings, for example as we mistakenly attribute our horse's failure to understand what we want to stubbornness or stupidity, when in reality it is more likely that we have simply failed to communicate properly!

Bridging the gaps

Having seen that horses are not so different from us in some respects, how can we try to bridge the gaps that remain? We have compelled the horse to live in our world, so it is up to us to find areas of mutual understanding, not the other way round. We can start to do this by the following means:

- Understanding what matters to our horses, rejecting dogma preached about certain aspects of training and management where it is irrelevant or potentially harmful (Chapters 3 and 4).
- Finding ways in which we can fulfil their needs and avoiding situations which create stress; contented horses are more likely to want to co-operate with us (Chapters 3, 4, 5, 13 and 14).
- Thinking about ways in which we can convey our wishes more clearly (Chapters 6, 7 and 8).
- If we are bringing up, or intend to bring up, young horses, giving them the best possible start in life (Chapter 9).
- Understanding the different priorities and needs of stallions, mares and geldings and tailoring our training and management to suit those (Chapters 10, 11 and 12).
- Remembering that our ambitions are largely irrelevant to horses, and putting their needs and welfare before those ambitions (Chapter 15).

The last point is of vital importance: if we are to train and manage our horses in a manner that is truly humane and ethical, we must learn to put their needs above ours. As the following chapters will show, that is only the start!

i Dr Marthe Kiley-Worthington, 'Are domestic equines easier to train than wild ones?' in *Equine Behaviour*, Issue 36, Summer 1997, p.7.
ii Andrew McLean, 'Training Psychology', *Today's Horse* (online publication, article archives).
iii Dr Marthe Kiley-Worthington, *Horse Watch – What it is to be Equine*, J.A. Allen 2005, p.123.
iv Marc Bekoff, *Minding Animals*, Oxford University Press 2002, p.17.
v Bekoff, *Minding Animals*, p.100.

Table 1 Some common problems caused by the way horses sense the world about them; possible causes, reemdial action, situations to avoid

Problem	Possible causes	Remedial action	Situations to avoid	Further reference
Horse is very spooky.	Tension; freshness and lack of exercise; overfeeding. May be related to vision, i.e. the horse may suddenly catch sight of something in his peripheral vision but be unable to define what it is.	Where tension is the cause, work on relaxation and gaining your horse's trust. Ensure that he is given plenty off freedom to let off steam and is given regular, steady work. Allow the horse to look around him when ridden. If shying is very frequent and severe, consult your vet regarding possible vision defects.	Feeding too much high-energy feed; allowing the horse insufficient exercise and freedom; irregular work patterns (if possible).	Chapters 4 and 13; Lesley Skipper, *Realize Your Horse's True Potential* Chapters 6 and 14.
Excitable and easily upset in windy conditions.	The noise of the wind means that horses cannot hear other sounds clearly or determine from which direction they are coming so they are likely to over-react to noises which would normally cause them no problems, or to behave as if they have heard noises which may not exist. The movement of trees, grass, bushes, etc. is also upsetting as it makes the detection of possible danger more difficult. Most horses may be affected in this way, including feral horses.	There is little you can do to prevent this as it is a normal reaction for a horse. Make sure that your horse's diet is not making things worse, i.e. check that he is being fed in accordance with the work he is doing. Excess energy will make him even more excitable.	If at all possible, try to avoid riding or working the horse in very windy conditions. It will be very difficult to keep your horse's attention in such conditions.	
The horse refuses to eat from feed buckets/drink from water buckets placed on the stable floor.	Even when a stable has been thoroughly mucked out the smell of urine and faeces is still detectable to the horse and the unpleasant smell may be putting him off eating and drinking. This is especially the case where a deep litter system is used.	Feed the horse in a manger hooked over the stable door; make water containers large enough so that the horse does not have to put his nose too near the floor to drink; clean out corners thoroughly and make sure there is plenty of fresh, clean bedding. Best of all, keep the horse out as much as possible.	Letting dirty bedding accumulate; having insufficient clean bedding; keeping horse inside for prolonged periods.	
Horse is very tense and often gets agitated in the stable; pulls faces for no apparent reason.	Frequent and/or prolonged loud or unpleasant noises; presence of rodents in stables causing rustling sounds and visible movements in the straw; biting insects.	Try to provide a quiet stable environment; if you must have music playing keep it soft and soothing. If rodent activity is suspected, get a cat to deal with mice and a terrier to take care of rats. Don't put poison down as other animals could eat it. Invest in insect repellents designed for horses and stables.	Loud, raucous music; too much maintenance activity (e.g. hammering and banging; prolonged use of tractors and other machinery) while horses are stabled; loud voices and shouting. Most horses will tolerate a degree of all of these things but too much noise will make even the most placid horse upset and nervous, so try to keep voices low and pleasant and if possible carry out maintenance activities when horses are not in their stables.	Abigail Hogg, *The Horse Behaviour Handbook*, Chapters 3 and 4.
Horse shies away and runs to back of stable when people approach him.	Memory of past ill-treatment or harsh management practices (e.g. horse being 'shown who's boss'); sudden and abrupt movements in his direction.	Approach the horse in a neutral, passive manner. Never make sudden movements or force your presence on him; wait until he accepts you in his personal space. Speak to him softly and in a soothing manner.	Walking straight up to the horse and immediately invading his personal space; making sudden movements in his direction; speaking loudly when near him.	Chapters 3, 4, 6, 7 and 8.

Chapter 3

In Harmony with Each Other

It ain't so much the things we don't know that get us in trouble. It's the things we know that ain't so.

Artemus Ward

In the Western world, especially in our current culture of 'market forces', we have been conditioned to think of competition as representing some kind of natural force. Even scientists such as evolutionary biologists, who should know better, tend to talk about natural selection as if it were some kind of competition. In reality, more and more zoologists and ethologists are starting to realize that, for most social species, tolerance and co-operation are at least as important as competition, if not more so.[1]

A competitive species?

In spite of this, much of the current popular literature on animal behaviour gives the impression that competition, whether for resources or for status, is as important to non-human social animals as it is in some human cultures. And all too many people in the horse world share similar beliefs, regardless of whether the evidence actually supports such beliefs. For example, many trainers believe that equine social organization is based on a 'pecking order', and that horses have a responsibility to challenge those above them in the pecking order for leadership. In the words of one trainer, 'there is always a challenge going on between leaders and those being led.'[i]

1 For a very readable discussion of this see Frans de Waal's *Good natured: the origins of right and wrong in humans and other animals*, Harvard University Press 1996.

Some trainers take this idea even further, stating that horses test their relationships with other horses by holding contests over valuable resources such as food, water, etc. In this way of thinking, once a horse has established dominance over another horse (i.e. when the other horse concedes) in respect of each resource being contested, he will go on to challenge other individuals within the herd until he has established himself as either dominant or submissive in respect of every resource, in relation to every horse within the herd.

I mean the above trainers no disrespect when I say that their statements appear to reflect the writers' own fantasies rather than any reality. I have searched the scientific literature and discussed this with people who, like me, have carried out systematic observations of groups of domestic horses, and I can find nothing to support the claims above. As this chapter will show, there is really very little for horses to compete over in the wild. Moreover, the notion that horses hold contests among themselves for status reflects a failure to understand what ethologists mean when they talk about 'rank' in social animals (in all fairness, sometimes even ethologists forget its true meaning). People who put forward ideas of this kind are not describing what actually happens, but rather what they think *should* happen.

Confusion about dominance and 'pecking orders'

Unfortunately, there exists a monumental amount of confusion regarding so-called pecking orders, dominance hierarchies and dominance relationships. It seems that such concepts are so deeply ingrained in some of us that they simply will not go away. They keep on popping up, distorting our ideas about horses and what is important to them. In this instance they plant the false impression in our minds that competition is not only natural to horses, but also an extremely important feature of their social lives. Yet, as we shall see, the evidence tells us otherwise: horses are in fact among the least competitive of social animals.

This is not often recognized because so much of the literature emphasizes aggressive encounters between horses. This may be partly because such encounters are so obvious in comparison with the more subtle interactions which make up the greater part of equine social life. It is also a relic of a time when animal behaviour scientists saw dominance hierarchies as the key to understanding animal societies. At one time almost all studies of animal behaviour were carried out in a captive environment, where human interference affected group size and gender distribution, and where highly unnatural conditions served to distort behaviour. It was not until ethologists started to observe animals in the wild, in their natural surroundings, that they began to realize that animal societies were far more complex than any simplistic model of 'dominance hierarchies' could predict.

What is a 'pecking order'?

Even so, much that was observed was 'shoehorned' into existing theories about hierarchies in animal societies; ethologists were still very much influenced by the pioneering work of the Norwegian scientist Schelderup-Ebbe in the early 1920s. Studying domestic chickens, Schelderup-Ebbe noticed that aggression between any two birds within a flock was a one-way process: if one bird pecked another, the other bird would not respond in kind. Schelderup-Ebbe therefore considered the aggressor to be the 'dominant' individual, and the one on the receiving end of the aggression was labelled the 'subordinate'. He believed that this open aggression was the key to social organization in domestic fowl.

Schelderup-Ebbe called this top-down social organization a 'pecking order', which is how we ended up with a much-misused term, often conjured up indiscriminately to describe virtually any animal society where the writer believes a dominance hierarchy should operate, regardless of whether this is in fact the case.

The 'alpha animal'

Another constantly misused concept which arose from early ethological studies of dominance hierarchies, and which is frequently invoked by trainers of dogs and horses alike, is that of the 'alpha' animal. This derives from a method used to determine dominance hierarchies in social animals. Ethologists using this method observe the number of aggressive interactions that take place within a specific period, then 'rank' the animals in order of the number of threats they have observed being made by each animal. The animal who has made the most threats is labelled the 'alpha' animal; the animal who made the next highest number of threats is classed as the 'beta' animal etc., all the way through the Greek alphabet to omega, if there are enough animals in the group to get that far. It should be obvious that this is an extremely crude and unsatisfactory way of looking at animal societies, not least because it tells us virtually nothing about how the animals in question interact in different social contexts. Nevertheless, it has proved exceptionally enduring, perhaps because it is so simple, and people (being people) like to latch on to simple explanations.

Unfortunately, this liking for simplicity has got us into a terrible muddle when it comes to understanding what is going on in animal societies. Ethologists have a regrettable tendency to write about 'high (or low) ranking' animals; lay persons and writers of popular books and magazine articles on animal behaviour have then latched onto this phraseology and used it as if it describes some equivalent of class in human societies. We even read of daughters 'inheriting' their mother's rank, when what is really being described is a simple 'ranking' in

The horse on the right is driving the other two away, but there is no evidence that he is doing so in order to get them to do anything or go anywhere specific – he may simply want them to move out of his personal space. (L. Skipper)

a hierarchy of aggression, as described above. As young animals will tend to take their lead from their parents, if (say) a mare tends to make a high number of threats towards other horses, then her daughters may well learn this behaviour from her! 'Rank' in this context means nothing more than this simple position in a hierarchy of aggression – and, as I have said, this really tells us nothing useful about how horses relate to each other in different contexts.

In spite of this, the idea of the importance of the 'alpha' animal persists. For decades it has formed the core of much dog training theory; the assumption is that since dogs are descended from wolves, their natural behaviour must parallel that of wolves. According to this theory, dogs would perceive the human family in which they lived as the equivalent of a dog pack. Owners were therefore exhorted to ensure that they achieved – and maintained – the 'alpha' status in the domestic 'pack'. Rigid sets of 'pack rules' were laid down to establish and maintain this status, and much problematical behaviour in dogs was attributed to the owner's failure to achieve and hold 'alpha' status.

However, this theory was based on inadequate observations of wolves in captivity. More recent long-term studies of wolves in the wild have established that wolf packs consist of a family group, that is the breeding pair and their offspring, and their behaviour is different in many key respects from that of the groups of mainly unrelated wolves generally observed in captivity. Hierarchy in such family groups is largely irrelevant. Furthermore Ray Coppinger, who has spent many years studying the behaviour of feral dogs as well as training working dogs for a number of different disciplines, has shown that the behaviour of feral dogs differs greatly from that of wolves, and that the whole concept of 'pack rules' is confused and confusing, not least for the dog.[2]

Towards the end of his life the late pet behaviour counsellor John Fisher, celebrated for his work with problem dogs, began to question much that had been accepted earlier about 'pack rules', and eventually discarded this way of thinking. As he put it in one of his later books, '...if it's how you want to live with your dog I have news that is going to disappoint a lot of people who have striven to reach this Alpha status – it all means diddly squat to your dogs.'[ii]

Like Coppinger, Fisher pointed out the confusion that can arise in a dog's mind when owners attempt to apply the 'pack rules' cited above, especially when these 'rules' are applied too rigidly. Belatedly, more and more dog trainers are starting to realize that this is rather a hit-and-miss way of training dogs, and are looking instead to training programmes based on positive reinforcement – which we shall look at in Chapters 7 and 8.

What about horse trainers, though? It seems that, so far from passing out of favour, training based on the concept of the 'alpha horse' is actually becoming deeply entrenched, thanks largely to the rather uncritical acceptance of this and other ideas about equine society by many trainers, training organizations, authors and equestrian magazines, and hence of the equestrian public. The concepts behind the dog training theory outlined above have basically been reinvented and applied to horses. Some trainers insist that, in order to communicate with horses effectively, we must become the dominant, or alpha, 'horse' of their herd, and that we must always maintain this position.

What is 'dominance'?

When trainers tell us that we must take the place of the dominant horse, it is often extraordinarily difficult to grasp exactly how they want us to do this. Part of the problem is that they do not define adequately what they mean by 'dominant'.

At its simplest, dominance simply means exerting control. Parents do this with their children, just as mares and stallions do with their foals and other youngstock; both may therefore be said to be 'dominant'. We exert control over our horses (or attempt to!), so at this very simple level, we could be said to dominate them. This does not necessarily imply aggression or the use of bullying tactics; domination can be achieved by many means, for example strength of personality, a confident manner, etc. Unfortunately the terms 'dominant' and 'dominance' are seldom used in this simple sense. They have become conflated with

2 See the Coppingers' remarkable book, *Dogs: A New Understanding of Canine Origin, Behavior, and Evolution*, University of Chicago Press 2002.

ideas about social hierarchies, especially about 'pecking orders' based on aggression. To an ethologist, a 'dominance relationship' is one in which one individual always responds submissively to another individual at the start of any aggressive encounter. A 'dominance hierarchy' is simply the order in which these dominance relationships arrange themselves; the idea is that this enables every individual to know his or her place within the society.

Sometimes this hierarchy is a linear one, e.g. A dominates B who in turn dominates C and so on. This is the classical 'pecking order' as described by Schelderup-Ebbe. However, in many animal societies a perfectly linear order is the exception rather than the generality. Thus one might find that A dominates B and B dominates C, but C dominates A; this is known as a 'triangular' relationship.

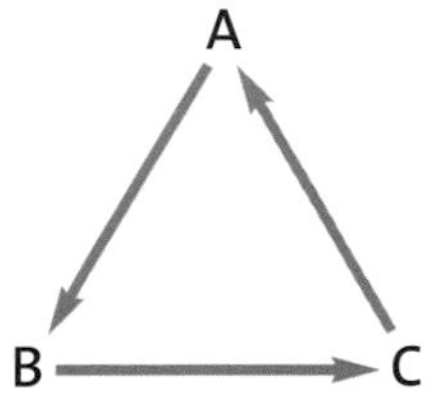

Or, the hierarchy might be partly linear (e.g. A dominates B who dominates C who dominates D; D does not dominate E but E dominates A (but not B, C or D).

This is where ideas about dominance hierarchies start to break down; once we get beyond simple linear or triangular relationships, it all begins to get rather too complicated, so that even trained ethologists with a battery of notebooks are often at a loss to decipher the complexities they find.

It is all too easy, when studying animal societies, to find dominance hierarchies where they do not actually exist; such hierarchies may appear to be a feature of the society in question, when statistically they may in fact represent random patterns of behaviour. Very often, observers see what they expect to see, and ignore anything that does not fit their expectations. There have even been cases where observers have been so convinced that a hierarchy must exist that they have 'tweaked' their figures until a recognizable hierarchy emerges! This is why textbooks on the study of animal behaviour frequently contain warnings to students to beware of being too eager to see such hierarchies in the behaviour they observe.

What role does dominance play?

So what purpose do dominance hierarchies serve? Assumptions usually made are that such hierarchies give dominant animals priority of access to potential mates, food, water, territory, personal space, etc. and serve to reduce levels of aggression within a group; once dominance relationships are established, physical aggression is replaced by threat displays from which the subordinate animal retreats

In addition, dominant animals are often assumed to be leaders – hence the emphasis, on the part of some trainers, on the idea of the trainer assuming the role of the 'alpha' horse.

These ideas do apply to some extent in certain animal societies, although societies based on hierarchies of aggression are by no means as widespread as was once thought. But how – if at all – do they fit into equine society?

Access to potential mates

Let's consider the first point, access to potential mates. The basis of equine society is the family unit, or band. This consists of one, more unusually two, mature stallions, up to five mares (rarely more; the usual range is between two and seven, with four or five representing the median), and their immature offspring. When colts and fillies reach sexual maturity they usually either leave the band voluntarily, or are expelled by the stallion; mares have occasionally been seen to assist the stallion in driving out sexually mature offspring, although this behaviour has not been commonly observed.[3] Sexually mature colts are therefore rarely likely to challenge the stallion for the right to mate with mares within the family group. There are, in any case, powerful inhibitions against mating with parents, offspring or siblings; this seems to be the result of familiarity, especially from an early age, acting to suppress sexual attraction.

This 'weeding out' of sexually mature males does not leave much need for a stallion to exercise dominance within a group in order to gain priority of access to mates. Therefore, the only real challenges to a stallion would normally come from outside the family group, usually from bachelors seeking to supplant the band stallion, less often from a stallion belonging to an existing band.

Writing about male-to-male interactions, i.e. between stallions belonging to different bands, or between stallions and bachelors, Joel Berger notes that '...only when an individual chased the other away was it clear that one was dominant at that time over the other. In 96.5% of the interactions among males I was unable to assign dominance status.'[iii]

So it would appear that stallions challenging or being challenged for access to potential mates are not trying to establish 'dominance' as such, but simply responding to a situation in which they either see an opportunity to acquire potential mates, or in which their family unit is being threatened.

Several studies of feral horse behaviour mention groups which had two

3 Andy Beck of the White Horse Ethology project has reported observing such behaviour in mares, as has Dr Marthe Kiley-Worthington.

Zareeba (left) ran out with his full sister Zarello (right) until he was two years old. (A. Chadfield)

stallions. These were instances where dominance relationships really were of importance, since in every case the nature of their interactions established that one stallion was clearly dominant over the other, and the dominant stallions invariably sired more foals than the subordinates.

So much for stallions and access to mates. But what about mares? Do they gain priority of access to the stallion through being dominant and, if so, how does this affect their reproductive success? To date no clear-cut correlation has been found between dominance and reproductive success. In fact, throughout his five year study of the Granite Range horses, Berger found that only one female in the entire Granite population retained her dominance status, and the number of foals she produced was neither better nor worse than the three other females with whom she associated for four years. Berger concludes that 'In Granite Range horses intraband dominance seems to be of little biological significance and had no effect on female reproductive success.'[iv]

Access to food and water

Very well, then, how about priority of access to food, water, etc.? For some species, food comes in discrete 'packages' (e.g. fruit for apes and monkeys), so one might expect challenges for access to food to be common. However horses' food is all around them, in the form of forage (grass, herbs, and less commonly shrubs and the leaves of trees) and is therefore freely available to all. Berger reported that 'Mares were not often aggressive to those with whom they were familiar...even in early spring when food was most limited and new vegetative growth had not yet begun, few feeding displacements occurred.'[v] This applied regardless of whether the forage was good or poor and these findings reflect those of other studies, i.e. that food shortages rarely increased antagonism among band members. So, left to their own devices, horses do not commonly challenge others over food; it is we who create artificial situations (limited access to grazing; concentrate feed in buckets; insufficient personal space, etc.) in which competition occurs.

Berger did note some jostling at water holes when water was frozen in winter or when it had partially dried up in summer, but in the main aggression between the mares in a band occurred when individuals approached too close to a newborn foal. This is similar to findings reported by Telané Greyling from her observations of the feral horses of the Namib Naukluft Park.[vi] Greyling concludes that 'Dominance in the Namib population ... seemed to be of little importance. No dominance hierarchies could be determined for the mares in groups or individuals in bachelor groups.'[vii] Greyling also notes that, although stallions were able to herd their mares away from other stallions, they were not domineering in any other way.

Food is scarce in the harsh envronment of the Namib Desert, yet the horses do not squabble over patches of grass. (Telané Greyling)

Reduction of aggression

So what role, if any, do dominance hierarchies play? Do they, as is often claimed, serve to reduce aggression? They may do so in some species, but it is debatable whether this is the case where horses are concerned. A dominance hierarchy could only reduce aggression if, once the hierarchy had been established, every animal within it not only knew their place but actually kept to it. This does not necessarily happen, as Chapter 5 will show. And Joel Berger reports that the same females were rarely the consistently dominant members of their bands. He says:

> Dominance relationships changed regularly and most often over periods that spanned a few days to several weeks. Because feeding displacements were rare and dominance changed among individuals, it was difficult if not impossible to assign a 'dominant female' status for intraband hierarchies. In fact the only periods when females consistently dominated others in their bands were after the births of their foals.[viii]

Yet in the popular literature we come up against more muddled thinking. We are told that it is every horse's responsibility to try to climb to the top of the rank ladder – as if they were so many human social climbers. But if, as a number of trainers insist, there is always a challenge going on between leaders and those being led, how can the dominance hierarchy serve to minimize aggression? Surely in such a case there would be continual conflict among the members of the group, which makes nonsense of the idea of a dominance hierarchy acting to reduce aggression. And, as we shall see in Chapter 4, feral groups, and well-integrated domestic groups, do not spend their time in perpetual conflict.

Aggression is often met with by retaliation; here Zareeba responds to aggression from Toska in kind. Human attempts to act like a 'dominant' horse may therefore be dangerous. (L. Skipper)

Identifying hierarchies

We may, if we feel we really must, identify hierarchies of aggression in groups of horses in a domestic setting. I can do so easily with regard to our own horses, by the simple (and very crude) test of making them go hungry, then presenting them with a bucket of feed and seeing who ends up with the bucket. This is how dominance hierarchies have largely been determined in groups of domestic horses. The scientists carrying out such tests are using a species' behaviour in extreme situations which, in the case of horses, would never be encountered in the wild, and then applying their findings to predict that species' normal behaviour. But everyday life is not lived at such extreme levels, so why should behaviour at those levels be cited as the norm?

Nevertheless, if I carry out such a test on my own horses, the resulting hierarchy would look something like this:

α	Imzadi
β	Kruger
γ	Kiri
δ	Tiff
ϵ	Nivalis
ζ	Toska
η	Roxzella
θ	Zareeba

This could certainly help me to decide who is turned out with whom in order to avoid conflict over food. However, it does nothing to inform me how these horses actually relate to each other socially in different contexts. A different situation could well see either a partial or complete reorganization of the hierarchy. For example, in the days before Nivalis fully realized what being a stallion meant, he was usually turned out with the rest of our horses. Now Kruger can be (not to mince words) a bit of a bully and Nivalis would regularly step in to protect his dam, Roxzella, from Kruger's bullying tactics. On one occasion Roxzella was drinking from the large water container in the field. Kruger came barrelling up to her, intent on driving her away from the water. Nivalis promptly stepped between them, his whole posture saying something like, 'Stop right there and there'll be no trouble. Come any closer and I'll pulverize you.' Kruger, who is a whole hand taller than Nivalis and powerfully built into the bargain, did indeed 'stop right there'; in fact, he actually went into reverse, so clear was the message

Kruger (right) is much bigger and more aggressive than Nivalis but, if sufficiently motivated, Nivalis does not hesitate to challenge Kruger. (L. Skipper)

Nivalis was sending out. Nivalis simply stood by until his mother had finished drinking, then quietly moved away, without giving Kruger another glance. So we would be unwise to rely on simple 'dominance hierarchies' derived from one context to predict how horses will behave socially in other situations. I give some examples of this in Chapter 5, when I describe what happened when our group was temporarily split up one year.

Leadership

There remains one possible role for dominance in equine society: the establishment of leadership.

We have here another muddle: the thinking that conflates 'dominance' and 'leadership' and assumes that the most dominant horse (or, if we must have it so, the 'alpha' horse) is the leader. Is there any truth in this?

We can define leadership in different ways, according to context. There is *social leadership*, which is concerned with the maintenance of harmony within the group, and its protection; this almost always falls to the stallion. There is also *spatial leadership*, which governs movement from place to place; a spatial leader decides when and where the group moves throughout its home range. So if the stallion normally takes care of group security, who decides group movements?

Findings vary from study to study. In some groups movement was initiated mainly by older mares, in others by the band stallion; in the latter cases the stallion would usually move the group by herding or actively driving them from behind. All we can really determine is that 'leadership' (however it is defined) may at various times be assumed by mares or stallions.

Regardless of sex, can 'leadership' be assigned to a dominant individual? Thirty years ago, ethologists were warning us not to confuse leadership with dominance: 'An important distinction is to separate true leadership from forcing, and from being first; just because a horse forces others out of his way does not mean that he is the leader, nor is the first one in a walking group necessarily in charge.'[ix] This is borne out by the findings of various studies of feral horses. Joel Berger says that among the bands he observed in the Grand Canyon:

> No one horse served consistently as a leader during walking patterns to or from the spring...the origin of a leader for a walking pattern frequently was the individual that merely assumed the initiative and walked. When others followed, the lead horse continued, but when there were no followers, which often was the case, the horse soon stopped.[x]

Feist and McCullough remark that 'We were unable to determine a hierarchy among the mares of a group with regard to position in movements. However, observed leaders were usually older mares or mares with foals or yearlings',[xi] while Berger, as in his comments quoted above, insists that 'At no time was complete leadership shown for any individual stallion or mare within a band.'[xii]

Various observers have recorded that if a group was alarmed they would all gallop away alongside one another, with no obvious leader; Berger says that when terrain was flat, horses did follow each other, though different horses assumed leadership at different times.

We do not even know whether any horse, setting off, say, on the trail to a watering hole, specifically does so in order to influence the actions of the rest of the band. They may have no such motive; it could simply be the case that they decide to move and the others follow them, possibly because they know from experience that certain horses know where water or the best food can be found. The only member of a band who normally shows unambiguous 'active' leadership (in the sense of deliberately moving the band members around) is the band stallion, although on odd occasions mares have been seen to do this. Otherwise the stallion does not dominate his mares, nor does he compete with them or his offspring for resources.

Submissive behaviour

In the kind of thinking that confuses leadership with dominance, much is often made of submissive behaviour on the part of the horse. However, apart from certain behaviours performed by foals and immature youngsters, horses do not show the kind of appeasement behaviour found in dogs (I will say more about this in Chapter 6). A horse faced with a show of aggression on the part of another horse will do one of two things: either respond to aggression with aggression, or simply move away. If a dominant horse is either met with aggression or avoided, how is this compatible with leadership?

CASE STUDY

Our stallion Nivalis and his mare, Tiff, spend most of their time together. Tiff is confident in her dealings with other horses, and if one really wanted to describe a dominance relationship between the two, one would have to say that Tiff was (marginally) dominant over Nivalis in most situations. She certainly will not take any nonsense from him, although competition between them over limited resources is almost non-existent: they drink from the same water bucket (often at the same time) and eat from the same pile of hay and from the same feed bucket, equally and without squabbles over who gets what. However, when it comes to moving about outside their compound (e.g. going from the compound to the field), Tiff invariably follows Nivalis. In fact we rarely lead her out; Brian tends to lead Nivalis and Tiff simply follows. If Nivalis moves up the field, Tiff goes with him. If he comes back towards the stables, Tiff runs after him.

Tiff and Nivalis live together in harmony; they share piles of hay, eat from the same feed bucket and drink from the same water bucket – often simultaneously! (L. Skipper)

Creating conflict

From all this we can see that horses exercise dominance only with respect to resources such as personal space or access to mates (although in a domestic situation, access to artificially limited resources such as concentrate feed may be an issue). Very often people will tell me that one mare (more rarely a gelding) in a group is 'the boss'. What they really mean in most cases is simply that this horse is the most aggressive! Dominant horses do make other horses move by threatening them, but usually this is simply to get them out of the way, not to get them to go anywhere or do anything specific (and certainly not to teach them anything other than, 'Get out of my way!'). So what exactly does Pat Parelli, for example, mean when he says, 'If more people knew how to relate to their horse as a dominant horse would, there would be a lot more happy horses and happy people'?[xiii] As we have seen, dominance does not equate to leadership, and dominant horses drive other horses away by means of threats – so just how is our behaving like a dominant horse supposed to make horses happy?

The conflict created by such an approach is illustrated by Abigail Hogg in her excellent book *The Horse Behaviour Handbook* (David & Charles, 2003). She points out that, in using the dominance hierarchy principle as a basis for training horses:

> We act aggressively and exert dominance *while keeping the animal with us*. The horse, whose first action is to move away from aggression and who understands that this is what is required of him by the situation, is actually being punished while at the same time being deprived of the ability to carry out the correct course of action.[xiv]

I am quite sure this is not what the trainers who advocate such an approach actually intend. Nevertheless, misconceptions about the nature of equine social relationships can either create problems or make existing problems far worse, by creating precisely the kind of conflict just described.

A muddled approach

Some trainers believe that if we allow horses to make the first move and initiate bodily contact with us, we are allowing them to dominate us. This is like saying that children should never be allowed to ask their parents for a cuddle. Is a child asking her mother for a hug trying to dominate her mother? I imagine that few people would see in the child's action anything more than a child's natural desire for comfort and affection. Horses like physical contact, too: is the horse wanting a scratch or a head-rub really trying to be dominant? People who believe this seem to think that to allow a horse to make the initial approach would be to abdicate our hard-won 'alpha' status and allow the horse to think that he is higher in the 'pecking order' than we are. This parallels the 'pack rules' described earlier in this chapter, and it evidently stems from the belief that when two horses indulge in mutual grooming, it is always the dominant horse who initiates the grooming. Is this true? In my experience it is not; much depends on the context and (as always) on the individual horses concerned. There is also the conflicting belief that mutual grooming is principally a way of reducing or avoiding aggression, so it will be the subordinate who initiates the grooming sessions; this shows how confused and confusing the whole issue really is. Many years ago I used to worry about this, and almost stopped initiating mutual grooming sessions with my horse. Thank goodness I did not, or I would have missed one of the most rewarding experiences one can have with a horse. I stopped worrying when I realized that the experts were in conflict on this matter, and began to suspect that, on this matter at least, few of them really knew what they were talking about! In fact, in most feral bands, virtually any horse may initiate grooming with any other horse and this is what I have found with regard to our own horses.

Our Arabian mare Tiff adores human company, and loves to rub her head all over us and lick not only our faces and hands, but our clothing as well. When she licks the backs of our necks, sticks her head over our shoulders, or rests her chin on the top of a head, is she trying to dominate us, or raise herself above us in some mythical 'pecking order'? Of course she is not. She is simply demonstrating her affection for us and showing us that she enjoys our company. By accepting her affectionate advances, are we relinquishing our place in the hierarchy? No, because there is no hierarchy for us to be part of; Tiff knows perfectly well that we are not horses, and since we are not in competition for a limited resource, there is really nothing to get hierarchical about.

Not just another horse

I do not believe that horses can ever think of people as just other (rather funny-looking) horses. This is not to say that they cannot become extremely attached to us, or that they cannot look to us for guidance and security. But if they were to look on us as conspecifics, all kinds of problems would arise; apart from anything else, it would be downright dangerous. (For more on this subject, see Chapter 9). It is surely far better to concentrate on looking at ways in which we can gain their trust and ensure their co-operation; this is exactly what we will be discussing in Chapters 4 and 5.

I hope this chapter has made it clear that, while we can often (if we look hard enough) identify dominance hierarchies within groups, these are not the social glue that binds these groups together. As we shall see in Chapters 4 and 5, social cohesion comes from bonds of friendship and affection, and from a strong spirit of co-operation. The dominance hierarchies that are so often observed in domestic groups are not an intrinsic feature of equine society, but a response to specific conditions, most commonly the kind of conditions which, through over-

Tiff loves to make contact with her human friends...

...but this is a sign of affection, not dominance. (L. Skipper)

crowding, compel horses constantly to invade each others' personal space. Yet they can still give us information; they can tell us when our management practices leave something to be desired, as well as helping us to decide which combinations of horses are compatible when turned out together. So how can we make use of what we know about equine social organization?

Avoiding conflict

Instead of thinking in terms of dominance and accepting social aggression as inevitable, we should consider how horses would choose to live if we left them to their own devices, and attempt to keep them in conditions which enable them to live in harmony. Wherever possible we should:

- Keep horses in small, compatible groups where they are given a chance to form long-term relationships rather than in large, anonymous, constantly changing herds.
- Ensure that the turnout area or permanent grazing is large enough to enable them to maintain their personal space without constantly having to invade someone else's.
- Make water troughs large enough so that horses are not jostling each other trying to get to the water; if necessary provide more than one trough.
- If hay or haylage is given out in the field, space the piles well apart and put extra piles out.
- If supplementary feed must be given, feed the horses in buckets spaced well apart.

We should also recognize that so-called 'alpha horses' are not usually leaders; they are more often insecure bullies who may make other horses' lives a misery if steps are not taken to prevent this. For more about bullies and anti-social horses, see Chapter 13 and Appendix II.

As far as our personal relationships with horses are concerned, we should bear in mind that – as I have already emphasized – it is highly unlikely that horses see us as other horses. There is no reason why they should attempt to dominate us; we are not in competition with them for some resource. By the same token, they are unlikely to understand any attempts we might make to dominate them and may well respond to such attempts with aggression. In Chapter 4 we shall see why horses usually misbehave and what we can do about it. We shall also see that co-operation, not competition, is the key to equine society, and consider how we can make this work for us.

i Bob Russell, 'Understanding Herd Mentality: Pecking Order', *Classical Riding Club Newsletter No. 14*, Summer 1998.
ii John Fisher, *Diary of a 'Dotty Dog' Doctor*, Alpha Publishing 1998, p.106.
iii Joel Berger, *Wild Horses of the Great Basin*, University of Chicago 1986, p.133.
iv Berger, *Wild Horses of the Great Basin*, p.159.
v Berger, *Wild Horses of the Great Basin*, p.157.
vi Telané Greyling, *The Behavioural Ecology of the Feral Horses in the Namib Naukluft Park*, MSc Thesis, University of Pretoria 1994.
vii Greyling, *The Behavioural Ecology of the Feral Horses in the Namib Naukluft Park.*
viii Berger, *Wild Horses of the Great Basin*, p.158.
ix D.A. Welsh, *Population, behavioral and grazing ecology of the horses of Sable Island*, MSc Thesis, Dalhousie, USA 1973 pp.205–206.
x Joel Berger, 'Organizational systems and dominance in feral horses in the Grand Canyon', *Behavioral Ecology and Sociobiology* no. 2, 1977, p.145.
xi James Feist and Dale R. McCullough, 'Behavior Patterns and Communication in Feral Horses', in *Zeitschrift für Tierpsychologie*, no. 41, 1976, p.358.
xii Berger, 'Organizational systems and dominance in feral horses in the Grand Canyon', p.139.
xiii Pat Parelli, 'Become a Natural Horseman with No Strings Attached', wwwparelli.com, article 12.
xiv Abigail Hogg, *The Horse Behaviour Handbook*, David & Charles 2003, p.87.

CHAPTER 4

Co-operation, not Confrontation

> ...you expect them to do your bidding...because you think you own them; you forget that they are alive, they have an intelligence of their own, and they may not do your bidding...
>
> MICHAEL CRICHTON, *Jurassic Park*

'Anyone who works with a number of horses recognizes how often horses tend to fight. The "togetherness" of horses is marked, above all, by competition and struggle.'[i] This statement by trainer Klaus Ferdinand Hempfling illustrates the way many people think about horses. But is this perception true? Do horses fight a lot, or do we tend to pay too much attention to aggressive interactions simply because they are so easy to spot, whereas more peaceful interactions may go unnoticed?

Analysis of the activities of feral groups shows that less than 1 per cent of the time is taken up by activities such as mating, giving birth, fighting and stallion interaction. And note that this 1 per cent includes all of those activities! This hardly paints a picture of an equine society held together by 'competition and struggle'. Indeed, it is hard to imagine such a society; togetherness does not come from competition and struggle (which tend to create disharmony), but from co-operation and mutual tolerance.

Increased levels of aggression in domestic groups are usually the result of overcrowding and other poor management practices. If the horses in a specific group fight a great deal, this would seem to indicate that something is radically wrong with the social lives of those horses. Rather than seeing this aggression as an organizing feature of equine society when clearly it is not, we should be looking at the management practices which make such conflict inevitable.

Group cohesion

For a prey species such as the horse, group cohesion is necessary for survival. The more experienced members of the group will have essential ecological knowledge, such as where the best feeding sites are, what plants are safe to eat, how to find water at different times of the year (including how to dig for water if necessary, as feral groups have been observed doing), the location of sites offering shelter in bad weather, etc. Social disharmony resulting from aggression among group members could severely hamper the transmission of such ecological knowledge.

Tit-for-tat

In the mid-1990s Dr Marthe Kiley-Worthington carried out a comprehensive, systematic survey of behaviour patterns among her own domestic group. She identified two aspects of this group's social organization which add far more to our understanding of horses than the usual rather rigid concepts of 'dominance': these are the 'tit-for-tat' response, which she likens to Charles Kingsley's famous maxim 'Be-done-by-as-you-did', and the opposite, which encourages co-operation: 'Do-as-you-would-be-done-by'.

Commenting on the findings of this study in her book *Horse Watch – What it is to be Equine*, Dr Kiley-Worthington says, '...the amount of behaviour related to cementing bonds and deflating potential splitting of the group, that is "sticking behaviour" [i.e. cohesive behaviour, L.S.] was 73% and behaviour related to "splitting" was only 26%. Every individual showed over 60% "sticking" behaviour.'[ii] Aggression was responded to mainly with avoidance or ignoring, but in 25% of cases the response was aggression. So it emerges from this study that the predominant friendly actions are what help to keep the group together.

Mutual grooming

Co-operation in horses takes various forms. One of the most obvious examples is that of social grooming, referred to by ethologists as *allogrooming*: this is literally a case of 'You scratch my back, and I'll scratch yours.' Social grooming sessions are among the most important social activities for horses, as indeed they are for many other species. Because of the degree of intimacy involved, social grooming helps to establish and strengthen bonds of attachment. Mothers groom with sons and daughters; siblings groom with each other; stallions groom with their mares and close friends groom with each other.

Such sessions usually involve two horses but, on occasions, three horses may be involved. Sessions may last from as little as a few seconds up to ten or more minutes; two of our horses, Zareeba and Roxzella, have been observed grooming each other for more than twenty minutes. Usually one horse initiates the session; if you spend enough time watching horses it becomes easy to tell when one is soliciting another to groom, as he sidles up to the other and presents the part of the body he wants the other to pay particular attention to. As the other horse responds, the initiator will reciprocate, and the pair will nibble at each other's

Brother and sister allogrooming: Toska (right) and Imzadi. (L. Skipper)

Close friends Zareeba (right) and Roxzella: mutual grooming is an extremely important part of equine social life. (L. Skipper)

coats quite vigorously, using their teeth and lips to remove dirt, loose hair and dead skin. They also use their very mobile muzzles in a side-to-side movement, massaging and stimulating the skin and underlying muscle.

Fly-swishing

A less intimate act, but also very important, is fly-swishing, where horses will stand nose-to-tail, swishing their tails to drive flies away from each other. Sometimes entire groups may be seen like this, often as they doze in the shelter of trees, where flies tend to congregate.

Swishing the tail helps to drive flies away. (L. Skipper)

below When standing in the shade of trees where flies may gather, groups of horses will often swish flies away from each other, like the Namib horses in this photograph. (Telané Greyling)

Keeping watch

When horses sleep lying down they are at their most vulnerable; their bulk makes it difficult for them to get up quickly, giving potential predators an advantage of precious seconds before the horse can make his escape. For this reason groups of horses seldom all lie down together (although I have occasionally seen this in stable domestic groups); usually at least one horse remains standing to keep a look-out for danger. Mares stand over foals, stallions often stand over sleeping mares and I have often seen individual horses standing guard over close companions.

These are the most obvious examples of how horses co-operate with each other to their mutual benefit. However, feral horses, and those kept in natural family groups, afford many more instances of co-operative behaviour.

Stallion alliances

One of the most intriguing examples found in feral groups is that of the two-stallion band, referred to in Chapter 3. During his five-year study of the horses of the Granite Range, Joel Berger recorded no less than seventeen instances of this phenomenon. He dubbed these stallion relationships 'alliances', since the

When a group of horses lies down to rest there is usually at least one horse who remains standing, probably acting as a lookout.

two stallions worked together to defend their group of mares from rivals. As mentioned in Chapter 3, these were instances where being the dominant member in a relationship really did pay off. This was not only because the dominant stallion was able to sire more foals, but also because the subordinate stallion invariably did more to protect the group from rival males than the dominant stallion did. This meant that the dominant stallion was less likely to be injured in aggressive encounters than the subordinate. Nevertheless, both stallions would risk injury to aid each other; they would form defensive alliances to protect their group against intruders.

In most cases the subordinate stallion had either very limited access to the mares in the group, or none at all. Yet these stallions risked injury to defend the group, even though they derived little or no benefit from doing so. This probably explains why most such alliances were short-lived; only two in Berger's study exceeded seven months in duration, while the remaining two lasted two-and-a-half years and at least four years respectively. Even so, the fact that such alliances exist at all tells us a great deal about horses' ability to co-operate with each other.

Other observers have noted similar alliances between stallions. Opportunities for such alliances among domestic horses are obviously rare, yet situations do occur in which one can see a faint echo of such a relationship. Our own stallion Nivalis was integrated into our group consisting of mares and geldings until he reached sexual maturity, when increased aggression towards the geldings meant that he had to be separated from them. It would have been better for him if we had been able to keep him with the geldings, well away from any mares; however with our set-up it was not possible, as the mares would always be too near for comfort. So for several years Nivalis was turned out on his own. However, he was not isolated; when in his stable he could touch noses with the mare Tiff and we frequently allowed Nivalis's dam Roxzella to move freely about the yard, at which time she would invariably wander over to her son to socialize with him. Although far from ideal, this arrangement did at least mean that he continued to have contact with his own kind, and he remained well adjusted and in good spirits.

However, he did tend to worry when the mares went out of his sight; he made this obvious by becoming restless and inattentive when we were trying to work with him. By monitoring his changes of mood closely, I discovered that if he knew that Zareeba, my Arabian gelding, was with the mares, he did not become agitated; it was as if he felt they were safe with Zareeba and therefore he could relax. I have speculated (although I cannot prove it) that he recognizes stallion-like behaviour in Zareeba (of which I shall say more in Chapter 12), and that he knows (having observed him do so on several occasions) that Zareeba will defend the mares from any real or perceived threat from intruders. So although this is not really the same kind of alliance as those observed by Berger and others, it does at least suggest that Nivalis considers Zareeba to be a possible ally.

In fact, stallions are among the most co-operative of all domestic animals. Andy Beck has written of his humbling experiences with the stallions who form part of his White Horse Ethology project in New Zealand; when population pressures made it necessary for Andy to separate some of the mares from the main groups, these stallions not only made no attempt to prevent him from doing do, but appeared to be actively assisting him in moving the mares about.

Co-operation among mares

Apart from mutual grooming and fly-swishing, co-operative behaviour among mares is not as obvious as that between stallions. Yet sometimes mares will put themselves at risk in order to protect other members of their group. In feral groups that have been taken over by a rival stallion, the new stallion may subject the mares to sexual harassment; this may be partly because so many males who take over existing bands are sexually inexperienced bachelors who have never held a group before, and so do not know how to go on. At such times the other mares will often come to the aid of the mare who is being harassed and drive away the stallion.

Baby-sitting

In domestic groups there is seldom any need for such assistance as just described, since such groups are hardly likely to be subject to a take-over by a stallion. However, mares may co-operate in more subtle ways. I have known of numerous instances of barren mares taking over the role of protecting the foals of other mares in a domestic group, as well as numerous examples of 'baby-sitting'; I described examples of this in my book *Inside Your Horse's Mind*. Among feral and free-ranging groups even colts will sometimes take over the baby-sitting role, and among our own horses Zareeba has frequently assumed such a role.

There is usually a limit to this baby-sitting role in that mares do not readily allow the foals of other mares to suckle them, and will often reject quite violently the advances of foals who have strayed away from their own mothers. Nevertheless, numerous exceptions to this have been seen in both feral and domestic groups. D.A. Welsh describes how a foal, separated from his group during clashes between several groups and bachelor stallions, joined another group. He tried to suckle from one of the mares and was initially rebuffed, but this mare later adopted him and in time was seen allowing both her own foal and the adopted foal to suckle.[iii] Also, a member of the Equine Behaviour Forum reported in 1999 that in ten years of breeding Quarter Horses she had never had fewer than two mares in any given season who would allow other mares' foals to take milk from them. On one occasion she observed a foal suckle from three separate mares![iv] Other members have reported similar observations, which tend to suggest that this phenomenon may be far more common than is generally supposed.

Adopting an orphaned foal

Andy Beck describes the adoption of Eric, an orphaned foal, by a bachelor stallion named Risqué in his experimental herd. To begin with Andy was unsure how this mature stallion would react to the companionship of a foal, but Risqué rose to the occasion magnificently. He took his responsibilities so seriously that he would abandon his grazing activities to stand over Eric, keeping watch over him as he slept after a feed. Andy Beck remarks, 'The two show every sign of having achieved a relationship very similar to that which occurs between sire and foal within a harem group, but with the extra element that, on occasion, it is Eric that stands watch over Risqué while he takes a nap!'[v]

The adoption of foals by bachelor stallions has been documented elsewhere. For example, the foal mentioned in Welsh's account cited earlier in this chapter was later observed to leave the band with another foal; these two were later adopted by a bachelor stallion. Telané Greyling notes a similar occurrence among the Namib horses: a four-week-old colt foal became separated from his mother; he was herded and accompanied by a bachelor stallion for a day before being reunited with his mother.

Guarding a mare and foal

Perhaps the most fascinating account of co-operative behaviour comes once again from Andy Beck, who describes the events following the birth of a foal in his free-ranging herd. The stallion, having kept watch over the mare all night, was resting on the ground; the mare and foal stood nearby, while one of the senior mares (sister of the mare who had just foaled) stood guard over the group. Eventually, all the curious youngsters were allowed to come and see the new foal, but this was done in an orderly manner, with each visitor taking care to keep back if the new mother showed any signs of annoyance at their presence. The mare and her foal stayed at the centre of the group for the rest of the day and during all that time the senior mares and the stallion continued to protect her from any possible threats.[vi]

This surely illustrates just how well the members of a fully integrated group get on together and interact, and demonstrates how the model of equine society as characterized by competition and struggle is at the very least inadequate and misleading.

Social facilitation

As we saw in Chapter 3, the old idea that equine society is controlled by one animal, the alpha or 'boss' animal who directs all a group's movements, is really hopelessly inaccurate, and in terms of explaining how horses co-operate with each other it is not very helpful. But, in the absence of such an animal, what social dynamic causes horses to move around as a group?

In *Dogs*, cited in Chapter 3, Ray Coppinger points out that sled dogs run because the other dogs in the team run. This is a phenomenon which ethologists call *social facilitation*; it can be observed in humans and most other social animals as well, and it is the reason why certain types of advertising are particularly successful. If we see someone eating or drinking something that looks delicious, we may find ourselves wanting to eat or drink even if we are not particularly hungry or thirsty. In other words, the actions of others influence us to want to do the same. This is more likely to be the case if the actions in question are in some way internally rewarding, or if they serve to get the animal or human out of trouble, for example in escaping from danger which may be perceived by only one member of a group.

Social facilitation helps to explain why horses tend to follow others (and us!). We can see this process at work when one horse in a group sets off to walk in a particular direction and the others follow. As we saw in Chapter 3, this movement can be started by any member of a group; however, among feral horses, the rest of the group are more likely to follow if the horse initiating the movement is either the stallion or an older, more experienced mare. Among humans, this tendency to follow the movement of a group has been explained by the probability that those following assume that those initiating the movement have some information which causes them to start moving in a specific direction. It is quite possible that the same applies to horses; this would explain why, when the horse initiating the movement is a younger, less experienced member of the group, the rest may follow only so far and then resume grazing; they may conclude that the initiator may not be worth following, perhaps being too inexperienced to have information worth acting on.

We can see, then, that rather than adopt an attitude of dominance, which would only make our horses want to remove themselves from our presence, we should work towards gaining their co-operation by building up trust and a liking for our company, so that they want to be with us, feel safe with us and regard us as beings whose judgement is to be relied upon. In order to do this we must first recognize that the way we behave towards our horses affects the way in which they behave towards us. In other words, behaviour breeds behaviour.

Behaviour breeds behaviour

This may sound like a cliché, but it happens to be true. If someone is rude or unpleasant, we tend to react negatively. Similarly, if we expect someone to behave badly, we ourselves will very often behave in such a manner that our body language, tone of voice, choice of words, etc. set up a reaction in the other person which provokes the very behaviour we expect. By creating the right conditions for this to happen, we bring about the very event we anticipate. This is often referred to as a 'self-fulfilling prophecy'.

We then feel justified in our prior belief that this person was bound to behave badly. This might or might not have been true, but by making it almost inevitable we have prevented any possibility of an alternative. It might well be that if we approached this person in a positive or even neutral manner we could defuse any tendencies for them to behave badly. This is, of course, by no means an infallible approach, because some people are unable to respond to positive approaches. However, it works often enough for us to adopt it as a working principle, and deal with those cases where it breaks down on an individual basis.

If all this is true of people, it is even truer of horses. Their phenomenal ability to read body language, even that of other species, is discussed further in Chapter 6. If we approach them in a bossy, coercive manner, we are likely to provoke a distinctly negative reaction! Since horses are naturally co-operative creatures it is up to us to create the conditions in which they want to co-operate with us. They seldom make mistakes in reading the behaviour of others, which makes it essential for us to approach them with the right attitude. This attitude is, above all, a positive one.

A positive attitude

Adopting this positive attitude involves discarding some of our ideas about horses. All too often, humans class a horse's failure to co-operate with them as 'naughtiness'. The horse does not want to move forward: 'He's being naughty'. 'She was naughty today; she bucked me off.' 'He was being really naughty today; he wouldn't pick his feet up for the farrier.' And so on. One definition of naughty is 'mischievous and disobedient'. Horses may often be disobedient, but are they necessarily being mischievous in disobeying? Is this an example of projecting human values and expectations onto them?

Take, for example, the horse who will not move forward under saddle. Is he being disobedient, and therefore naughty? If we take the view that horses are under an obligation to obey our wishes, and that they should realize and accept this, then the answer is probably 'Yes'. But are they under any such obligation? Do we really have the right to demand, and expect, obedience from them? More and more people are starting to question the extent to which we should exploit animals just because we can. But even if we believe (as some people do) that we have some God-given right to dominate horses and bend them to our will, how can the horse be expected to know this? We have seen how very unlikely it is that horses have any concept of anyone being the 'boss'; that being so, why on earth should they give us their obedience just because we want them to do so?

So instead of saying, 'He's being naughty' when our horse won't pick his feet up, move forward, stand still to be mounted, etc., we should be asking *why* he is refusing to do these things.

CASE HISTORY

An Arabian gelding showed severe behavioural problems under saddle. His bucking fits and nappy behaviour appeared to be caused by a bad temper and lack of willingness, but veterinary examination revealed that he had bone spavin (a degenerative disease of the hock) in both hocks and so was in considerable pain when ridden. This horse was fortunate that his owner was not prepared to accept assurances from so-called experts that his behaviour was simply naughtiness and an unwillingness to work, and he is now on the way to becoming sound again.

First rule out physical pain

The rule followed by all genuine equine behaviour experts is this: always consider and if possible rule out physical pain as a cause before seeking psychological explanations for difficult and unco-operative behaviour. Any animal in pain is likely to be difficult; even cats, with their high pain threshold, can be extremely awkward patients. Horses generally have a much lower pain threshold than cats and, unlike dogs, they do not vocalize their pain – it might be better for them if they did yelp like dogs when hurt!

Horses tend to respond to externally-produced pain by withdrawing from whatever they perceive has hurt them. So, for example, a horse who has been hurt by harsh use of the bit is likely to try to avoid being bridled; in the same way a horse hurt by an ill-fitting saddle may try to avoid having the saddle put on. In some cases difficult behaviour may be caused by the *memory* of physical pain. A horse previously ridden on a harsh contact or with a severe bit may still try to avoid contact with the bit even when he is later ridden by a sensitive rider with gentle hands; in cases like this gradual re-education is the answer. This might seem obvious when put like this, but it is surprising how many people will automatically assume, not that the horse is in pain (or remembers and anticipates pain), but that he is just being difficult!

Be realistic

In spite of – or perhaps because of – all the new training methods that have sprung up in the last few decades, it seems that many people are not content with accepting the horse *as a horse*. As Emma Kurrels puts it, 'There are more problem horses today or to put it correctly horses with problems than there have ever been. Why? It could be argued that the demand for 'bomb proof' or totally desensitized horses is on the increase which has opened a Pandora's box of "methods".' [vii]

No matter how great the degree of understanding there might be between you and your horse, never forget that he is still a horse, and that you have on your hands a creature endowed not only with very acute senses but with an extremely highly developed sense of self-preservation and lightning-fast reflexes.

Some of the methods demonstrated by certain trainers have sometimes resulted in unrealistic expectations on the part of devotees of those trainers. Many of them end up believing that, unless their horse behaves perfectly at all times, they have somehow failed. We certainly want our horse to have good manners and to be calm and confident, so that he does not continually spook at imaginary monsters in the hedge, or panic whenever anything unusual happens. But reactivity is so much a part of the horse's psychological make-up that the only way we could overcome it completely would be to suppress every aspect of behaviour that makes a horse a horse and not some other mammal. Attempts to create the 'super-obedient' horse can result in the use of oppressive methods even where such oppression is not the intention. Horses trained by such methods can end up in a state of perpetual anxiety, unable to relax for fear of making a mistake; thus they may perform mechanically, with all spontaneity trained out of them. A horse is not a machine – and indeed we would not want him to be!

Laying down the basis for liking, trust and co-operation

Horses like a quiet life. They dislike confrontation and seek to make life as comfortable as possible for themselves. If they are asked to perform a task that they find difficult, frightening, uncomfortable or incomprehensible, they may either resist (if that is easier than complying) or do nothing (even easier). If we accept that they have no concept of us as 'boss' and there is no reason why they should feel a sense of obligation to us, then we can see that they do not resist or fail to comply with our demands simply to annoy us or make us look foolish; they do so because it is the easiest option for them. So, if we want them to co-operate with us in ways that make life more challenging for them, we must find some means of making their co-operation rewarding for them. Methods of doing this are given in Chapters 7 and 8, but before we can make use of them fully we have to lay the foundations for training by establishing a good relationship. We can do this by establishing ourselves as someone the horse can trust. This means:

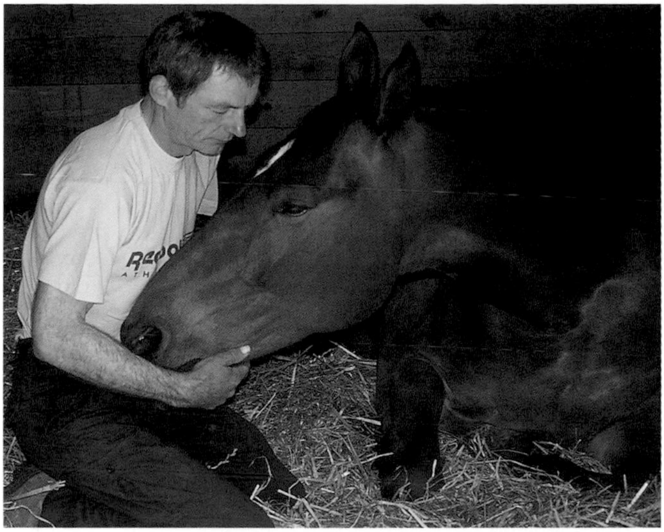

Horses are at their most vulnerable when lying down, so allowing another horse (or, in this case, a human) to approach this close is a great sign of trust. Toska is devoted to Brian, who was present at his birth and has looked after him all his life. (L. Skipper)

- Behaving towards him as we would like him to behave towards us, with consideration and respect for personal space, never treating him roughly or with impatience.
- Remaining calm and confident, even in a frightening situation.
- Making it easy for him to co-operate with us by understanding what he finds difficult and helping him to overcome difficulties.
- Never 'ambushing' him by asking him to do something for which he is unprepared.
- Never insisting that he does something which frightens him without first tackling the reason for the fear.
- Being fair: never punishing him unjustly, i.e. for doing something he could not avoid, such as bucking because he lost his balance (giving him the benefit of the doubt is never as bad as injustice).
- Being clear about what we are asking; *we* may know what we mean but does the horse?

If you are experiencing a problem with getting your horse to co-operate, first of all – after having eliminated pain as a cause – try to break the problem down into its component parts. Ask yourself:

- What you are trying to achieve.
- How you are going about trying to achieve it.
- Whether you are looking at the problem from a human point of view rather than the horse's.

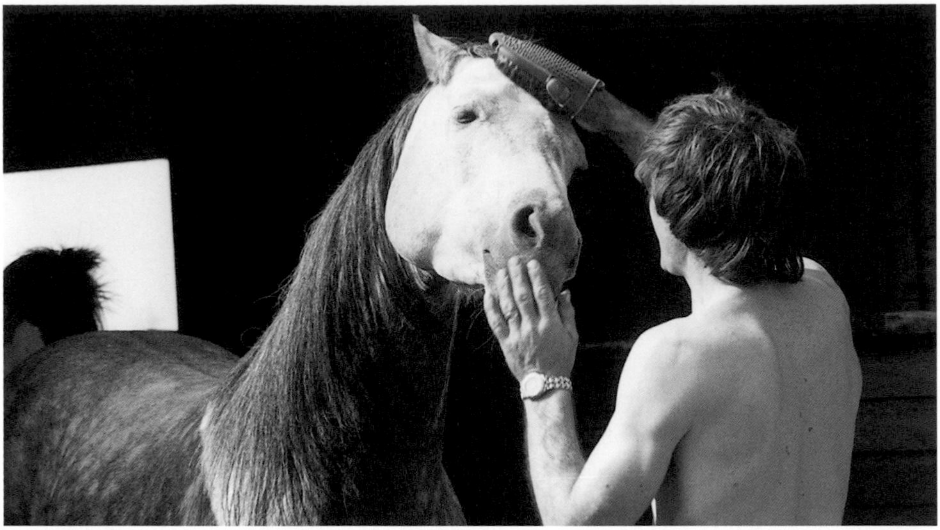

Nivalis's relationship with Brian means that he will stand to be groomed in the stable yard without any kind of restraint, even though there is a very attractive mare in the stable behind him! (L. Skipper)

You need to have great faith and trust in your horse in order to do something like this, especially with a stallion! Please do *not* try this yourself; Brian and Nivalis have a special relationship based on mutual trust and respect but there is still a considerable risk involved in actions like this. (L. Skipper)

- How the horse might see the problem.
- What actions he has to perform in order to comply.
- Whether these actions might be difficult for him.
- How you are asking him to perform an action or behaviour – if you were asked to carry out a specific task by someone speaking a foreign language which you did not understand, how successful do you think you would be? Chapters 7 and 8 give guidance on *shaping* actions and behaviours.

Tables 2a and 2b (see pages 66–69) list some common problems that arise out of co-operation issues, and suggest possible causes and some possible solutions.

Some commonly experienced problems and possible solutions are also given in Appendix II. These are by no means exhaustive, as discussion of all the possibilities would take a book in itself. However, by applying the problem-solving principles outlined above, and using the information gained in this and other chapters, as well as other sources, you should be able to analyse problems not covered here and develop a logical approach to dealing with them.

You will see that I have included in the tables columns for 'Possible causes' and 'Possible but less likely causes'. I have deliberately not included a column for 'Impossible causes' (i.e. factors that can be ruled out), because we simply do not know enough about what may be going on in horses' heads to be able to rule out possibilities. (By this I do not mean that all things are possible, just that we do not yet know for sure what the full range of possibilities may be.)

Avoiding problems

So many of the problems people experience with horses could be avoided or eliminated if only they would realize that a lack of co-operation usually stems from ignorance about what we are asking, fear, discomfort or actual pain. Horses try to tell us, in the only ways they can, that they simply cannot perform as we are asking them to. Confrontation leads to tension and stress, which in turn makes learning difficult and creates resistances. As Marthe Kiley-Worthington observes:

> The remarkable thing about equines is that, if there is sufficient knowledge and sensitivity about what annoys them in their associations with humans, and efforts are made to reduce the irritation, they become extraordinarily co-operative. Instead of being passive sufferers having to perform particular tasks by domination and fear, as many believe they are, they can become willing volunteers, participating in activities together with humans with enthusiasm, sometimes even making informed judgements to improve the way to achieve certain goals...If however no effort is made by humans to recognize and to try to reduce the cause of irritation, they will quickly become more and more difficult and unco-operative – just like humans.[viii]

i Klaus Ferdinand Hempfling, *Dancing With Horses: Communication by body language*, (tr. Kristina McCormack), J.A. Allen 2001, p.51.
ii Kiley-Worthington, *Horse Watch – What it is to be Equine*, J.A. Allen 2005, pp.269–270.
iii D.A. Welsh, *Population, behavioral and grazing ecology of the horses of Sable Island*, p. 220.
iv Amy Coffman, 'Stranger Things have Happened', *Equine Behaviour*, Summer 1999, p.4.
v Andy Beck, White Horse Ethology Project website, www.equine-behavior.com.
vi Andy Beck, White Horse Ethology Project website.
vii Emma Kurrels, www.companyofhorses.com, article, Problems and Perceptions.
viii Kiley-Worthington, *Horse Watch – What it is to be Equine*, pp.208–209.

Table 2a

Some common problems with handling and management; possible causes, less likely causes; some possible solutions

Problem	Possible causes	Possible but less likely causes
Aggression towards other horses.	Fear of other horses (inadequate socialization or bad experience with another horse).	Innate viciousness (rare, although rogues do occur).
Agression towards humans	Pain or discomfort; previous bad experience.	Innate viciousness (rare); lack of respect for handler.
Barging or turning in when being led.	Horse has never been taught to lead properly; insecurity; over-eagerness to go somewhere.	Lack of respect for handler; attempt to dominate handler.
Biting.	Fear; insecurity; bid for attention; boredom; lack of basic manners.	Lack of respect for handler; attempt to dominate handler.
Difficulties with clipping.	Fear of clippers; dislike of the sensation; memory of pain or discomfort caused by clumsy clipping in the past.	
Difficulties tacking up/head shyness.	Pain, or the memory of pain; sensitivity; previous rough handling when being tacked up.	Lack of respect for handler.
Kicking stable wall/banging on door.	Excitement; impatience, usually at feed times; frustration at being cooped up in stable.	
Problems leaving companions.	Insecurity.	
Pulls back when tied up.	Horse has never learned to accept being tied up; fear of being tied up; insecurity.	Lack of respect.
Pushing/crowding.	Horse has never learned proper manners; insecurity.	Lack of respect for handler; attempt to dominate handler.
Refusal to load into horsebox or trailer.	Bad previous experience, either loading or travelling; fear of confined spaces; fear of slipping on ramp; fear of, or dislike of, unstable surface.	Lack of respect for handler.
Refusal to stand still for the farrier.	Previous bad experience with farrier; lack of balance; fear of, or dislike of, having feet picked up and held.	Lack of respect for handler.

Remedial action	Further reference
Re-socialization.	Chapter 13 and Appendix II; Dr Marthe Kiley-Worthington, *Horse Watch: What it is to be Equine*, J.A. Allen 2005, Chapter 12.
Have the horse thoroughly checked over by a vet for possible causes of pain or discomfort; build up trust (see Chapter 4) and use positive reinforcement to make the horse's experience with humans as pleasant as possible.	Chapters 4, 7 and 8 (see under Positive Reinforcement in Chapter 7).
Lead bargy horses out before other horses so that they do not become too excited; behaviour modification (see Chapter 7); see also Chapter 9, where I describe teaching foals to lead.	Chapters 7 and 9.
Extinction; behaviour modification (but always try to discover and eliminate the cause – see Chapter 7).	Chapters 7 and 8; Karen Pryor, *Don't Shoot the Dog*, Bantam Books 1999.
Teach horse to accept clippers very gradually, using habituation together with positive reinforcement.	Chapters 7 and 8 (for Positive Reinforcement); Alexandra Kurland, *Clicker Training for Horses*, Ringpress ed. 2001; Kelly Marks, *Perfect Manners*, Ebury Press 2002.
Check tack fitting, especially saddle; have the horse's back, neck and legs checked over by a vet; have his mouth examined by an equine dentist to check for pain caused by tooth problems or bitting problems caused by mouth conformation; take great care and be tactful when tacking up.	Lesley Skipper, *Realize Your Horse's True Potential*, J.A. Allen 2003 Chapter 7.
Extinction; behaviour modification (but always try to discover and eliminate the cause – see Chapter 7); change in management routine to reduce frustration.	Chapters 7 and 8.
Habituation (see Chapter 7); increase horse's confidence about leaving his companions.	Chapters 4, 5 and 7.
Establish trust and mutual respect (Chapter 4); learn to read the signs that he is about to pull back (increase in tension) and untie him before he reaches that point. Teach him to tolerate being tied up for very short periods, working up to longer spells (habituation; see Chapter 7).	Chapters 4, 7 and 9
Establish trust and mutual respect (Chapter 4); teach horse to touch a target (Chapter 7) then use this to get him to move around and to step away from you as described in Chapter 8 (read Chapter 7 first).	Chapters 4, 7 and 9.
Try to establish the root of the fear or dislike and remove or minimize the cause; make it easier for the horse to go into the horsebox or trailer.	Appendix II.
See Appendix II; also Chapters 7 and 8 for ideas about teaching the horse to accept having his feet picked up using positive reinforcement.	Chapters 7 and 8 (for Positive Reinforcement) and Appendix II.

Table 2b

Some common problems with training; possible causes, less likely causes; some possible solutions

Problem	Possible causes	Possible but less likely causes
Bucking.	Over-freshness; pain or irritation under the saddle; loss of balance.	Naughtiness; thinking of the rider as a predator on the horse's back.
Cold-backed.	Sensitivity; vaso-vagal syncope (fainting).	Back problems.
Crookedness.	Lack of suppleness and schooling.	Conformation (all horses are crooked to some degree but in most cases this can be minimized by correct schooling).
Ducking out of jumps.	Fear of jumping; over-faced; over-jumped, leading to sourness.	Naughtiness.
Head-tossing.	Discomfort from bit; pain from teeth; ear abscess or infection; pain in back and neck.	Naughtiness; unwillingness to work.
Hollowing.	Poor rider position; lack of strength in back and neck; badly-fitting saddle.	Basic conformation.
Napping.	Insecurity; fear of leaving companions and security of familiar ground.	Naughtiness; lack of respect for rider.
Not standing still to be mounted.	Previous experience of rider's toe prodding horse's side when mounting; saddle pulled out of position when rider mounts.	Naughtiness; thinking of the rider as a predator on the horse's back.
Opening mouth.	Pain or discomfort from bit.	Conformation of mouth.
Pulling.	Discomfort from bit; poor rider position.	
Rearing.	Pain, especially in the mouth, neck or back; over-freshness; unwillingness to go forward (see under Refusing or reluctance to go forward).	Naughtiness; stubbornness; lack of respect for rider; innate viciousness.
Refusing or reluctance to go forward.	Pain (almost anywhere in the body); fear of loss of balance under rider (especially in green horses or those recovering from injury); lack of energy.	Naughtiness; stubbornness; lack of respect for rider.
Resistance to the bit.	Pain from bit; pain from teeth; lack of strength in neck and back.	Stubbornness; mouth and other conformation problems.
Resistance to the leg.	'Switched-off' because of poor/contradictory use of rider aids.	Stubbornness.
Won't stop.	Poor/contradictory use of rider aids causing confusion over what is required.	Naughtiness; lack of respect for rider.

Remedial action	Further reference
Check tack fitting, especially saddle; have the horse's back, neck and legs checked over by a vet; go back to basics on the lunge to build up muscle strength and tone and improve balance; ensure that horse's diet gives him sufficient energy; if bucking is linked to freshness, ensure the horse has sufficient exercise and regular work; check rider position and capability.	Susan McBane, *The Illustrated Guide to Horse Tack*, David & Charles 1992; Lesley Skipper, *Realize Your Horse's True Potential*, J. A. Allen 2003 Chapter 9. .
Walk around in hand or lunge lightly before tacking up, to raise the heart rate slightly; take extra care when tacking up, doing the girth up very gradually; if symptoms persist ask vet to check horse's heart for irregularities.	
Correct riding and schooling.	Chapter 8; Sylvia Loch, *The Classical Seat*, Horse's Mouth Publications, 2003; Sylvia Loch, *Dressage in Lightness*, J. A. Allen 2000; Karin Blignault, *Successful Schooling*, J. A. Allen 1997; Lesley Skipper, *Realize Your Horse's True Potential* J. A. Allen 2003.
Give the horse a complete rest from jumping for several months. Go back to basics and start by working over poles on the ground, progressing to small cross-poles, and building up very gradually to higher jumps.	Lesley Skipper, *Realize Your Horse's True Potential*, J. A. Allen 2003 Chapter 9.
Have teeth checked and make sure the bit is fitted correctly; correct riding and schooling.	As for Crookedness, above.
Improve rider position; check fitting of tack, especially saddle; have the horse's back, neck and legs checked over by a vet; go back to basics on the lunge to build up muscle strength and tone and improve balance.	As for Crookedness, above.
Build up trust between horse and rider; increase horse's confidence about leaving his companions.	Chapters 4 and 5.
Take care when mounting not to dig your toe in the horse's side or pull the saddle out of position; use a mounting block or have a leg up wherever possible; retrain your horse using positive reinforcement.	Chapters 7 and 8; Alexandra Kurland, *Clicker Training for Horses*, Ringpress ed., 2001.
As for Head-tossing, above.	Lesley Skipper, *Realize Your Horse's True Potential*, J. A. Allen 2003 Chapter 7; see also under Hollowing.
Have teeth checked and make sure the bit is fitted correctly; correct riding and schooling.	Lesley Skipper, *Realize Your Horse's True Potential*, J. A. Allen 2003 Chapter 7; see also under Hollowing.
Check fitting of tack, especially saddle; have the horse's back, neck and legs checked over by a vet; go back to basics on the lunge to build up muscle strength and tone and improve balance; ensure horse's diet gives him sufficient energy (or reduce high-energy feed if horse is over-fresh).	Lesley Skipper, *Realize Your Horse's True Potential*, J. A. Allen 2003 Chapter 7; see also under Hollowing.
As for Rearing, above	As for Rearing, above; Lesley Skipper, *Realize Your Horse's True Potential*, J. A. Allen 2003 Chapter 7 for suggestions about bitting.
Have horse's teeth checked; check the fit of the bit and that it is not too severe; go back to basics to build up muscle strength and tone and improve balance.	Lesley Skipper, *Realize Your Horse's True Potential*, J. A. Allen 2003 Chapter 7.
Correct riding and schooling.	Chapter 8; as for Resistance to the bit.
Correct riding and schooling.	As above; Lesley Skipper, *Realize Your Horse's True Potential*, J. A. Allen 2003 Chapter 10.

Chapter 5

Friends and Companions

Horses are forever saying goodbye.

Richard Adams, *Traveller*

When horses are left entirely to their own devices (i.e. with minimal or no interference from humans), equine society is far more dynamic in structure than many people realize. It is certainly not the static organization beloved of many trainers!

Family bonds

On our small private yard we are fortunate in having several family groups. Although – with one exception – these are not directly comparable to the kind of family groups found in feral horses, they do enable us to observe the dynamic nature of the relationships between stable groups of closely related horses. The exception is the family group consisting of the stallion Nivalis and the mare Tiff (Mikenah) and their colt foal, Tariel. Although this group is smaller than the average feral family band, families of this size do occur, especially in places like the Namib Desert.

The family relationships are shown in Figure 5. All of these horses have been together for most or all of their lives, apart from Tiff, who came to us in 1998 at the age of seven. She fitted in straight away, with only a very minimal settling-in period. All the horses accepted her without fuss and within a matter of days it was as if she had been with us for years.

Family bonds can endure for many years. Dr Marthe Kiley-Worthington cites the case of her stallion Oberlix and his daughter Shemal, who have lived together on and off for more than four years. Because of the inhibitions against incest

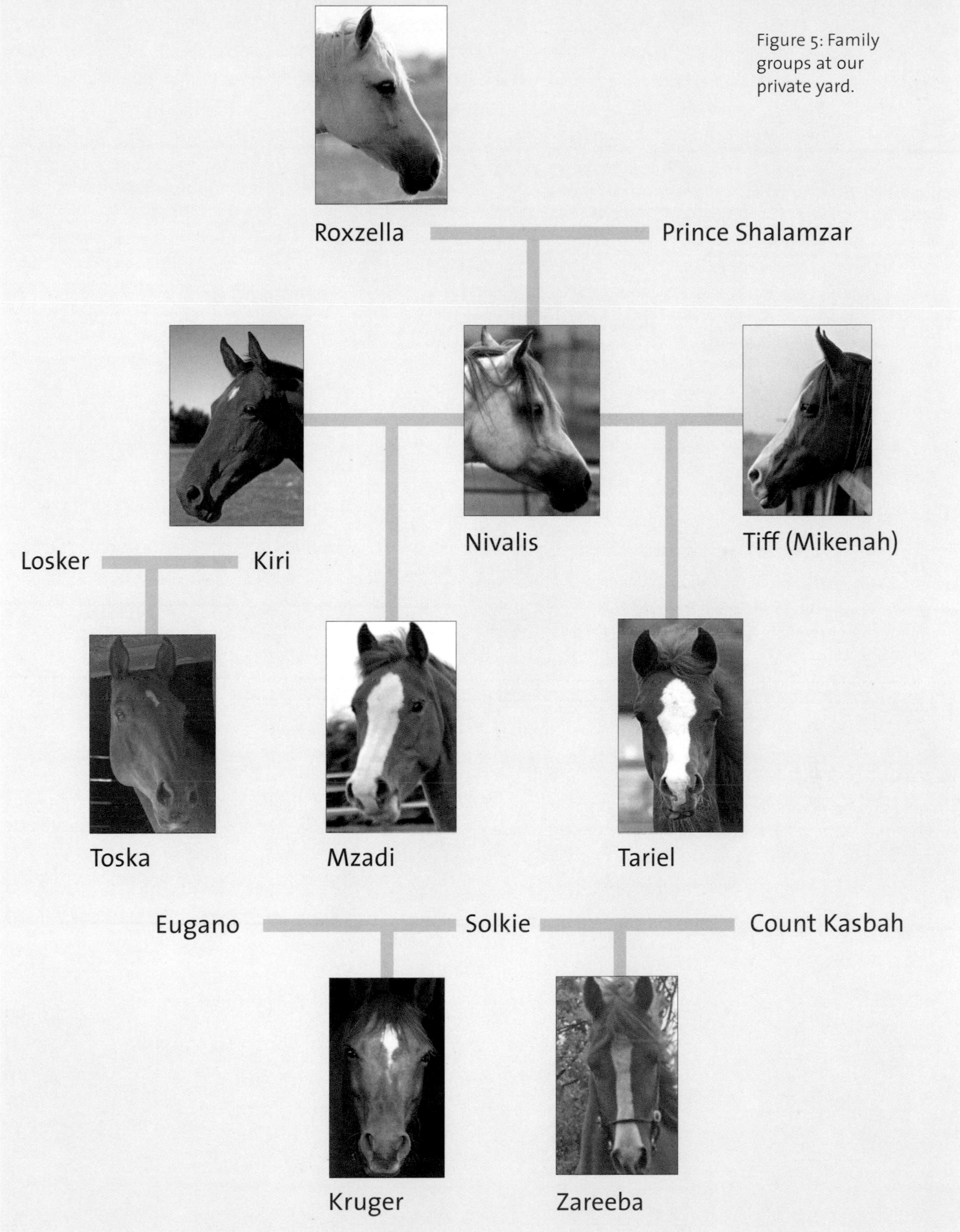

Figure 5: Family groups at our private yard.

referred to in Chapter 3 they are not particularly attracted to each other sexually, but they remain close companions and friends. If our stallion Nivalis is in one of the stables when his dam Roxzella wanders into the yard, she will usually go straight over to him to say hello and sometimes to indulge in some mutual grooming. Our home-bred mare Imzadi is still very attached to her dam Kiri – so much so that she was still taking milk from her mother at the age of five! Imzadi's half-brother Toska is also still fond of his dam and when the horses are

Mothers and sons may groom each other: Nivalis and Roxzella indulge in mutual grooming over the stable door. (L. Skipper)

Mares and their offspring may retain strong bonds of affection; Imzadi and her dam Kiri are still very close to each other. (L. Skipper)

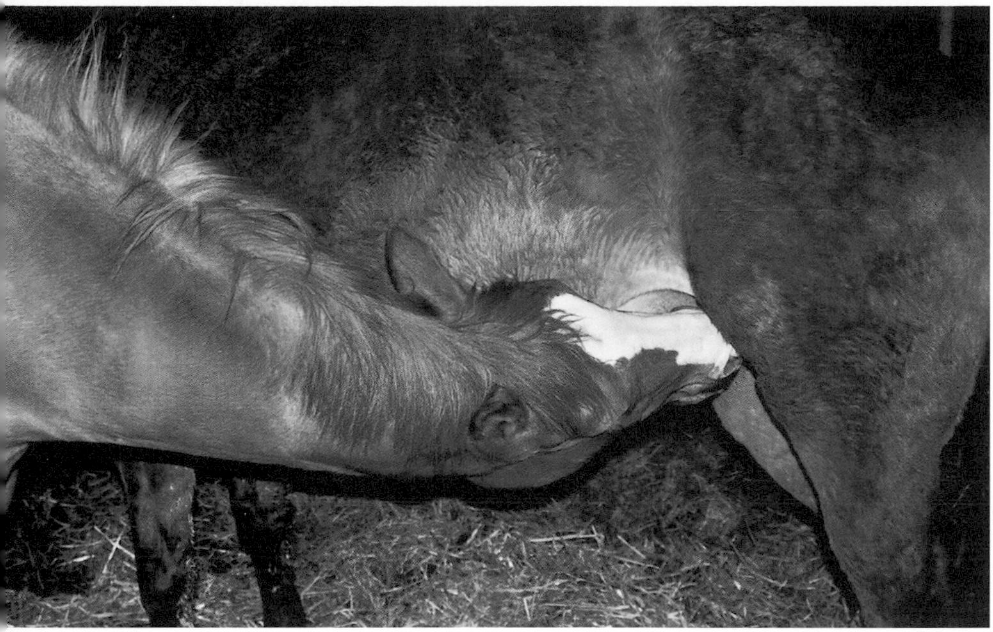

Imzadi was still taking milk from her mother at the age of five. (L. Skipper)

turned out at night in the summer Kiri and Toska will often lie down close to each other.

Such bonds of affection frequently survive prolonged separation. I acquired my Arabian gelding Zareeba when he was two years old; his half-brother Kruger came to us two years later when Kruger was three years old. Before they were separated they were always together; on the day we brought Kruger home he and Zareeba appeared overjoyed to be reunited. A friend bought Anna, an Arabian filly, direct from her breeder. Several years later she acquired Anna's dam; when the latter and her daughter were reunited it was as if they had never been apart.

Pair bonds?

This raises the question of a term frequently encountered, especially in the pages of popular equestrian magazines and Internet discussion groups: *pair bond*. The received wisdom in such circles seems to be that horses will pair-bond (some sources say for life) with another horse of the same sex and similar age, although the phenomenon is sometimes reported as occurring between members of the opposite sex, i.e. mares and geldings. But is this use of the term accurate?

One dictionary definition of 'pair bond', which seems to correspond to the sense in which an ethologist might use it, is 'the exclusive relationship formed between a male and a female, esp. in some species of animals and birds, during courtship and breeding'.[i] According to this definition, it would only occasionally apply to horses. However, it all seems to depend on who is using the term and in what context!

If it is used to mean nothing more than the fact that horses do become very attached to other individuals, and spend much of their time grazing and grooming, and doing all the other things horses do when at liberty with that other individual (or individuals), then we would have to say that yes, horses do pair-bond; but that is using the term in a very loose and possibly misleading manner. If it is used to mean that horses associate exclusively with one other individual, then that certainly occurs sometimes, but seems to be a response to local conditions or traumatic events rather than something that occurs normally in feral horses. Writing about the Namib horses, Telané Greyling observes:

> I have seen strong bonds occasionally between a specific mare and stallion, two bachelor stallions, some youngsters, etc. These bonds or rather friendships are strong but not inseparable (like in humans) and mostly formed due to specific circumstances. Some last for long periods (10 years in my study this far) with 'break-ups' from time to time, others last for shorter periods of 2–4 years, especially young bachelors…horses form friendships which differ from horse to horse regarding the intensity, in other words some horses like to have a close friend and others are 'loners'.[ii]

My observations of our own horses bear out Telané's conclusions; several of them have very strong ties of affection with one or more of the others, but in no way could one describe these relationships as 'exclusive'. So when trainers teach that horses 'pair-bond', they should really define what they mean more clearly –and use the term correctly! Andy Beck of the White Horse Ethology Project has suggested that 'social bond' might be substituted for 'pair bond'; I think this would be a far better, and more accurate, term to use.

Excessive attachment

One of the biggest problems for horse owners arises out of this equine need for friendship. The problem pages of equestrian magazines abound with pleas for help regarding horses who exhibit signs of great distress, sometimes amounting to hysteria, on being separated from a close friend. In some cases this reaction may occur even if the separation is of quite short duration, say only a very few minutes. One prominent 'natural horsemanship' trainer recommends habituating horses to separation from their companions by tying them up for between four and eight hours. I find this suggestion disturbing, not to say dangerous. I know that in the days of being used for transport horses frequently had to stand tied up for long periods, but the fact that it was done then is no reason why it has to be done now, especially in the name of lessening distress! The trainer concerned does not specify whether any forage or water is to be made available, or whether he expects someone to observe the horse during this time to check for signs of distress and to be on hand in case of an accident.

All our horses accept being tied up very well, but they get bored after a relatively short time; Kruger and Toska in particular are past masters at untying knots and wandering off in search of food and/or entertainment. Furthermore, a horse tied up is extremely vulnerable to accidents; I have heard of horrific accidents in which a tied-up horse has been frightened by something, pulled back and broken his neck (or, in one case, snapped his rope, fallen on concrete and fractured his skull). No matter how much one tries to anticipate such accidents, and remove possible hazards, a tied-up horse (no matter how well behaved) is an accident waiting to happen if left for more than a very short time.

When Kruger sustained a temporary radial nerve paralysis some years ago, we had to leave him tied up (on the vet's advice) for several nights to prevent him from lying down and being unable to get up again, until he was able to move his foreleg once more. We were so worried for his safety that we spent some sleepless nights making frequent checks on him! This is virtually the only occasion when I would leave a horse tied up for any length of time, i.e. when circumstances make it absolutely necessary. In the context of habituating a horse to being separated from his companions I cannot see that it would do anything other than replace one kind of distress with another, so please, think twice before trying this or any similar 'remedies'!

CASE HISTORY

I was once asked for advice on this very matter by a lady with a mare who was extremely insecure. The mare had been a broodmare and it was possible that her foals had been taken away from her too early and too abruptly. If taken away from the other horses she became extremely anxious; when brought in from the field to her stable on her own she called loudly and kicked the stable walls. If left in the field on her own she galloped around and sweated up until one of the other horses was put in with her.

I made the following suggestions:

- Bringing another horse in from the field with her and keeping that horse close by within sight.
- Not leaving her in the field on her own, at least initially; another horse to be kept with her until the others returned.
- Putting her in an adjoining paddock, first of all with another horse and then, if she reacted well, on her own, so that she remained in sight of the other horses.

- Once she had become accustomed to that, and was happy to be separated from them but within sight of them, moving her out of sight of them for very brief periods.
- When she realized that she was not going to be permanently separated from the other horses, she would hopefully grow accustomed to the idea that being apart from them was not such a bad idea after all. The periods when she was separated from the other horses could then be gradually extended until she was spending longer and longer away from them.
- As she became used to being away from the other horses for extended periods, she could be put out in the field on her own, again for very brief periods to begin with, and again making sure that at least one other horse was turned out very soon after the mare was put out. These spells in the field on her own to be extended little by little until her confidence in this respect was built up.

I stressed the importance of doing all this very gradually and that the main thing was to reassure her that she and her companions were not going to be separated permanently.

Five months later the mare's owner informed me that she had taken my advice and the mare was now confident enough to stand in the yard on her own. It may take longer to restore her confidence fully, but this does show how adopting a gradual, sympathetic approach can work even with extremely anxious horses. To make this even more effective, we add positive reinforcement. This would involve something that the horse found pleasant, e.g. every time the mare in the case cited remained quiet when separated from her companions for a specific period, she could be given some food, a scratch or whatever gave her pleasure. This could then be extended until she was only being rewarded for being quiet for longer periods (see Chapter 7 for a fuller discussion of this).

Losing a companion

If horses can form strong attachments and remember each other even after long separations, how do they feel when they lose a companion? It is widely assumed, not only by scientists but by horse owners generally, that horses do not grieve over dead companions. Indeed, animals in general are thought to have no concept of death, this being (we are told) a uniquely human attribute.

However, as with so many assumptions, this one becomes less and less convincing the more we learn about animal behaviour. Elephants appear to have some concept of death; they have been observed covering the bodies of other elephants who had just died in something akin to a burial ritual, and whenever they come across the bones of an elephant they always stop and examine them, as if trying to recognize the deceased as an individual. It may be that other species, too, behave in such a fashion; it could simply be that we have not yet observed such behaviour.

Equine grief

As far as horses are concerned, their apparent lack of grief following the death of a companion (or, in the case of a mare, at the death of a foal) is generally taken to mean that they do not feel such emotions. However, the fact that horses do not display overt grief does not mean they do not feel it. There is a considerable amount of anecdotal evidence to suggest that mares, in particular, and sometimes stallions too, do feel the loss of their offspring very keenly. In my earlier book *Inside Your Horse's Mind* I cited the case of a stallion who showed great distress when the mare he was running with gave birth to a premature foal who died almost immediately. When the farmer whose field the horses lived in went to bury the foal, the stallion tried to protect the body by preventing the farmer from carrying out the burial.

Andy Beck, of the White Horse Ethology Project in New Zealand, tells of a remarkable event that can only be described as bereavement behaviour. Andy is a careful observer, not given to flights of fancy, who evaluates evidence critically and as objectively as anyone can. During the second year of the Project, three foals died within seventy-two hours of each other; all three were only a short distance apart. Andy, deeply distressed by the deaths, made long and frequent observation visits to the group over the next few days, on the lookout for any signs of illness among the remaining youngsters. He describes what he saw during his visits:

> The dams of the dead foals, the stallion and all mares that did not have a foal at foot, surrounded the dead foals at a distance of some four to five meters, and there they stayed. For three consecutive days and nights, the group remained in watch over the bodies, leaving only to drink, after which they returned to take up their vigil once again. At no time did I witness any of the group taking time off to graze. At the end of three days, the group dispersed and went back about their normal activities, and at this stage I moved in with a spade and buried the small remains.[iii]

Such behaviour in the wild could be dangerous because, as Andy points out, the smell of decomposing bodies could well attract scavenging predators. Furthermore, if the illness had been contagious, it would put the rest of the group at risk. However, the similarity between elephant bereavement behaviour and that shown by Andy's horses was remarkable; the whole group participated, and the behaviour lasted for approximately the same length of time. Andy was struck by the fact that in many human cultures the mourning period was very similar. This made him wonder whether this meant that, in many species, it may take around three days for individuals to come to terms with their loss.

Andy began to ask other breeders whether they had observed similar behaviour in mares who has lost foals, but found that in most cases the foal was taken away and buried almost immediately following the death. However, two breeders did confirm that they had seen such behaviour in mares; they added that at the end of the period the mares seemed to have accepted their loss and were no longer visibly depressed.

As Andy points out, vets would normally advise removing the dead foal and burying it immediately, and of course if there is a risk of infection spreading, this would be the correct course of action. If, however, horses need to mourn for a few days in order to come to terms with their loss, Andy suggests that it might be kinder to leave the body until the mare (or companion) no longer shows an interest in it. As he further points out, if the dead foal is taken away too quickly, the mare may come to associate its loss with the person removing it.

Looking back to the case of the stallion who tried to prevent the farmer from burying his foal's dead body, one wonders whether he, too – and his mare – simply needed time to mourn the loss of their offspring. Andy Beck goes on to say:

> All the circumstances of the three deaths in the herd left me with unanswered and, quite possibly unanswerable, questions about equine behavior, but I well remember, and always will, the atmosphere of mutual grief and support for the three mares, and I have never witnessed a human funeral that touched me more deeply. Such gentle, civilized creatures, such palpable and dignified grief. Any glib assumptions about equine society that I may have been prepared to make beforehand were banished forever, and I was left feeling humbled, chastened, and greatly privileged to have been allowed to share in their grieving process.[iv]

Separating friends and family

All of this should make us think very carefully about the many ways in which we routinely break up equine families and separate devoted companions. This is a fact of equine life; even in the wild, where families may stay together for many years, some separations are necessary, for example when colts and fillies leave the family group. However, this is not necessarily an abrupt separation and there is always a chance that they will meet their families again. This is seldom the case in a domestic situation. When we separate foals from their mothers or adult horses from their companions, they may feel acute distress. Horses who move around a lot in their lifetime may learn to accept this separation from friends; in some cases they do not stay in the same surroundings long enough to form deep attachments. Just like humans, certain horses cope with this much better than others. Those who do not cope well may become withdrawn and may seem to lack personality. Sometimes they develop behavioural problems which are often misdiagnosed as being caused by a defective temperament.

Horses moving to new homes deserve consideration. Being uprooted is traumatic for them; in the process they lose everything that is familiar to them. Before I acquired my Arabian gelding Zareeba, then two years old, he had never left the place where he was born or been parted from his sister and half-brother. Going to a new home was therefore quite traumatic for him. On first being turned out he raced up and down, calling out in the hope of hearing a familiar voice in reply. With tactful handling and a suitable companion he soon settled in, but I shall never forget his initial distress on arriving at a strange place. Tiff, on the other hand, travelled more than 400 miles from Cornwall and settled in almost immediately. Even so, we made every effort to ensure that she felt comfortable in her new surroundings, and did not ask anything of her until she was properly settled.

Re-establishing a social order

Part of the mythology surrounding the idea that equine society is shaped by 'dominance hierarchies' is the notion that every time horses are added to, or removed from, a group, the whole 'pecking order' has to be sorted out again. Some people go so far as to maintain that this is the case even when a horse is taken out of the field for a relatively short time, say an hour or so, and that this is a major source of disruption among domestic groups.

It is certainly true that in yards where horses are constantly coming and going, the resulting social disruption can cause problems. However, this does not seem to be the case where the groups in question have been stable for a considerable time and where all the horses in a group know each other well. I have observed the horses belonging to livery clients of the riding stables next door for many years now. Most of them have been together for a number of years, they all know each other well and there have been comparatively few subtractions from or additions to the group. When one of the horses is taken out of the field to be ridden, his return is greeted with interest, but certainly not with any kind of aggression. In fact in twelve years of systematic observation of the horses next door, I can honestly say that I have not seen anything remotely resembling the re-establishing of the social order referred to above.

The same is true of our own horses. In 2002 one of our geldings, Toska, went away on loan to a young eventer who hoped to accomplish great things with him. At the same time we were offered the use of a field just across the road from our yard, an offer which we took up eagerly, being (like so many people in the UK) short of grazing land. Three of our mares (Kiri, Roxzella and Tiff) were put in the field over the road; this left four horses in the yard. Our fourth mare, Imzadi, was then on box rest because of a bout of laminitis; at night she had the company of her father, Nivalis, while the remaining geldings Kruger and his half-brother Zareeba were turned out together. That year Kruger and Zareeba re-kindled their early close relationship, and for several weeks the two of them were out at pasture – the first time in almost twelve years that they had been out together without any other horses.

Once Imzadi had recovered from her laminitis she was allowed very limited access to grazing, so we turned her out with Kruger and Zareeba. The latter, normally the most peaceful, easy-going horse one could find, immediately went for her, and chased her with real aggression. Every time she attempted to go near Kruger, Zareeba would chase her away, ears flat back and teeth bared. Imzadi who, as we saw in Chapter 3, is normally the most aggressive of our horses, simply fled. Zareeba's behaviour was so out of character that it would have been puzzling, except for the fact that he was so obviously trying to protect Kruger, just as he had done many years before when Kruger first came to us. This overrode his previous relationship with Imzadi; whereas at one time he would have simply avoided her, he now challenged her with such force that she immediately backed down.

My husband, concerned about the mare, brought her in again and turned her out away from the boys. Then, a couple of weeks later, we put Zareeba and Kruger out with the mares in the field across the road, as the grazing was better there. This time it was Kruger who was aggressive towards the other horses, driving them away every time they attempted to go near Zareeba. If Zareeba strayed too close to the others, Kruger would step in and herd him away from them. Eventually they settled down and Kruger allowed the other horses to get near Zareeba, but there was no sign of the original groupings I had observed over a period of years.

When the autumn rains came, we moved the horses back to our own land. On being turned out together again, they ran around excitedly for a while then settled down to graze. Zareeba and Roxzella, who had stayed apart from each other while in the other field, resumed their previous close friendship, engaging in mutual grooming for prolonged spells. However, when Imzadi made a move towards her grandmother Roxzella with the apparent intention of grooming, Zareeba immediately went for Imzadi, just as he had done several weeks earlier. Every time she attempted to approach the group, Zareeba chased her away aggressively and would not let her near any of the other horses. The interesting thing is that he would let her graze near him, and at one point they were grazing side by side; he would just not let her near the others. However, the next day, when they were all turned out together again after being in all night, Zareeba completely ignored Imzadi, and the horses all resumed their former relationships.

Shortly after this, things got even more interesting. Toska had then been away on loan with his young eventer for four months. Because the eventer had sustained a serious injury, Toska came back to us prematurely. He was born at our stables and prior to going away on loan had never left our yard, so he grew up with all but one of our horses from birth (the exception being Tiff, who came to us when Toska was three years old). According to the theories referred to earlier, Toska's return to the group after such a length of time should have resulted in a major disruption of the group, as they would then have to re-establish their 'pecking order'. So what happened when we turned Toska out with the others again? Absolutely nothing, except that one by one the others all came up to him to make sure it was really him – after a quick sniff (which was not accompanied

Imzadi (left) remains indifferent while Roxzella and Zareeba look on as Toska settles back in to his former life after an absence of four months. They accepted his return without fuss but with obvious curiosity. (L. Skipper)

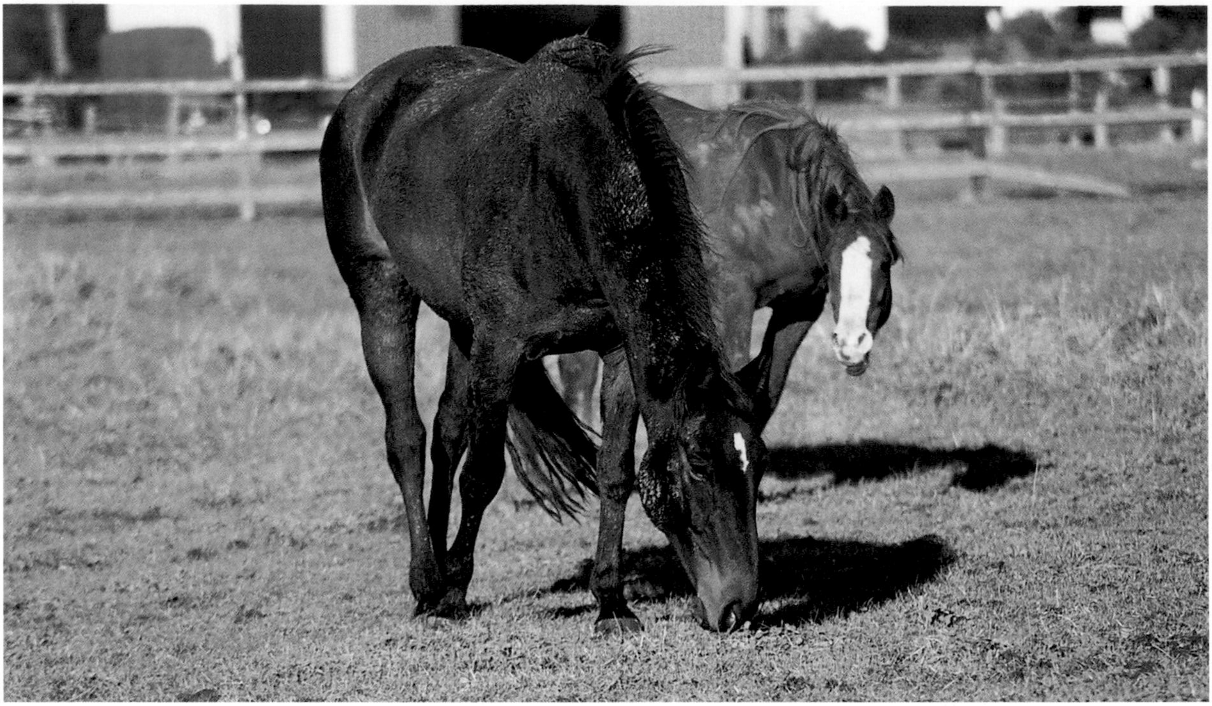

Toska's return after an absence of four months: Tiff looks at him as if to say, 'Is it really you?' (L. Skipper)

by any aggressive overtures, not even any squealing), they all settled down to graze together as if Toska had never been away.

These events reinforce the view that equine social relationships are far too complex to fit into some simple-minded 'hierarchical' scheme. It also suggests (a point also made by zoologist Telané Greyling) that a different environment has an effect on relationships: the relationships changed when the horses were in a strange field, and reverted to their previous forms when the horses returned to their normal environment.

Keeping disruptions to a minimum

What can we learn from all this? If we want our horses to remain healthy, we should keep disruptions to a minimum if we can. Such disruptions, if they happen too frequently, cause stress, which can have a detrimental effect on a horse's health. If changes are unavoidable, we should make them as gradual as possible, and – as always – take into account each horse's personality. The longer a group has been together, the more likely it is that they will get on well together and that minor disruptions will not affect them too much. On the other hand, major changes may cause them a great deal of stress. This does not mean that we should keep moving horses around so that this does not happen; that would be worse than anything. It just means being aware of what change can mean to such long-established groups.

Allowing time to adjust

It can be very traumatic for a horse to move from one home to another, especially since people may have widely differing ideas about how horses should be managed and trained. Horses are adaptable: this is one reason why humans have found it so easy to tame and train them. However, this adaptability is not limitless and horses can still suffer while they make the necessary adjustments. If you are acquiring a new horse, or moving one from one yard to another, I would suggest that you try as far as possible to find a yard where the regime (if there is one!) is as similar as possible to the one the horse is leaving (unless of course he has been kept in bad conditions), and make any changes slowly. This may be difficult or even impossible in some cases, but I think we should make the effort to render any major changes as gradual as practical. Some horses appear indifferent to change; these are very often the ones who have had numerous owners or a variety of different stabling arrangements. However, others who change owners or livery yards a lot can be made quite anxious and insecure by so many changes: as always, get to know your horse (and, as far as possible, his past history) before making any assumptions about what will or will not suit him.

I would certainly allow horses a lengthy period of adjustment before expecting them to do any demanding work. Problems often surface after a horse has been in his new home for two or three weeks; people find that the calm, steady horse they tried out before purchase has turned into a bucking, rearing monster. Suspicion falls on the vendor: was the horse doped when being tried out? This suspicion may very occasionally be justified, but the horse's change of personality is much more likely to be caused by the trauma of being moved. The initial reaction may be apathy, sometimes followed by something like the explosive behaviour just described. Before assuming *anything* in such a case, I would give the horse the benefit of the doubt and allow him time (several weeks at least, although some horses need several months to a year before they really settle in) to grow accustomed to his new surroundings.

It pays to find out as much as possible about how a new horse has been managed, trained and ridden in the past; one may not always get completely frank answers, but it is always worth trying! The more one finds out, the easier it will be to introduce the horse (gradually, of course) to a different way of doing things.

Contented horses

The natural gregariousness of horses and their ability to form close, often long-term relationships, can work for us. If they are contented in their relationships with other horses they are more likely to remain healthy and to feel relaxed enough to work well with *us*. They may not see us as other horses but they are capable of seeing us as friends and companions, whose company they enjoy and whom they like to please. We should take the time and effort to let them do this; horses with whom we have taken the trouble to forge relationships seldom forget us. My friend Joanne was very close to our stallion Nivalis when he was a foal, as

When Nivalis was a foal, he and Joanne were devoted to each other; Nivalis was just five months old when this was taken. (L. Skipper)

Now that Nivalis is a mature stallion, he and Joanne retain their affection for each other. (L. Skipper)

the photograph on page 84 shows. When the time came to back him, it was Joanne who first sat on his back and it was with her that he took his first steps under saddle. He may not see her for years at a time, but whenever she appears at the stables he greets her with every appearance of delight in welcoming an old friend. Relationships matter to horses!

i *Collins Dictionary of the English Language*, 2nd ed. 1986, p.1104, entry under *pair bond*.
ii Telané Greyling, personal communication 2004.
iii Andy Beck, White Horse Ethology Project website, www.equine-behavior.com.
iv Andy Beck, White Horse Ethology Project website.

CHAPTER 6

Talking Together

'When I use a word,' Humpty Dumpty said, in rather a scornful tone, 'it means just what I choose it to mean – neither more nor less.'

LEWIS CARROLL, *Through the Looking Glass*

A look at the various training methods purporting to be based on natural horse behaviour shows that they are all, to a greater or lesser extent, founded on communication using the horse's language: by this I mean *body language.*

Psychologists have been interested in body language and what it conveys for decades. However, they have mostly concentrated on human body language. Ethologists, for their part, are more concerned with how animals communicate with conspecifics; comparatively little work has been carried out on cross-species communication. In spite of claims made by various trainers, equine body language is still poorly understood, with varying interpretations being put forth to explain different gestures and expressions. Some interpretations are clearly far-fetched, while others may be influenced by prior assumptions. So can we really use body language to talk to our horses? And if we can, how do we know whether what we are conveying to them is actually what we think we are saying?

Equine vocalizations

In Chapter 4 I said that in some ways it might be better for horses if they yelped like dogs when hurt. In a domestic situation this could certainly be the case; however, in the wild it could work against them, as a predator hearing a horse call out in pain would be alerted to the possibility of prey in distress. Horses in extreme agony do sometimes scream; perhaps by that time they are in such a bad way that, in the wild, a relatively swift dispatch by a predator would be better than prolonged suffering.

Unlike many other animals, horses make comparatively little use of their voices, in spite of the variety of neighs and whinnies that film and TV programme makers seem to feel obliged to include in their soundtracks whenever horses are featured. They do, however, have a wide range of vocal sounds – but how and when these are used depends very much on context and so they defy attempts to classify them neatly and assign specific meanings to them. Neighs and whinnies, for example, seem to be used mainly to communicate when horses are out of sight of each other. Each horse has a distinctive voice, and in my earlier book *Inside Your Horse's Mind* I speculated that this might serve as a form of identification, so that horses hearing the voice of another horse they know well enough can recognize that individual. I can always tell which of our horses is calling out, even from two fields away! This is not to say that I know exactly what they are saying to each other; it may be the equivalent of, 'Is anybody there?', 'Who's there?', 'I am here', or it could be a form of greeting. Several of our horses always whinny to us when we arrive at the yard; it may mean nothing more than 'About time, where's my bloody breakfast?', but it is still pleasant to have one's presence acknowledged. Horses may give soft nickers when they want to attract attention; when my husband is sorting out the haynets, the stallion Nivalis invariably gives a low nicker to let Brian know he wants some more hay, even though he already has plenty!

Equine body language

In general, though, equine communication is carried out by means of subtle body language. Anyone who spends any time around horses quickly learns to interpret the more obvious signs, for example the flattened ears which denote annoyance and, when accompanied by rolling eyes and bared teeth, mean real aggression and a possible bite or kick. Less apparent are the signs of tension and distress; these may be nothing more obvious than a tightening of the skin around the eyes and mouth. On the other hand, if the horse is feeling good he will look generally alert, with bright eyes and ears pricked. Ears flopping sideways are usually a sign of relaxation; ears turned slightly back (as opposed to flattened back) indicate attention to something behind or slightly behind the horse; this is often seen in ridden horses, where it is sometimes mistaken for annoyance or fear. The horse's entire bearing must be taken into account before you make any judgement regarding this! (For comprehensive descriptions of equine communication, with splendid photographs and drawings illustrating many nuances of equine body language and facial expressions, see George H. Waring's *Horse Behavior*, first published in 1983 but reissued by the publishers in the late

Signs of tension are apparent in this horse's expression: the head is raised, his eyes rolled back and his muzzle is tight and extended. This Welsh Cob stallion was alarmed by the presence of another stallion close behind him. (L. Skipper)

The older horse on the right is clearly saying to the bumptious colt (Nivalis as a yearling), 'Go away!' (L. Skipper)

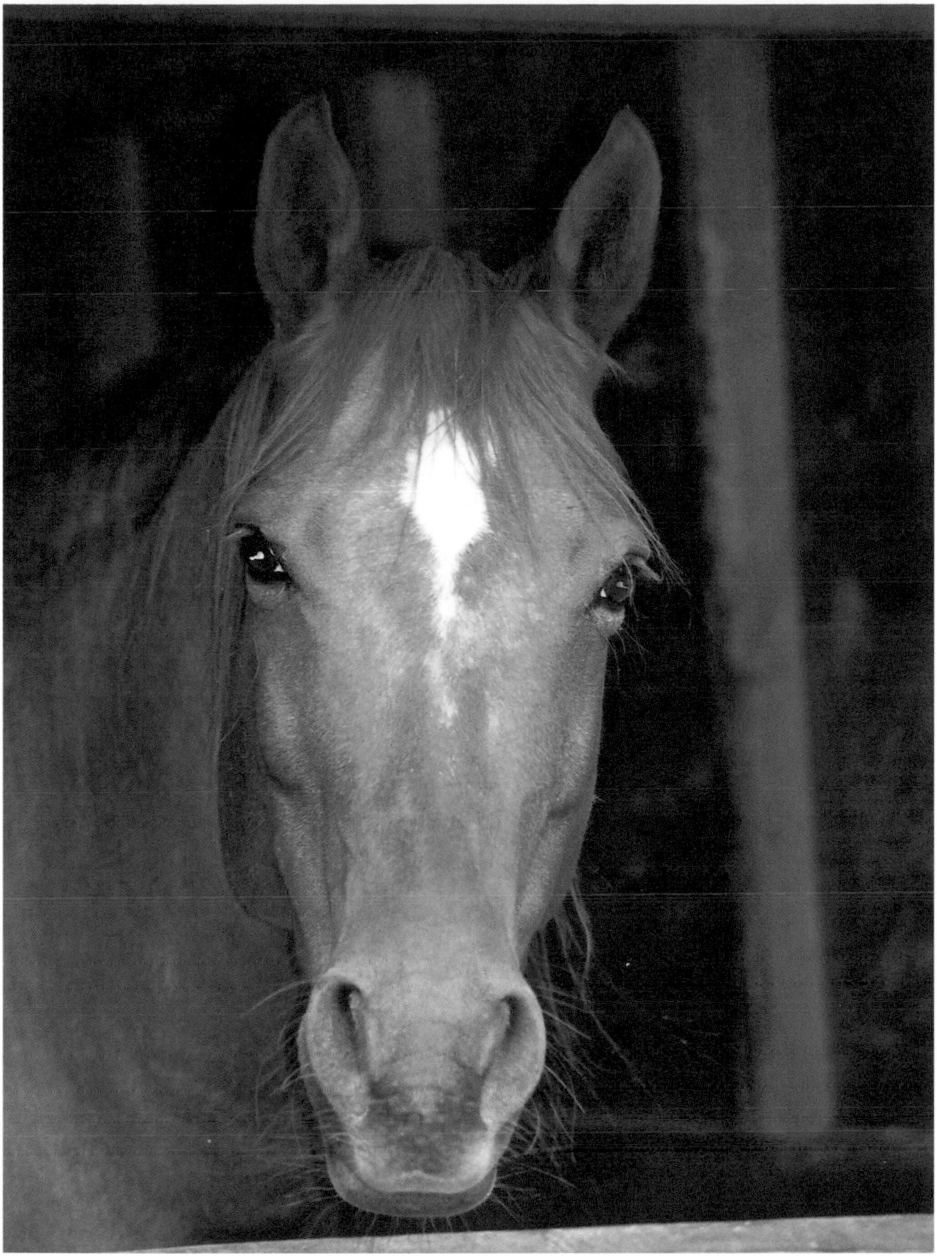

Kruger's whole expression is bright and alert. (L. Skipper)

1990s,[1] and another excellent book, *A Practical Guide to Horse Behavior* by Sue McDonnell.)

All of these basic gestures are obvious in what they convey. But what about the kind of body language that could be used in training? Are the interpretations often assigned to some of this body language correct? Some postures and facial expressions are often interpreted in ways which may not be accurate, and which may give rise to misleading ideas about what is going on.

1 Some of these drawings were reproduced, by kind permission of Dr Waring, in *Inside Your Horse's Mind*.

The positioning of this mare's ears indicates that her attention is divided between something ahead and slightly to her right, and what is happening to the left and behind her. (L. Skipper)

below This stallion's ears are turned back towards his rider; this shows that he is paying attention to her. (L. Skipper)

Can horses read the body language of other species?

In Chapter 2 I mentioned the idea that humans appear permanently aggressive to horses because of our 'pinned-back' ears. This is not a new idea; it has been appearing in equestrian literature for several decades and has been put forward by such people as Michael Schäfer and Desmond Morris, as well as trainers such as Pat Parelli. The idea seems superficially plausible, but how likely is it that horses read our appearance in such a manner?

To be able to do so, they would have to be able to generalize from their anatomy to ours and to know that our ears corresponded to theirs. Until recently, this idea would not have been generally accepted by scientists. However, experiments conducted independently by me and by Dr Marthe Kiley-Worthington, involving horses imitating our actions,[2] suggest that horses can indeed generalize in this way.

If this is true, does this mean that the assumptions of Schäfer, Morris, Parelli, etc. are correct, and that horses do indeed see us as permanently aggressive, because they are able to recognize the correspondence between our ears and theirs? My own observations lead me to think that this is highly unlikely. Even if they do understand that the funny-shaped things attached to the sides of our heads are ears, they are quite capable of learning through experience that in our species their pinned-back appearance does not denote aggression. Indeed, most horses learn to read the body language of other species extremely well.

Clever Hans

Just how well they can read human body language is brought home to us by a story involving a horse, his owner and a perceptive psychologist. Anyone who has studied psychology or animal behaviour, as well as a great many people who have not, will have heard the story of *Kluge Hans*, Clever Hans. Hans belonged to a German, Wilhelm von Osten, who believed he was an equine genius. Hans could respond to various questions either by pawing the ground a certain number of times, or by indicating letters of the alphabet with his hoof. Experts who examined Hans could find no evidence of trickery or of cues being given by von Osten; Hans would still give the right answer if von Osten was not present. However the psychologist Oskar Pfungst felt that it might be more profitable to study the *questioner* rather than the horse. Pfungst discovered that Hans could not give the right answer if he could not see the questioner, or if the questioner did not know the right answer. Furthermore, he would *always* give what the questioner thought was the correct answer, even if the latter tried to remain quite still and

2 See Chapter 11 of *Inside Your Horse's Mind*; see also Kiley-Worthington, *Horse Watch – What it is to be Equine*, Chapter 3.

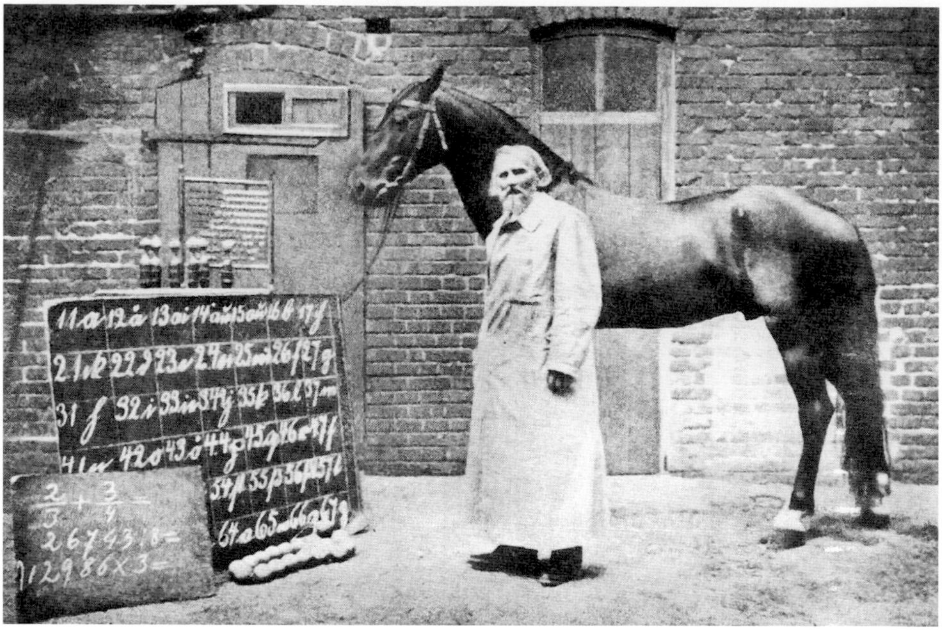

Clever Hans, the horse whose cleverness lay in his amazing ability to read the most minute changes in human body language.

not give any 'cues'. It became clear that Hans was reading the most minute changes in the questioner's breathing, facial expression (even the tiniest involuntary twitch of the nostrils or of the eyebrows), general postural tone, etc. and deducing the correct answer from these almost imperceptible changes that took place as the correct answer was reached. In other words, he was interpreting body language with a perception and accuracy that almost defies the human imagination and from this he was working out when to give the desired response. The truly remarkable thing about this story – and the one which is most often overlooked – is not just that Hans was able to distinguish and interpret, with such devastating accuracy, the body language of his audience. It is that, among all the jumble of signals which the audience were quite unconsciously sending (by which I mean all the inadvertent twitches, shifts of position, etc. that anyone will make even while attempting to sit still), Hans was able to distinguish and read those that were truly relevant to his task.

Not all horses posses this ability to the same degree as Hans; even so, most of them can read us so accurately that it is very difficult indeed to fool them. This may explain why so much of their body language goes unnoticed by us; it is so subtle that we miss it completely, although it may be glaringly obvious to them.

Using body language with horses

Much of the body language that we make use of with horses is not at all subtle, although we sometimes like to think it is. One of the most effective uses of body language is simply guiding them where we want them to go. When older horses move ahead and turn in when being led, we are often told that this is a sign of the horse attempting to assert dominance. In fact it is based on the kind of 'blocking' movement that foals use when they want their dams to stop so that they can take milk. They simply move in front of and across their mothers, who then stop and allow the foals to suckle. The led horse doing this is doing nothing more than he did when he was a foal, except that the handler takes the place of his dam. He is not being 'dominant' in the social sense, any more than the foal is (except in the very loose sense of influencing what happens). He may not want to go where we are taking him; he may not want to go anywhere at all. He could be unsure about whether it is a good idea to go where we want him to (perhaps we have not convinced him that we are trustworthy), in which case we have some work to do to gain his trust (see Chapter 4).

We can make use of this kind of 'blocking' movement when we want to guide horses in a specific direction. For example, when lungeing a horse or working him loose, we can slow or stop his forward movement by simply moving across and slightly in front of him. (Take care not to actually get in his way; if you are not sure how he will respond it is always best if you can use vocal cues as a back-up – see later this chapter for use of the voice in training.) Also, if the horse is excited allow him to let off steam before attempting any serious work; calmness is essential if he is to learn anything of value.

If we want to calm an angry or frightened horse, we adopt a neutral, non-threatening posture, turning slightly away, with arms and head lowered, breathing slowly and deeply and – no matter how scary the situation might be – preserving our calm demeanour. The horse knows then that we are not a threat to him. If we simply stand still in this posture most horses will eventually come over to investigate and we can then proceed – reading the horse's own body language as we do so – to try to make friends with him. If he will allow us to step into his personal space we can try a stroke or a scratch on the neck or withers. We do *not* make a grab for his headcollar or try to cram a halter on his head! Instead, we proceed very gradually, not fussily and tentatively but with confidence, calmly and quietly, until the horse will tolerate us actually taking hold of him. Be careful when trying something like this with a really angry or frightened horse; always watch his posture and facial expression, even if only out of the corner of your eye. Be ready to get out of the way quickly – and if possible wear a hat![3] If you are at all unsure of your ability to handle a situation like this, it is much safer to admit this and let someone more confident take over.

There are other, more subtle ways in which we can use body language with horses. Their ability to interpret human body language accurately means that

3 Some horses who have had bad experiences under saddle will run away from anyone wearing a hat, so in these cases you might need to disguise protective headgear.

Brian makes his posture neutral, with lowered eyes and arms. The foal is happy to be with him as he is not threatening in any way. (L. Skipper)

they quickly learn to associate facial expressions with mood. They are quite capable of understanding that a frown, a tense posture and an angry, raised voice means that a human is not in a good mood; conversely they can recognize that a relaxed posture, smiles and a pleasant tone of voice denote a good mood. If you want to improve your relationship with your horse, speak to him politely and pleasantly and smile when you look at him. As we saw in Chapter 4, behaviour breeds behaviour and horses respond according to how we behave towards them!

Equine submission

Much of the lore that has grown up about the use of body language in training is based on the idea of *submission*. As we have seen, horses submit by moving away, which is not very useful if we want them to stay with us so that we can train them. In any case, as Abigail Hogg points out in *The Horse Behaviour Handbook*, the fact that horses do this does not necessarily imply that by moving away they have accepted the other horse's authority over them[i] – it just means they have got out of the way!

There is no equivalent in the equine behaviour repertoire of the kind of appeasement behaviour shown by, for example, dogs, who will cringe, lie down and roll over, etc. Even the 'foal-face', which every horse owner who has had much to do with foals will have seen, and which used to be regarded as appeasement, is now no longer seen as a gesture of submission. This gesture is often called 'snapping' in equine behaviour literature; the foal or young horse extends the neck and head and opens and closes the mouth without bringing the teeth or lips together. It is usually interpreted as being intended to prevent more mature horses from acting aggressively towards an immature horse; Zeeb, who first described it in 1959, called it *Unterlegenheitsgebärde* (submissive gesture). However, there are several problems with this. First of all, in the majority of cases it does not actually do that; a number of studies have shown that it has little or no effect with regard to inhibiting aggression on the part of older horses. A three-year study carried out on the developmental behaviour of foals during their first twenty-four weeks of life showed that, far from preventing aggression, snapping sometimes triggered it. In addition, foals often approached older horses and snapped to them, initiating an encounter rather than simply reacting to one. I have seen a foal and a yearling (Toska at three weeks and Nivalis aged one year) snapping to each other, and I have read reports from several people who say they have observed mature stallions snapping to foals.

The authors of the studies mentioned above concluded that snapping was ritualized suckling behaviour (i.e. the gesture was very similar to that of a foal suckling), and that it could occur as a displacement activity in situations where the foal is excited or subject to conflicting emotions. For example, the foal might be curious about other horses and wanting to seek them out, but lack the social skills to be able to approach them in an acceptable manner (much like a child whose manners with adults may be rather awkward). Similarly, if other horses approach him he may not know how to deal with them – again like a child who lacks the confidence to talk to adults. In the case of the yearling and the foal snapping to each other, they may both have been unsure how to deal with the situation: Nivalis had never seen another foal and Toska had never seen another

Rather than being a submissive gesture, 'snapping' may be a displacement activity on the part of socially naïve youngsters. Here Imzadi snaps to her father Nivalis. (L. Skipper)

yearling! The mature stallions observed snapping to foals are another matter; there may be something else altogether going on here. What is clear is that this is far from being the simple submissive gesture it is usually said to be.

'Licking and chewing'

In view of this, what do we make of the 'licking and chewing' that is supposed to indicate submission or, at the very least, a willingness to co-operate with us? This is the interpretation that is often used when a horse is worked in a round pen; the horse may stop, lower his head and lick his lips, sometimes champing slightly as he does so ('chewing'). However, it could mean any one of a number of things. It could be a sign that the horse is anxious; I have often seen this in horses who are apprehensive about something. It might be a displacement activity similar to snapping, for example if it occurs during round pen training the horse might be feeling conflicting emotions about the situation he is in. On the one hand, he might want to run away (although he cannot, as he is confined by the pen), but be tired of running and wanting to stop, but unsure if it is safe to do so. On the other hand, it might be a sign that now he knows no harm is going to come to him he is starting to relax. It is our responsibility to learn to read the basic signs that tell us whether a horse is tense, relaxed, etc, which involves looking at the whole horse, not just his head or any other single part – so that if we see these signs during the course of training we can tell whether they are evidence of anxiety, conflict or relaxation. If the horse is showing signs of anxiety or stress, we back off. These signs might be: tension in the muscles of the jaw, muzzle and around the eyes, head raised, neck and back muscles tense and stiff, and tail clamped. While these are all indications of tension and anxiety, not all of them have to be present before we can tell that all is not well. If the horse is genuinely relaxed (floppy ears, fluent movement, relaxed neck and back and tail swinging freely) we can proceed without causing him distress.

Using the voice

Although I have made much of the fact that vocal communication is of secondary importance to horses, this does not mean that we cannot use our voices to communicate with them. Oddly enough, this is one area in which natural horsemanship and conventional training come together: both tend to disparage, or discourage, the use of the voice in training.

Some (not all) of the 'naturals' insist that we should use only body language because use of the voice is not 'natural'. However, this seems unnecessarily restrictive. If we want to hold rigidly to what is 'natural' we would not be training horses at all!

In some disciplines, such as dressage, the use of the voice is banned for other reasons which will be discussed in Chapter 8. However, in the Classical Riding Club Training Tests (mentioned in Chapter 15) the *discreet* use of the voice is allowed. The idea is that the rider can use the voice to encourage the horse but not to give directions such as 'Canter at X!' – again, we shall see the reason for this in Chapter 8. But could we, in any case, teach a horse something as complex as that? We all know that horses can learn to respond to single words; are they also capable of learning entire phrases? Could we indeed use these as instructions?

Given that circus and stunt horses can learn vocal instructions without too much difficulty, there is no reason why horses in general should not learn to respond to phrases such as 'Trot at A' as long as we have taught them to associate 'Trot' with the gait (as we would do when teaching the horse to lunge) and 'A' with the location of the letter A in the *manège*. It is not even very difficult to do this; it simply takes time, patience and an understanding of the training principles which will be discussed in Chapter 7. Marthe Kiley-Worthington and her partner Chris Rendle have taught their horses (and various other animals) all manner of tasks and manoeuvres using whole phrases and sentences rather than just single words; she expands on this theme in Chapter 7 of her book, *Horse Watch – What it is to be Equine.*

We can certainly make use of the voice in many ways. Every horse should be taught to respond to his name. I am always rather startled when I hear or read a statement to the effect that horses do not learn to do this. All of our horses know their names and will come when called (unless there is something else going on which is too fascinating to ignore, when they can sometimes become selectively deaf!).

As suggested earlier, even when we make use of body language it is always best to be able to use the voice as a back-up if necessary. A horse who is excited or upset may respond better to vocal cues than to body language; we have found that ours respond to the word 'Steady' spoken in a calm, soothing voice, drawing the word out so that it becomes 'Steeeadeeee'. Others may respond to different words; you simply need to experiment to find out what works best with individual horses.

Speak clearly

When using the voice we have to speak clearly and not mumble, or horses will not be able to distinguish individual words from the jumble of sound. If we do speak clearly they will often pick up certain words and phrases and learn to associate them with specific events or objects. Zareeba has a very distinctive 'dinner call' which he makes when he knows dinner is in the offing: a deep, forceful noise in his throat which often rises to a high-pitched, melodious whinny, almost like a coloratura soprano. Having heard me say 'I'll do the dinners now' for many years, he now makes his dinner call whenever he hears the word 'dinner'. In view of the belief, held by many scientists, that horses do not copy each other, it is interesting that several of our other horses have now developed their own version of Zareeba's 'dinner call', even though none of them previously made any such calls!

Using words and phrases

We can make use of this facility for picking up words and phrases in all manner of ways. Most of us already do this; we say things like 'Stand!' or 'Stand up!' 'Move over', etc. in our everyday dealings with horses. If I want Zareeba to lift his off fore I just say, 'Last one please!' because that is what I have said for years when picking his feet up, the off fore always being the last to be picked up. If we ask Nivalis to lift one of his forelegs, then put it down, and then ask 'Other one please' he knows that we want him to lift the opposite foreleg to the one he has just lifted, regardless of whether the latter was the off or the near fore.

Remember that if you want to teach your horse words and phrases you must wait until he is performing an action and time the words to coincide with that action. He will eventually make the association, but if your timing is wrong he may never understand what you mean (see Chapter 7 for more about this). Horses are not born understanding English, or any other language!

Once we understand the learning principles which will be outlined in Chapter 7 we can ask horses to do all manner of things using words and phrases. For example, we can get them to open gates, provided the latch is not too difficult for them. A horse we had some years ago was so good at this that we just used to say, 'Open the gate please' and he did; if the latch was awkward we just needed to undo it for him and he would push against the gate to open it. We can teach horses to retrieve their dinner buckets from inside the stables, using the kind of conditioning techniques described in the next chapter – in fact using these techniques we can teach them anything of which they are physically capable. As we shall see in Chapter 7, we do not necessarily have to use the voice; any cue will do as long as it is clear. However, vocal communication comes much more easily to humans than does the deliberate use of body language, so if we can sometimes make ourselves clearer by using the voice then why not do so? Horses seem to enjoy hearing us talk and ours will often amble over when they hear us having a conversation nearby. Rather than get stuck with one mode of communication, we should try whatever works; if this happens to be vocal communication then use it!

i Abigail Hogg, *The Horse Behaviour Handbook*, pp.88–89.

CHAPTER 7

Learning

In nature there are neither rewards nor punishments –
there are consequences.

ROBERT GREENE INGERSOLL, *Lectures & Essays*

As I mentioned in Chapter 1, so-called 'traditional' horsemanship has been much criticized in recent years. We are usually told that traditional methods of training horses (a phrase to which people often bring their own definitions) rely mainly on 'negative reinforcement'. The implication is usually that this involves the use of a greater or lesser degree of force and/or punishment, and that more natural training methods can eliminate this use of force. Many people appear to accept this without question, but is it an accurate perception? Some traditional methods do rely on the use of force; some do not. Thinking on this matter is muddled, to say the least, because (as we saw in Chapter 1) one person's equestrian tradition may not be another's. The muddle becomes even greater when we throw in the claims, made by many modern 'natural' horse trainers and so-called horse-whisperers, that their methods reject the use of force and rely on the establishment of a harmonious relationship between horse and trainer. However, many of the critics of 'natural horsemanship' feel that the latter, too, relies on negative reinforcement to a degree not generally realized by its devotees.

The problem is that very often the methods in question are extremely vaguely defined and when one reads books and articles which supposedly describe these methods, they very often remain obscure and difficult to grasp. Even after attending demonstrations of a particular trainer's work, many people end up wondering exactly what is going on. The fact that there are now so many different training methods makes it extremely difficult for the horse owner to decide which, if any, of these methods would be best for their horse.

In this chapter and the next I want to try to unravel the principles behind these methods. In order to understand these principles, we need to know how horses learn. All mammals (including, of course, humans) learn in pretty much the same ways. The strengths of some species may lie in different areas of learning than others, but essentially the processes are the same. Different modes of learning have been identified; in this and the following chapter I have concentrated on those which are of most use to us in training horses. (For an in-depth discussion of all the other learning modes, see Chapter 3 of Dr Marthe Kiley-Worthington's book *Horse Watch – What it is to be Equine*, J.A. Allen 2005).

Alpha intelligence?

There is one idea which I should like to dispose of before going any further. The obsession with dominance has led a number of people astray when it comes to assessing a horse's 'trainability'. Just as many people assume that the most dominant horse is going to be the leader, there is also a tendency to assume that dominance equates to intelligence. One trainer asserts that 'The dominant horse is the most intelligent, and as a result they are usually quick learners.'[i] There is no definition of 'intelligent' given here, but however one defines intelligence, is there any truth in this writer's assertion? Scientific studies carried out so far have found no correlation between social dominance and learning ability. Out of interest I carried out a survey of our own horses to see if I could determine any correlation between dominance and intelligence. Defining 'intelligence' rather crudely as capacity for learning, quickness of understanding and ability to adapt to novel and demanding situations, I was able to construct (admittedly in a rather subjective manner) a rough hierarchy as follows:

α Zareeba
β Nivalis
γ Imzadi
δ Kruger
ϵ Roxzella
ζ Toska
η Tiff
θ Kiri

This does not quite represent a complete reversal of the previous 'hierarchy' table given in Chapter 3, but it does demonstrate very well how little correlation there really is between position in a dominance hierarchy and intelligence – however one defines the latter! I do not think it is at all helpful to make prior assumptions about intelligence and learning ability; any assessment of trainability must be based on knowledge of the individual horse and not on unexamined dogma.

Habituation

Horses, like other animals, have to learn what elements in their environment are worthy of their fear, and what may be safely ignored – in other words, they grow accustomed, or *habituated* to things which would otherwise cause constant alarm. Habituation can be an extremely useful tool in training horses; by gradually introducing a horse to scary objects such as rustling bags, washing flapping on clothes lines, tractors with the engine running, etc. we can get him accustomed to the idea that they are not so scary after all and eventually he will ignore them. I habituated my gelding Zareeba to traffic by taking him and his companion, a Connemara foal, for walks down the lane to a wide grass verge bordering a busy road. They learned to ignore the traffic while grazing happily and both were subsequently very good in traffic. If this process is carried out too quickly the reverse may occur and the horse, instead of getting used to scary objects, sees them as an object of even greater fear; this is known as *sensitization*. Care must therefore be taken not to rush the habituation process.

Disconnected brains?

Horses may appear not to connect something they have seen, say, on their left, with the same object when they pass it again on their right. Many people believe that the two halves of the equine brain are imperfectly connected, and that the two sides of a horse's brain do not communicate effectively. So, we are told, we have to teach the horse everything twice, once for each side. In fact, there is no physiological reason why the two halves should not communicate just as well as they do in human brains. Indeed, experiments carried out by Dr Evelyn Hanggi in the USA have shown that horses can certainly transfer information efficiently from one side of the brain to the other. The apparent disconnection between their left and right may have more to do with the way they see things than with anything else. Because their range of binocular vision is limited in comparison with ours, it may well be that they do not immediately make the connection between an object seen from one side, and later from the other (try looking at a reversed image of a familiar scene, and you too may experience an initial lack of

The equine brain, seen from above

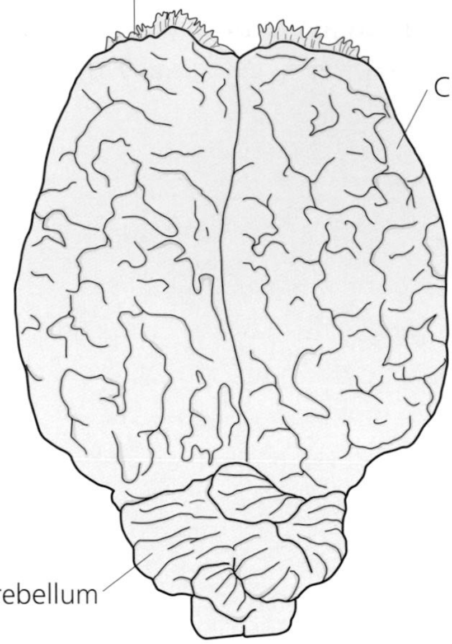

Although the equine brain is divided into right and left hemispheres, just like the human brain, there is no physiological reason why the two halves should not communicate perfectly well. Experiments have shown that in fact information does cross over efficiently from one half of the equine brain to the other.

Figure 6: The two sides of the equine brain are not imperfectly joined, as many people suppose; horses are perfectly capable of transferring information from one side of the brain to the other.

recognition). Or it could be that they did not pay sufficient attention to it in the first place!

In addition horses, like humans, are usually right- or left- 'handed': that is, they are more supple on one side than the other. In this respect, it is one-sidedness, not an imperfectly joined brain, that prevents them from performing equally well on both reins.

Flooding

The technique known as *flooding* is sometimes used in the treatment of human phobias; it involves exposing the person to whatever their phobia is centred on, without possibility of escape, until they become habituated to it. An example might be making someone suffering from a phobia of spiders hold a large spider in their hand, or submit to having spiders crawl all over them, until they become desensitized and no longer fear spiders. This technique can be successful in some cases, but it appears to work mainly with people who were not very anxious about their phobia in the first place. With others, if the anxiety level is too high, the subject may either terminate the session or simply 'switch off'. This means that the phobia is not cured, it is just being temporarily 'shelved' and may break out anew in a sufficiently frightening situation. It therefore carries its fair share of risks when used on humans and these risks are compounded with animals, as they cannot tell us just how anxious they really are in the first place. Flooding can therefore actually increase the degree of fear, sometimes to the point where the animal collapses. Because of these dangers it is not generally recommended in the training of animals, although some trainers do make use of it (see section on Imprint training in Chapter 9). Gentle habituation to potentially frightening objects and situations is far preferable.

Conditioning

Learning theory revolves around a process known as *conditioning*. For some people, such as trainer Karen Pryor, this process is akin to a law of nature; however, it is not simply a question of eliciting automatic responses. Animals (and humans) must still think about the conditioning process and they can, if they so choose, resist it. Conditioning is therefore based on a set of principles, not physical laws. Having said this, these principles, as Pryor points out, underlie all learning-teaching situations. Conditioning represents the single most powerful tool we have in the training and management of animals, which is why I have devoted so much space to it.

Classical conditioning

Many people will have heard of the Russian physiologist I.P. Pavlov and his famous experiments with dogs. Pavlov trained the dogs to associate being fed with the ringing of a bell, and eventually the sound of the bell alone was sufficient to make the dogs salivate in anticipation. This is known as 'classical conditioning' and it can occur naturally. For example, a horse who has happily gone past a gateway for years may have a frightening experience there – perhaps a dog rushes out barking, or a plastic bag in the hedge flaps and gives the horse a fright. The horse subsequently refuses to approach that gateway, even though whatever frightened him may no longer be there; he has been 'conditioned' to fear it. (Humans, too, can be affected like this; they can develop a dislike of certain places, sights, sounds or smells because they are associated with some unpleasant experience.) Understanding this helps to explain a great deal of equine behaviour.

Operant conditioning

The other kind of conditioning is known as 'operant conditioning'. This type of learning works on the basis of stimulus-response. The stimulus (or cue) could be almost anything: in the case of a ridden horse, the stimulus or cue might be a touch of the rider's leg, with moving (forward, sideways or back, depending on the context) being the required response. The idea is that all such responses have to be *taught* by means of conditioning. For many people, this forms the basis of training horses and to a large extent this is true. However, it is very far from being the whole story – as we shall see in Chapter 8.

Reinforcement

To be effective, the type of learning involved in operant conditioning needs to be *reinforced*. Karen Pryor defines a reinforcer as '... anything that, occurring in conjunction with an act, tends to increase the probability that the act will occur again.'[ii] There are two categories of reinforcement: *negative reinforcement*, and *positive reinforcement*. These are often abbreviated to -R and +R and I shall use these abbreviations throughout the rest of the book.

The 1990s and the early years of the twenty-first century have seen some very heated debates on the subject of -R. The word 'negative' is usually taken to mean that something unpleasant is involved and indeed this can often be the case. However, some trainers who profess to use only +R have implied that -R is *always* unpleasant for the horse, which is not true at all. I confess that I have also fallen into that trap in the past, but further researches have shown me that I was mistaken, and that good trainers make use of a number of tools, of which mild -R is only one.

-R is often confused with punishment (which I shall deal with separately later in this chapter), which is one reason why many people who have studied learning theory do not use the words 'punishment' or 'reward'; instead, they point out that -R and +R are simply terms used to describe the conditioning process involved.

It is important that we understand this, because the debates referred to above have caused a great deal of confusion in the minds of many horse owners. It is also important to avoid the use of emotive language, because this adds nothing to our understanding and may actually hamper it by clouding our judgement.

Negative reinforcement (-R)

This consists of applying some stimulus or cue; once the animal has responded as we wish, the stimulus is removed or the action forming the cue ceases. This removal of the cue or stimulus is what *reinforces* the desired behaviour, making it more likely that the horse or other animal will repeat the action.

Many people believe that this removal of the stimulus constitutes a reward, but this is not the case. This is part of the confusion referred to above; it is far better to think of -R in terms of taking something away – hence the term 'negative'.

Positive reinforcement (+R)

This takes place *during* the desired response; the horse is rewarded by a food treat, a stroke or pat, or verbal praise. In +R the animal has a choice: if the behaviour is offered freely, it is rewarded; if the wrong behaviour (or no behaviour) is offered it is simply ignored, in which case no reinforcement takes place.

Punishment

-R is often confused with *punishment*. But because punishment occurs *after* a particular behaviour has taken place, it can have no effect on *that* behaviour. However, it might have an effect on future behaviour, e.g. if we are fined a substantial amount of money for speeding in a car, we might be less inclined to speed in future. Nevertheless, it does not *guarantee* this, it only makes it *less likely* that we will behave in this way – we might simply take greater care not to get caught! As a deterrent, punishment is not actually all that effective; witness the number of criminals who go on to offend again after release from prison, and the number of children who keep on being naughty no matter how often they are punished. Where animals are concerned it may be even less effective. As Karen Pryor says, 'Learning to alter behaviour in the future in order to avoid consequences in the future is more than most animals can understand.'[iii] For this reason its uses in training are very limited.

Getting the timing right

Whatever type of reinforcement we are using, it is essential to remember two very important things. First, in order for behaviour to be reinforced we must introduce the reinforcement the very instant the desired behaviour is occurring, or the animal has no means of knowing exactly what action we are approving. If we reinforce the behaviour of, say, moving back when the horse has already stepped back and stood still again, we are actually reinforcing standing still! Second, behaviour that is not occurring cannot be reinforced. We either have to wait for the behaviour we want to reinforce to occur naturally, or we have to create conditions in which it can occur. If we are using +R we pair a specific behaviour as it is occurring with a reinforcer; the behaviour might be something like stepping back if the subject is a horse, or sitting in the case of a dog. When the desired response occurs we give the reward. If we are using -R, we introduce something the animal wants to avoid – with a horse this might be pressure on a headcollar to make him move back; with a dog it could be pushing his hind end down to make him sit. As soon as we get the desired response we remove the pressure. In both cases – whether we use +R or -R – we have *reinforced* the desired behaviour.

What we can do then is introduce a cue or signal at the same time as we reinforce the behaviour. In the examples given, this might be 'Back!' or 'Sit!' respectively, but it can (and usually will) be something that, in itself, is initially meaningless to the animal. (For example, a horse does not understand that 'Walk on!' means just that, until we teach him to associate the phrase with the act of walking on.) The actual words used do not matter as long as we use them consistently; we tend to use words that mean to us what we want them to mean to the animal because it is easier for us to relate words to actions in this way. This pairing of a reinforcer with a cue or signal enables us to ask for a specific behaviour without either having to wait for it to occur naturally or inducing it by some means. So if we have paired 'Back!' with either a reward or, say, pressure on the headcollar, the horse knows that we want him to step back, just as 'Sit!' tells the dog we want him to sit.

Conditioned reinforcement

We can then take this a step further. It may be that, because of the nature of what we are doing, we cannot give the reinforcer in time for it to coincide with the exact behaviour we want to reinforce. Say we are lungeing a horse and want to reinforce breaking into canter. We cannot get to the horse to give him a reward, so what do we do? We pair some kind of signal, which could be a verbal one such as 'Good!', or a click using a clicker box (see photograph on page 107), or anything else that can be clearly heard or seen, with the reinforcer. This enables the animal to understand that 'Good!' (or a click, or whatever) means that a reward is forthcoming, and that it was for performing *that* specific action and not some other. This is called *conditioned reinforcement*. The timing of the conditioned reinforcer has to be just right but correctly used it is a very powerful training tool indeed.

Clicker training

Conditioned reinforcement forms the basis of clicker training, which is now becoming more and more widely used in horse training. I must confess that when I first learned about clicker training I disliked the idea, feeling that it smacked of mindless teaching by rote. Now that I know more about it I freely admit that I was wrong and in fact I had been using a verbal equivalent of the click for many years without even thinking about the fact that it was basically the same thing! The click is only a *marker*, used to tell the horse that he has done something correctly as described above. It is useful because it is a clear, discrete sound which enables very precise timing of the conditioned reinforcer.

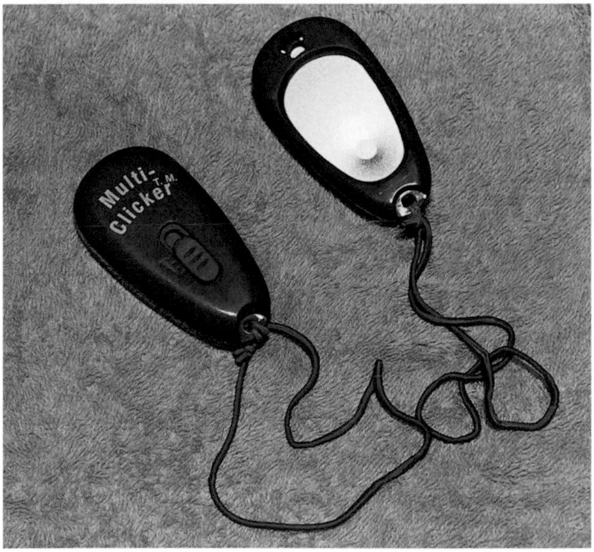

The clicker is a simple piece of equipment which, as the name suggests, makes a distinct click when pressed. This particular model has adjustable settings which make the click louder or quieter to suit individual animals. The click is simply a marker to tell the animal when an action is correct. (L. Skipper)

Target training

In clicker training the horse is typically introduced to the marker by being taught to touch a target, which can then be moved around to encourage different behaviours. However, targets can be used regardless of whether one uses the clicker or some other marker. The target can be anything you choose, as long as it is large enough for the horse to see properly: Alexandra Kurland often uses a small plastic cone; I generally use a piece of wood. If you hold the target close enough to the horse's nose (without actually pushing it at him), he will eventually touch it, either because he is curious or simply because it is positioned so that at some point he is bound to touch it. The instant this happens, click (if you are using a clicker) or say 'Good' or use whatever other marker you choose, and give your horse a tiny mount of food (grain, pieces of carrot or whatever the horse likes). Eventually he will work out that every time he touches the target he gets some food; he will also learn to associate the marker (clicker, voice or whatever) with the food. Soon he will be deliberately touching the target, because he knows that this is the way to get something he enjoys. Once he is confirmed in this behaviour you can start moving the target around. Do this in very small steps (a principle which we apply to any training situation); for example if you want the horse to touch the target while it is on the ground, you do not simply lower it to the ground or the horse will become confused and discouraged. Instead, lower it a little at a time – just a few centimetres – and eventually you will find that the horse will readily reach out to touch it when it is on the ground.

When you are satisfied that the horse will touch the target whenever it is presented (i.e. because this behaviour is now confirmed as part of his repertoire), you can introduce the cue. You present the target and say, 'Touch!' The horse

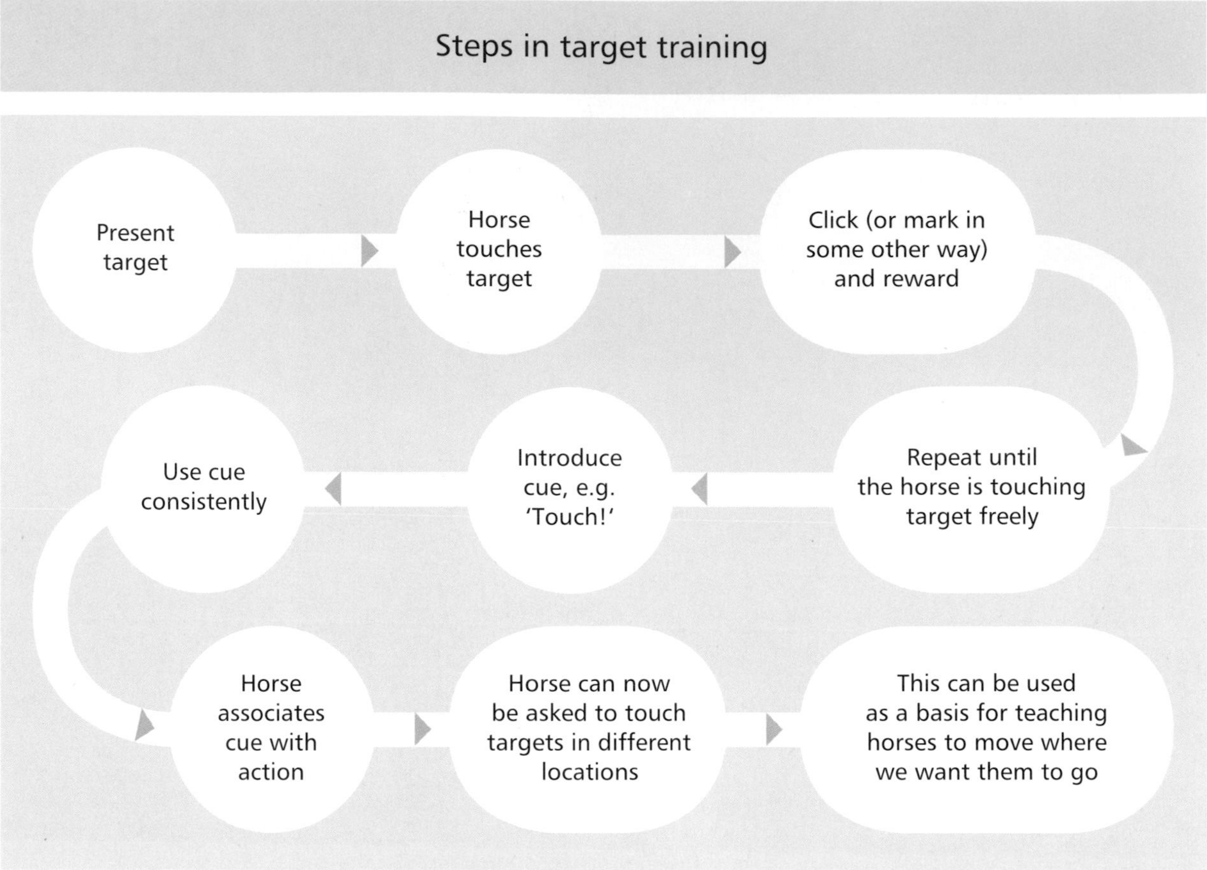
Steps in target training
Present target
Horse touches target
Click (or mark in some other way) and reward
Repeat until the horse is touching target freely
Introduce cue, e.g. 'Touch!'
Use cue consistently
Horse associates cue with action
Horse can now be asked to touch targets in different locations
This can be used as a basis for teaching horses to move where we want them to go

Figure 7: Steps in the process of target training.

knows that the presence of the target means you want him to touch it, and if you say 'Touch!' every time you present the target, the horse will soon associate the cue with seeking out and touching the target. Most horses respond to this willingly and enthusiastically. You can then use the target to move the horse around without laying a finger on him – which gives him a choice and ensures that he is complying of his own free will, without any element of coercion. (For more about how you can use target training, see Alexandra Kurland's *Clicker Training for Your Horse*, Ringpress ed. 2001.)

Shaping and selective reinforcement

If we are using +R it may seem as if we will have to go on rewarding a behaviour or the animal will simply stop producing it. However, this is not the case. It is only in the very early stages of learning that constant reinforcement is needed. Say we want to teach a horse to 'shake hands'. The photographs on page 109 show my husband Brian in the process of teaching our mare Imzadi to 'shake hands' by reinforcing a slight raising of the leg when it occurred naturally. Once she was

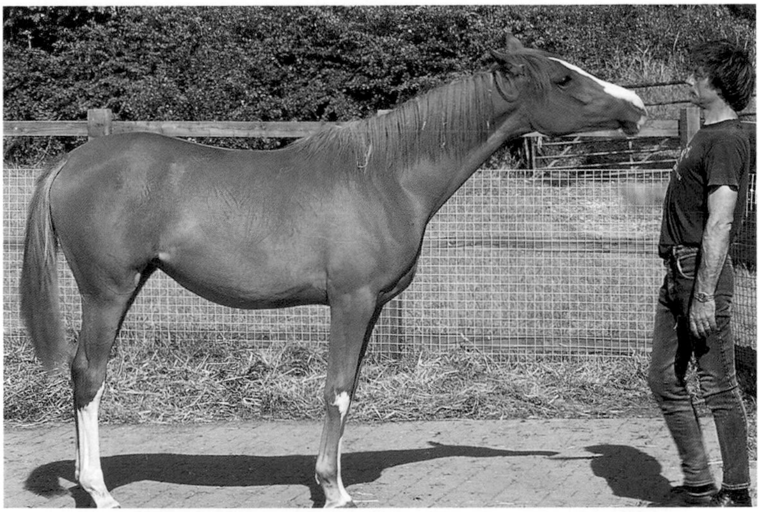

Brian asks Imzadi to stand up for him in order to gain her attention. (L. Skipper)

Once she has raised her foreleg for him and allowed him to hold it, Brian reinforces her behaviour with a titbit. (L. Skipper)

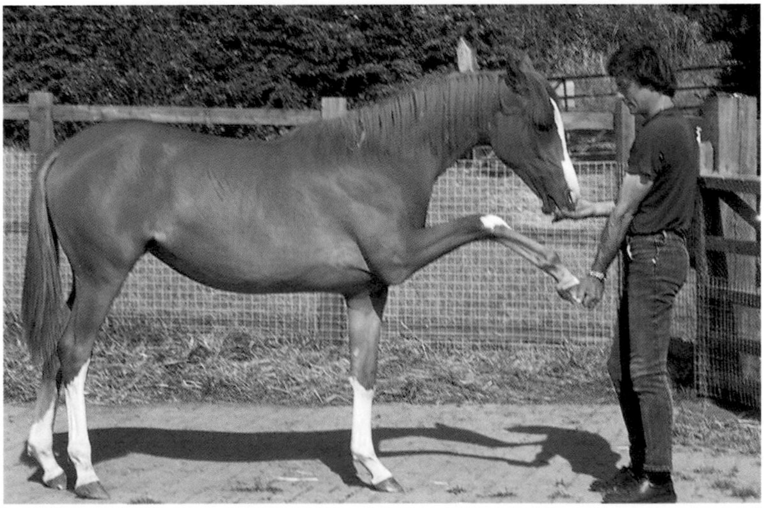

Finally, Imzadi progresses to 'shaking hands'. Each step has been offered freely and reinforced using +R. (L. Skipper)

raising her leg for him on request, Brian moved on to reinforcing only when Imzadi raised it higher. Gradually Brian was able to get her to raise her leg to a level where he could 'shake hands' with her, by reinforcing only when she raised it a little higher than before. This process is called *shaping* and that of selectively reinforcing some responses and ignoring others is called a *selective schedule* of reinforcement. Now that it is ingrained in Imzadi's behavioural repertoire, we have no need to reinforce it every time she does it for us; if we only reward her for it now and then she is more motivated to produce the behaviour for us ('This time I might get a reward') than if we rewarded her every time. (For more about schedules of reinforcement and why they have such a powerful effect, see Karen Pryor's *Don't Shoot the Dog* and *Smart Horse* by Jennifer M. McLeay – two very useful guides to the principles of training through conditioning.)

Hitting the jackpot

Another useful tool, and one that is very rarely mentioned, is the concept of the *jackpot*, described by Karen Pryor as 'a reward that is much bigger, maybe ten times bigger, than the normal reinforcer, and one that comes as a surprise to the subject.'[iv] A jackpot, says Pryor, may be used to mark a sudden breakthrough. She cites the case of a horse trainer who, when a young horse executes a difficult movement for the first time, leaps from the horse's back, untacks and turns the horse loose in the arena. The jackpot in this case is complete freedom and, says Pryor, it often seems to make the new behaviour stick. This is not to say that horses need find their work so onerous that being ridden is something they cannot enjoy. However, complete freedom is something that horses, like most humans, certainly find refreshing and rewarding.

Bribery

Many people seem to be put off the idea of +R because they think – or have been taught to think – that rewarding a horse is somehow *bribery*. This is not the case; bribery is something which people use in an attempt to reinforce behaviour which has not yet occurred – and, as we have seen, such behaviour cannot be reinforced. This is not to say that we cannot or should not use something very like bribery on occasion; we can use food, for example, as a *lure* or an *incentive*, to elicit a specific behaviour (such as walking forward). The main problem with this is that the lure can be very distracting. In ordinary +R, the animal has to think about which behaviour results in a reward. If a food lure is used, the animal (whether a horse or a dog or whatever) is not concentrating on the behaviour but on the food; this distraction may make it much more difficult for him to understand what you want.

Food rewards

A reward must consist of something the subject wants. Food rewards are not likely to be reinforcing if the subject has just eaten, or if he does not like the food being offered. In the case of horses, a stroke or a scratch on the withers may sometimes be just as effective as food. Objections to food rewards often centre around the fact that horses do not give each other presents of food, and as their food is all around them in the form of grass, giving them discrete packets of food is meaningless to them. However, this misses the point: if a horse likes a particular food it is just as effective as any other type of reinforcer – sometimes more so. This is why the *bereiters* of the Spanish Riding School carry sugar lumps around in the pockets of their tail-coats! The argument that it is not a natural part of the horse's lifestyle likewise misses the point: as I suggested in Chapters 1 and 6, if we are to stick only to what is strictly 'natural' then we will not get very far. It is also untrue that food rewards make horses nippy. They will only do this if food treats are given indiscriminately and for no reason (in which case they are meaningless). We use appropriate food rewards all the time and do not have any problems.

Accidental reinforcement

Sometimes we can inadvertently create and then reinforce behaviours. When my gelding Zareeba was a youngster I taught him to take a mint gently from between my lips. Because the nature of equine vision means that horses cannot see directly in front of their noses, Zareeba had to tilt his head in order to see the mint. This gave him a very comical appearance and, as he was being given a mint, this reinforced his behaviour of tilting his head. He now tilts his head to solicit goodies from humans, who find his expression so irresistible that they invariably comply! Having paired this behaviour with the phrase, 'Tell me what you want' I now have only to say this and Zareeba tilts his head.[1] This is a harmless and amusing example of what can happen with inadvertent reinforcement, but it underlines how careful we need to be that we are not accidentally reinforcing the wrong thing!

Extinction

If a behaviour is not reinforced to the point where it becomes ingrained, or not reinforced at all, it will cease completely. As I am writing (or rather attempting to write) this, our Border Collie x GSD pup is trying to get me to play with him

1 Interestingly, two of our other horses have started doing this, even though they have not been taught to do so. This is surely an example of horses learning from each other.

Zareeba soon learned that his comical expression could be used to coax goodies out of humans; his behaviour was thus reinforced. (L. Skipper)

by pawing at me and attempting to nibble at my fingers. I am ignoring him so, after a very short while, he goes away. If, on the other hand I push him away or start shouting at him, he thinks that's great: he has got a reaction and effectively I am reinforcing his behaviour of trying to get me to respond to him.

Similarly, when our stallion Nivalis was a youngster and wanted attention he would grab at my sleeve or nudge me. It was tempting to respond with irritation but I ignored him and eventually the behaviour stopped because it was not being reinforced. This process is called *extinction*.

Changing unwanted behaviour

Using conditioning to cure certain types of problem behaviour is a far more effective approach than punishment. One method involves training an animal to perform a behaviour that is physically incompatible with the unwanted behaviour. For example, Nivalis, like many stallions, could be quite nippy as a youngster. To counteract this we taught Nivalis, using +R, to stand still when requested. He could not stand like this and continue to nip; we thus got rid of the nipping without resorting to punishment.

We can also try what Karen Pryor calls 'putting behaviour on cue'. Suppose your horse persistently bangs his door at mealtimes. Using +R, you teach him to bang on cue, by reinforcing the behaviour when it occurs, then pairing the behaviour with a cue such as 'Bang!' (or any word you like). Once you can get the horse to bang on his door by giving the cue, and it has become an ingrained part of his behavioural repertoire, you have effectively put the behaviour under the control of the cue. Then you simply never give the cue! This technique is often used to cure dogs whose barking has become a problem; like all training it requires time and patience but it is actually a very effective way of getting rid of unwanted behaviour and it illustrates just how powerful conditioning techniques can be.

First do no harm

Great care should be taken when attempting behaviour modification. Some experts in learning theory maintain that it is pointless trying to understand the underlying cause of behaviour in animals; it is enough to be able to modify it. I think this can be a dangerous approach. Take the example of the horse who bangs on his door. If this is only done at mealtimes we can ignore it (extinction) or put it on cue; the horse will still get his dinner once he stops banging. However, if the horse bangs on his door out of frustration at being cooped up in a stable, then eliminating or modifying the behaviour does nothing to ease the horse's frustration, which may be intensified and expressed in a different manner, possibly through stereotypical behaviour (such as weaving) or aggression. So always investigate the cause of unwanted behaviour! In some cases you can do this yourself, by observing and analysing the horse's actions; in others you may need to call in an animal behaviour specialist.

I have done no more than give a very basic outline of the principles of conditioning; there is so much more to these principles, and their ability to shape behaviour in the training of animals (and humans!) is so powerful, that anyone who really wants to learn more about these principles – and I suggest that every horse owner would do well to learn more – should go on to read the books mentioned earlier in this chapter. Furthermore, in making use of these principles, we must never lose sight of the fact that horses have thoughts and feelings of their own and that, for the learning to be fully effective, we must engage those thoughts and feelings by making learning both interesting and worthwhile for the horse – hence the emphasis on +R.

Is negative reinforcement always bad?

However, -R also has its place. For many years a great deal of animal training relied on -R, so clearly it is effective or people would not use it. However, +R is very much more pleasant than -R, both for the trainer and the animal. Prolonged use of strong negative stimuli has been shown experimentally to cause neurosis in animals. So the use of -R should be as mild as possible and kept to a minimum. But does this mean that the use of -R is always bad?

Some writers (including Karen Pryor) have stated that -R always contains an element of punishment: '...all negative reinforcement, by definition, includes a punisher'.[v] Yet on the same page she appears to contradict herself, saying that 'Negative reinforcers can be benign',[vi] citing their use in the taming of shy llamas (referred to in Chapter 8). So which is true? As Pryor points out, the strength of an aversive (i.e. whatever is introduced that the animal wants to avoid) can only be judged by the recipient; we may think it is mild but the animal may regard it as very severe. However, it all depends on the aversive; in horse training all may not be as it seems.

In Chapter 8 I will explain what is really happening in good horsemanship (which is the only kind we are interested in here). In the meantime I leave you with a question: What is the difference between a cue and an aid? Before you read the next chapter I would like you think about this question. The answer lies in the words themselves!

i Mark Hudson, 'Wake up call', *Horse & Rider* March 2004, p.48.
ii Karen Pryor, *Don't Shoot the Dog*, Rev. ed., Bantam 1999, p.1.
iii Pryor, *Don't Shoot the Dog*, p.105.
iv Pryor, *Don't Shoot the Dog*, p.11.
v Pryor, *Don't Shoot the Dog*, pp.111–112.
vi Pryor, *Don't Shoot the Dog*, p.112.

CHAPTER 8

Accentuating the Positive

> You must reward the horse each time he does what you ask of him, but never ask more than he is capable of giving. This will make him your friend and not your slave.
>
> NUNO OLIVEIRA

Having looked at the principles of learning theory in the previous chapter, we can now see how it can be put into practice. We learned in that chapter that:

- A specific behaviour must actually be occurring for it to be reinforced.
- We cannot reinforce something that has not happened.
- A reinforcer must be given at the correct time or the wrong behaviour may be reinforced.
- Punishment is not a very effective training tool: it can only be used to tell the horse what *not* to do; it can never tell him what he *should* be doing.

This being so, how do we get the horse to perform the kind of behaviour we want to reinforce?

Invoking a behaviour

We can do this by setting up situations which make the horse more likely to offer the behaviour we want (for example, as we saw in Chapter 7, if we want the horse to touch a target, we place it so that he is almost bound to do so when he moves his nose to investigate it). However, if we decide we will use only +R, how do we get the horse to perform certain behaviours under saddle? Suppose we want him to move forward. We can reinforce a spontaneous movement in the right direction using +R as described in Chapter 7; we then shape this behaviour until the horse is moving forward freely on request. But what happens, for example, when he is already moving and we want him to change gait? How do we tell him what we want him to do? On the lunge, or working the horse loose, we can make use of body language to encourage him to move forward (although this is really mild -R); if he changes gait voluntarily, we can pair this with a vocal cue (e.g. 'Trot!' if he has started trotting, 'Canter!' if he has popped into canter, etc.). But what do we do under saddle? We can use vocal cues as we have done in our work on the ground. However, it has been established over many centuries that more subtle and precise cues can be given by astute use of the rider's seat and legs (where the cues also constitute aids). If we are using these as we have been taught to do, how can we avoid the use of -R?

Positive or negative?

By using +R we can shape behaviour in ways that are not only easier for the horse, but also more pleasurable for him, so he is more willing to co-operate with us. Some people will insist that they use only +R in riding and this is theoretically possible. However, it raises practical problems. We can use exclusively +R on the ground, but the moment we sit on the horse's back we are influencing him with our own body, whether we like it or not. Every tiny movement we make on a horse's back, whether intentional or not, could be classed as -R, because all but the most insensitive horses will react to such movements in some way. The only way we could avoid absolutely any element of -R in riding is either to remain completely immobile on the horse's back (physically virtually impossible) or, better still, not get on his back at all! Since riding is the reason why most of us have horses in the first place, this is not a very satisfactory option, so it seems we are stuck with an element of -R. Is this necessarily a 'bad' thing?

We can easily get the horse to walk, trot and canter using the verbal or other cues we have taught him when working from the ground. We can also, by means of shaping techniques, teach the horse all the other things we want him to do under saddle. We can even, if we are skilled enough, teach him *how* we want to perform an action. However, we should take care here because the approach that relies solely on cues does nothing to assist the horse physically. We must also pay attention to the many ways in which the rider interacts with the horse, influencing his responses and either assisting or hampering his efforts.

Aids and cues

In the previous chapter I asked readers to think about the difference between a cue and an aid. A cue can sometimes also be an aid, and an aid can often also be a cue. However, the two terms are not automatically interchangeable; some cues are definitely not aids! A cue is an action performed to tell the horse what we want him to do. I am sure many people will have ridden riding school horses or ponies who canter when the instructor says 'Canter!' and not because of anything the rider has asked of them; that is a response to a verbal cue. You can teach a horse to halt by shouting 'Whoa!' (or 'Ho!' in some parts of the USA); in some countries riders use a whistle or some other vocal cue. An aid, on the other hand, is something that is supposed to *help* the horse, rather than simply telling him what to do. This is what I meant when, at the end of the previous chapter, I said that the words themselves would tell you the difference between a cue and an aid. 'Aid' in this sense means exactly what it does in everyday life, to help or assist – the old English word for an equestrian aid was indeed 'help' and this has simply been superseded in equestrian parlance by the French equivalent, from *aider*, to help.

Using cues

In theory (and in practice) we can teach the horse almost anything we want him to do by use of cues; indeed, many competition dressage horses are trained this way, which explains why a cleverly trained horse can sometimes make a poor rider look very much better than they really are. For example, you can teach a horse to *piaffe* quite easily by tapping his legs with a stick and rewarding every correct response, building up the movement step-by-step; this is the process known as *shaping*, which we came across in Chapter 7. The problem with this is that, used on its own, it bypasses gymnastic development. If you set out to teach the horse 'movements' in this way, out of their proper developmental context, you have missed the point, and the result is often a travesty of what it should be. All too often the give-away is the fact that the horse's hind feet lift higher than his forefeet, which means that he is on his forehand, and what he is performing is not a *piaffe* but a *piaffe-like* movement. Does it matter? Yes, it does. The whole point about advanced movements such as the *piaffe* is that they are supposed to represent the pinnacle of training under saddle: the point where the horse is so well balanced and can collect himself with such ease that every movement we ask him to make is carried out with minimum effort on the horse's part. Asking the horse to perform advanced movements before he is confirmed in collection may result in physical damage; many of the horses we see taking part in dressage competition, even at the highest level, are not properly collected, and are therefore unable to perform advanced movements correctly.[1]

If a horse is physically ready to perform advanced movements, then provided the training and riding have been correct, he will start to offer the beginnings of

1 For more on this subject, see Chapter 8 of my book *Realize your Horse's True Potential.*

them spontaneously and that is the point at which we begin to reinforce them. These movements do, after all, occur naturally – albeit not necessarily with much polish, as they often arise from excitement. Naturally, some horses find them easier to do than others and performing them under saddle, calmly and under the weight of a rider, is a completely different matter, requiring the proper gymnastic development referred to above.

This does not mean that we cannot teach the horse all kinds of things under saddle. However, we need to consider whether he is physically capable of doing whatever we are trying to teach him. It should never be simply a matter of teaching the horse to perform a movement just because we can!

It is, in any case, rather arrogant of us to presume that we can actually teach the horse anything when it comes to movement. As I said in an earlier book:

> They can run, jump, move sideways, backwards, pirouette, trot in circles, perform *piaffe*, *passage*, or just about anything else we might ask them to do. They already know how to be horses! Every movement we could possibly ask them to perform, they already know how to do. They do not have to be taught what to do, any more than a foal has to be taught how to stand up and run about... All we can really teach them is a better way to make use of their natural abilities.[i]

Cues may tell the horse *what* we want him to do, but not *how* we want him to do it. For example, halting in response to a verbal command is a very useful thing to teach horses, but it is not an aid; it is a cue. It may get the horse to halt, but it does nothing to *help* him to halt efficiently. So although halting a horse by using vocal cues is wonderful in an emergency, it is no substitute for correct riding!

The rider's body as an aid

Contrary to what many people believe, the aids are *not* 'mere conventions'.[ii] The greatest masters of equitation, who have contributed to the ethos of equitation known as *classical*, realized centuries ago that there are various ways in which we can help the horse to perform under saddle. These involve positioning the rider's body in such a way that the action we want the horse to perform flows naturally from that positioning, together with the use of the legs to stimulate the muscles which propel the horse forward, and the hands to receive and direct the impulsion thus produced. These aids evoke natural responses, not learned via a series of cues. We are using our own body to tell the horse what we want him to do with *his* body, and making it easy for him to do so. (For a fuller understanding of these natural responses see Karin Blignault's *Successful Schooling*, Chapters 1 and 4. See also *A Classical Riding Notebook* by Michael J. Stevens, *The Classical Seat* by Sylvia Loch, and *Invisible Riding*, also by Sylvia Loch. See also my earlier book, *Realize Your Horse's True Potential*. Details of these books are given in the Bibliography.)

Nuno Oliveira, one of the great masters of equitation, was renowned for his ability to use the aids with great subtlety, in ways that helped every horse he rode to perform beautifully under saddle. (From *Lusitano: Son of the Wind* by Arsenio Raposo Cordeiro, courtesy of Sr Raposo Cordeiro)

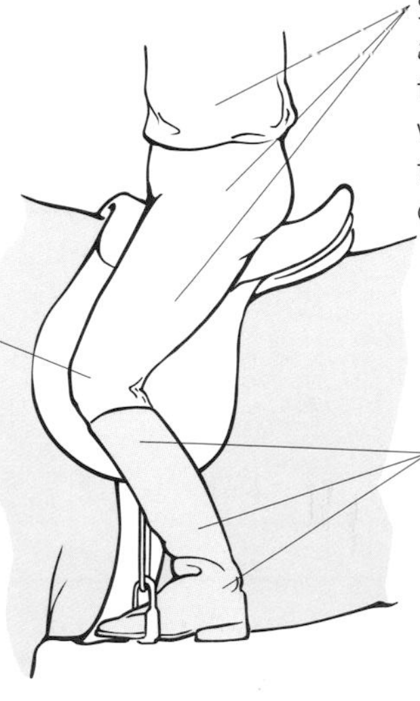
Subtle shifts of weight and muscle tone not only tell the horse, very precisely, what we want him to do, they actually help him to carry out our requests
Gripping with the knee (as opposed to holding it firmly against the saddle – there is a difference) acts to block the horse's forward impulse: light pressure here can be used as a stopping aid
Light, 'electric' touches of the rider's leg at these points stimulate the horse's abdominal muscles to raise his back and bring his hind limbs forward

Figure 8: The rider's body can be used, very subtly, as an aid.

The role of negative reinforcement

But surely this means we must still make use of negative reinforcement? It does, but as I said in Chapter 7, the use of 'negative' in this context need not mean anything unpleasant; it is simply a description of the process involved. The reason why so many people have come to view *any* use of -R in an adverse light is the way in which it has been described in various books and magazine articles. Unfortunately many of the authors (and this includes some very experienced horse trainers!) seem to have an extremely crude idea of what the aids entail. For example Karen Pryor says that 'The horse learns to turn left when the left rein is pulled, but only if the pulling stops when it does turn. The cessation is the reinforcer. You get on a horse, kick it in the sides, and it moves forward; you should then stop kicking (unless you want it to move faster).'[iii] Pryor repeats her statement, cited in Chapter 7, about -R inevitably containing a punisher: 'When you pull on the left rein, until the moment that the horse turns, you are punishing going straight ahead.'[iv] However, she is using as her example the crudest form of riding there is. In the various classical schools of riding, the idea of pulling a horse around by his head in order to turn would be regarded as violating one of the most basic principles of classical riding. By this I mean the idea that one rides the horse from back to front. The rider does not turn the horse by pulling him

Rider Elaine Herbert asks Lusitano stallion Prazer to turn using her body position and subtle shifts of weight. Prazer complies willingly because Elaine has made it easy for him to do so. (L. Skipper)

around; on the contrary, the turn is merely *indicated* by the hand. I was always taught to 'lead the way' with my thumb, in other words the hand is merely rotated outward slightly. The sensation felt by the horse should never be more than very mild indeed; no more than the sensation felt when someone touches your elbow to guide you in a specific direction. The rider turns their body in the direction of the turn (shoulders and hips are parallel with the horse's shoulders and hips), and the horse, mirroring the rider, turns in the same direction. This ensures that the horse actually bends his body as opposed to simply bending his neck in the direction of the turn.[2]

In this way of riding the negative aspect is confined to the fact that the rider asks for the turn by changing the positioning of their body; the horse, wanting to stay in balance beneath them, turns his body accordingly, and the rider stops asking for the turn. Where is the element of punishment in that? The alternative is not to change our weight distribution at all. Say we ask the horse to turn (using a verbal cue) but stay in exactly the same position in the saddle as we were in before the turn. What do you think is going to happen? The horse is being asked to go one way but our weight distribution does not change to allow for this and, as a result, serves to hamper the horse's ability to turn efficiently. Effectively, we are no longer in harmony with the horse and in fact could be said to be riding *against* him.

The classical way

It helps if we think of the horse and rider as a pair of dancers in traditional ballroom dancing: one leads, and the other follows. The leader does not just push or pull his partner around; it is more a matter of indicating to the partner where to go by subtle changes in balance. The rider must also be subtle, and this is the art of riding. As Karin Blignault says:

> We explain to the horse, with our body, what to do with his body. Thus it is a body language which explains, very specifically to the horse, which muscles to contract. We use the aids in a very specific way to influence the horse's natural balance and righting reactions and therefore facilitate the movement we want.[v]

To reiterate: the aids do not only tell the horse where we want him to go, they *help* him to achieve what we are asking. This is the basis of classical riding.

Attempts to train the horse without paying sufficient attention to the rider's position in the saddle and what they are doing (often subconsciously) with their body are responsible for a great deal of physical and mental damage to horses.[3]

2 The horse who does this is not using his body correctly; he is disconnected at the base of his neck, out of balance and difficult to steer. Indeed, horses who have been ridden like this for any length of time are often wooden and very uncomfortable to ride, because they are not supple enough. This is the fault of the training and riding, not the horse!

This is why the use of the clicker (or any other marker) should never be used as a replacement for correct aiding; it is an additional training tool, not a substitute for good riding. The rider must still develop a feel for what is happening under the saddle and at the end of the reins, and listen to the feedback the horse is giving by way of his physical responses. We are never for one moment relieved of the need to practise good horsemanship!

In this context, then, 'negative' does not mean anything unpleasant for the horse, it simply means that when the rider stops applying the aids, they are *removing* the stimulus (-R). In classical riding we use this very mild -R in combination with lots of +R. I think that effective – and humane – training under saddle combines +R with the mildest kind of -R. The latter does not have to be unpleasant for the horse; on the contrary, it can help him immensely by making it easy for him to comply with what we ask of him.

We can (indeed, should) still use +R in the course of our ridden work. My husband and I did this for many years before we knew anything about the principles of conditioning, simply because it seemed right and logical to do so. For example, when a horse performs a movement well we say, 'Goood,' or 'Yes, that's the way' and the horse knows by our tone of voice that he has done well and that a treat (food, a stroke, a scratch or whatever the horse likes) will be forthcoming when the session ends. The advantage of the clicker (or a more discrete vocal sound used as a marker) is that it can mark with greater precision the exact point at which the horse has performed correctly, whether it is a correct canter transition or some other aspect of movement.

Using negative and positive reinforcement on the ground

Suppose we want to teach the horse to step back. There are several ways of doing this. Perhaps the commonest, unthinking method is to approach the horse waving our arms and shouting, 'Get back!' The sensitive horse may well shoot away; very few horses will stand still while people wave arms in their faces. Some horses might think that such shouting and arm-waving is a prelude to a physical attack, and as a result they could become nervous whenever people approach them. They might also develop a degree of head-shyness; I have seen this happen with a number of horses subjected to this treatment. A less sensitive horse might ignore the shouting and arm-waving completely, which leaves the arm-waver with very little to fall back on short of actual physical assault to make the horse move back.

Another common approach, which often meets with a degree of success, is to

3 For an understanding of why this is so, see my earlier book *Realize Your Horse's True Potential*; see also Sylvia Loch, *The Classical Seat and Dressage in Lightness*, and Mary Wanless, *Ride With Your Mind*.

physically push the horse in the chest until he moves back. Again, this may work with more sensitive horses, and if paired with the exclamation 'Back!' may result in a horse who steps back as soon as he hears the command 'Back!' However, it is not so successful with the horse who simply doesn't feel like stepping back; you could push and shove some horses all day and they would not move (many Warmbloods are like this, but such horses can be found in all breeds). It also smacks of physical assault, albeit of a very mild nature, and some horses may take exception to this.

One method used by some trainers to get horses to back up from the ground consists of waving or twirling a long line at them. This is effective because no horse likes having things waved or waggled in his face. However, although this technique has its place, in its more extreme forms it is not exactly a pleasant experience for the horse. At the same time as the horse is stepping away from the waggling line, he is also raising his head to avoid the line, which acts to hollow his back. Horses *can* back up with a raised head and hollowed back, but the process is difficult and may actually be painful for them, and they may become predisposed to head-shyness as a result of trying to avoid the line.

All the above methods rely on *aversion*; if the action the horse wants to avoid ceases as soon as he backs up, then the horse's behaviour (i.e. backing up) has been reinforced. They are all examples of -R. As we have seen, this can either be quite unpleasant for the horse (as above), or it can be relatively benign. An example of benign -R is a method which involves taking hold of the horse's headcollar (or a rope attached to the centre ring of the headcollar) and exerting mild pressure on either the headcollar or the rope; the horse steps back to avoid the pressure, which is instantly released.[4] Although there is certainly a degree of pressure involved, most horses accept this method quite readily, and it does not seem to have any of the unpleasant side-effects associated with the other methods mentioned.

Do we have to use -R at all, though? What method can we use that is actually pleasant for the horse as well as being physically comfortable? We can wait until the horse steps back of his own accord and then reinforce the behaviour as it occurs (+R). Alternatively, we may set up a situation in which we can elicit the behaviour we want. Before trying the following exercise you will need to make sure that your horse has been taught to touch a target as described in Chapter 7 and has been confirmed in his response to being asked to do so.

Hold the target (which, as previously explained, can be anything you choose) fairly close to his chest, high enough so that he cannot simply bend his neck and touch it; make sure he knows it is there. Say 'Touch!' and you will find that in

4 This is the basis of the technique known as 'pressure and release', used effectively by trainers such as Alexandra Kurland and Kelly Marks.

order to touch the target he has to step back. The instant he takes the first step, reinforce his action with a small amount of food, a scratch or whatever he likes. Once he is confirmed in stepping back you can introduce the cue; this will typically be 'Back!' When he is stepping back consistently as soon as you say 'Back!' you can build on this as described in Chapter 7 and get him to take progressively more steps backwards; you do not reward him until he takes another step back, and so on until eventually you only have to say 'Back!' and he automatically takes the required number of steps backwards. This is only one method of teaching a horse to step back; you may be able to think of many others. The main thing is that we understand the principles used in the example given; once we have this understanding, we can start to apply these principles to many other situations.

Some people maintain that +R and -R should not be combined, but many very good trainers do make use of a combination of mild -R with +R, with excellent results. However, it is important that we understand when we are, in fact, using -R and do not confuse it with +R. Its use should never be oppressive or forceful, or we will be negating the effects of any +R that we may also be using. Remember that we are only truly using +R when we reinforce a behaviour that is freely offered, with the horse under no restraint and able to go away if he so chooses. Anything else is -R, whatever trainers choose to call it. Whether the -R is benign or oppressive depends on how it is used, the individual trainer's approach and on the sensitivity of the horse. Well used, mild -R can provide the horse with clear, unambiguous indications of what we want. Used oppressively,

Brian encourages Nivalis to put his forefeet on the bale of straw. Nivalis offered this behaviour freely, starting with pawing at the bale and progressing to putting his feet up on it. NB: if you are trying something like this, use a more stable, solid base, as straw bales tend to tip over and additionally the horse could get his foot caught in the baling twine. (L. Skipper)

Once Nivalis has both forefeet on the bale, Brian uses +R (in this case a Polo mint) to increase the horse's willingness to repeat the action. This kind of training is not only fun, it also benefits horses; by doing new and different things they learn how to learn, and their world is enriched by new experiences. (L. Skipper)

it can sour a horse, create stress and lead to behavioural problems. Whatever method you use, remember that stress is the enemy of true learning, which cannot take place if the horse is tense or frightened. Treat the horse as an individual, and never become so bound up with the method that you stop listening to the horse!

Underlying processes

From all this we can see that training methods which often seem to give spectacular results do so because they are based on an understanding of learning processes. Sometimes this understanding may be intuitive; there are many perfectly good trainers who get excellent results without ever really knowing exactly what they do to achieve those results; some 'natural horsemanship' trainers as well as many traditional trainers come into this category. Writing about the evident success of techniques such as 'approach and retreat' Karen Pryor observes:

> Trainers who use these techniques often have superstitious explanations for what is happening; and while many have formed the habit of making some sound or motion that functions as the marker signal or the conditioned reinforcer, few are consciously aware of doing so. Nevertheless, it is not magic at work; it is the laws of operant conditioning.[vi]

What happens in the process cited by Pryor? As she explains, it is often used with animals who are very shy, such as llamas. Any attempt to approach them directly would result in instant flight, so the trainer approaches as far as possible before this flight reaction kicks in. This approach constitutes a mild negative stimulus; if the llama stands still, the trainer then retreats, removing the negative stimulus (the presence of the trainer); this removal acts as a reinforcer (-R). The trainer gradually gets closer and closer until the llama will tolerate his presence without running away. A positive reinforcer (say a bucket of food) is then introduced and the llama realizes that standing still in the trainer's presence might be a good thing after all. It is important to realize that the negative or aversive stimulus here (i.e. the presence of the trainer) is very mild and relatively benign, and the animals soon realize that the trainer's presence is not harmful: in other words, they become habituated, as described in Chapter 7.

However, some other methods commonly used by the new wave of trainers may not always be so benign. This is not to say that the intention behind them is not good; it is the use of such methods without an understanding of how they really work that can create problems. This includes certain techniques for gaining control of the horse's feet; the idea is that by controlling the feet we gain control of the whole horse. There is much truth in this, but anyone using such methods needs to take care that they are not sending out conflicting messages to the horse. As we saw in Chapter 3, if we adopt an aggressive attitude (and this might mean nothing more than mildly aggressive body language), we are telling the horse to go away while at the same time preventing him from doing so (e.g. because we have hold of him on the end of a rope). This can create serious conflict and, depending on how the technique is used, can even introduce an element of punishment. This does not mean that we should never use such methods. With some horses, especially bumptious young colts who – perhaps because they have been isolated from normal equine society – have never learned appropriate behaviour and how to respect personal space, the technique of (for example) swinging a rope to induce the horse to move away and keep his distance can be very useful.[5] However, such techniques should be used very carefully, and with due regard to the temperament of the horse in question; used indiscriminately, such techniques could – by introducing the elements of conflict and punishment already referred to – render a timid horse neurotic or a bolder one dangerous.

Criticisms have also been levelled at the use of round pens in training, and for similar reasons; if the horse feels under too much pressure in the round pen, he may well react explosively. Responsible trainers apply only mild pressure and know when to back off; it is the less responsible trainers who have given rise to criticism of round pen techniques.

5 Abigail Hogg gives a very good example of this in her *Horse Behaviour Handbook*, cited in Chapter 3.

Learned helplessness

Overuse of methods which create conflict could possibly induce in certain horses a state of what is known as 'learned helplessness'. This term was introduced by the psychologist Martin Seligman in the 1970s. Seligman demonstrated that animals placed in an experimental position in which they cannot avoid something unpleasant (such as an electric shock) no matter what they do, will later generalize their experiences in situations where they are powerless to situations in which they *could* act to avoid unpleasantness, or even life-threatening situations, but they fail to do so. In other words, they have been trained to be helpless.

Seligman's theories have not gone unchallenged, especially as other experiments have shown that learned helplessness may be a temporary state, which resolves itself after a comparatively short time (sometimes as little as forty-eight hours). Some other researchers believe that learned helplessness is produced by some form of debilitation induced by stress, and that it is a short-term physiological imbalance that is self-correcting with the passage of time.

Even so, it is easy to see how the concept of learned helplessness could apply to certain horses, subjected to the kind of situation described above, especially if the trainer employs aggressive body language but gives the horse no opportunity to move right away (for example because he is held on a rope or confined in a pen, round or otherwise). Such horses could well fall into a state of learned helplessness. This would mean that their natural flight responses would be suppressed, resulting in a horse who, to all outward appearances, is exceptionally obedient, but who is in fact in a state of induced helplessness. I do not mean to suggest that all such methods carry this risk, or that all horses are likely to be so affected, but it is something to be aware of if trying such techniques.

The same warnings could apply to many more conventional training methods; the advantage here is that it is much easier to see what is going on, and to take appropriate action. Take, for example, the horse who is ridden on a harsh contact, with the reins held short and tight, while the rider tries to boot the horse into submission in the hope that 'riding him into the contact' in this manner will somehow induce the much sought-after head carriage.[6] Apart from the fact that this is physically injurious to the horse, it is also illogical – the equivalent of driving a car hard with the handbrake on. Some – perhaps most – horses simply cannot produce the required 'outline' without prior suppling and gymnasticizing exercises, not to mention sympathetic and well-balanced riding. Such horses, repeatedly subjected to the kind of riding mentioned above, may also fall into a kind of 'learned helplessness', and take on a 'spaced out' look, with glazed eyes

6 For more about the elusive 'outline', see Chapter 8 of my earlier book, *Realize Your Horse's True Potential* (J.A. Allen 2003).

and the kind of vacant expression which people often describe by the saying, 'The lights are on but no one's at home'.

Frozen watchfulness

Early in 2004 a series of articles in a popular equestrian magazine introduced the idea that certain training methods were inducing in horses a state of what was called 'frozen watchfulness'. It was suggested that horses affected in this way might display hyper-vigilance towards their trainers, constantly watching for cues in the trainer's body language; crowd their trainers; perform many appeasing behaviours and displacement activities and be quiet and withdrawn outside the training session.

These articles created quite a stir in some equestrian circles, together with a great deal of confusion. However, I have already raised the question of training-induced anxiety in horses in Chapter 4 and in the paragraphs above on learned helplessness. And, as we saw in Chapter 6, appeasement behaviours are not really part of a horse's behavioural repertoire. Furthermore 'frozen watchfulness' is a psychological term defined as 'An alertness or even hyper-vigilance that is maintained despite an overall inhibition of motor activity that may include mutism' [vii] and it is used specifically to describe a condition common in abused children. It is therefore inappropriate to apply it in regard to horses and its use seems to be another example of the misappropriation of scientific terms. I have only mentioned it here because so many people have been alarmed or confused by its use in the articles referred to, and this confusion seems likely to remain with us for some considerable time.

Evaluating methods

No one system of training is infallible and no one system will suit every horse, no matter what anyone says. The thing to remember is that training methods are *tools*, which like any tool can be misused, or they can be a valuable part of the trainer's toolkit; this applies whether one uses +R or -R. For example, round pens have been used in the training of horses for at least two thousand years. Used well, they can be a helpful way of working with horses in a safe enclosure in which no one can get trapped in a corner if things go wrong.[7] Used badly, they can make a horse feel trapped and induce feelings of panic, which the horse may either suppress or act upon.

To take another example, it is possible to abuse clicker training by using it to

7 I have seen a round pen used very effectively in the rehabilitation of a sensitive Lipizzaner rendered psychotic by mistreatment.

The round pen can provide a safe environment in which to work without the risk of anyone getting trapped in a corner if things go wrong. Here, Kelly Marks is allowing a youngster to let off steam while keeping things under a degree of control. (Courtesy of Kelly Marks)

overcome a horse's reluctance to perform an action. We may congratulate ourselves on having trained our horse to do whatever we want by means of a humane method, only to find that his reluctance to perform was caused by pain or discomfort, or that he was not yet physically ready to perform that particular movement. This does not mean that the method is wrong; it just means that we have not made proper use of it.

One way in which we can evaluate the effects of a specific method is by observing horses being trained by that method. This is most commonly by means of public demonstrations; however, some trainers hold 'open days' on their premises for visitors to see them at work. If you have the opportunity to watch trainers at work using different methods, you may be able to see how those methods actually work, as opposed to claims made about how they work. It is essential to keep an open mind because sometimes, especially at demonstrations, there is an element of showmanship involved, and it is easy to be seduced by this and to overlook what is actually going on. Learn as much as you can by observing horses who are obviously contented and relaxed in their work, so you can recognize whether horses being trained by a particular method are actually responding positively or whether they are tense, withdrawn and unhappy about the whole process.

Ultimately, all we can really do is expand our knowledge as much as possible, so that we understand the principles of training, are aware of the effects of what we are doing and can anticipate and avoid the kind of actions that result in distress to our horses.

i Lesley Skipper, *Realize Your Horse's True Potential*, J.A. Allen 2003, pp.144–145.
ii Pryor, *Don't Shoot the Dog*, p.75.
iii Pryor, *Don't Shoot the Dog*, p.9.
iv Pryor, *Don't Shoot the Dog*, p.7.
v Karin Blignault, *Successful Schooling*, J.A. Allen 1997, p.10.
vi Pryor, *Don't Shoot the Dog*, p.7.
vii Jane E. Edgerton, *American Psychiatric Glossary, 7th Edition*. Washington, DC: American Psychiatric Press 1994.

Chapter 9

The Best Start in Life

When you're a foal, you've got to larn to respect your elders and behave right.

Richard Adams, *Traveller*

Most of us find foals irresistible. There is something about those enormous, liquid eyes, that velvet-soft coat and those impossibly long, wobbly legs that appeals to something deep inside us. This appeal is so strong that it is all too easy to forget that it takes time, effort and resources to raise a foal. Then, when the foal has grown up, you have a mature horse on your hands, whom you either have to be prepared to care for yourself, or else find a good home for him.

It is not at all uncommon for people to buy mares without realizing that they are in foal. However, increasing numbers of ordinary horse owners are either buying foals or breeding their own, because they like the idea of bringing up their own youngster.

This is an exciting prospect but it carries with it enormous responsibilities. As we have seen, an animal's character and temperament are shaped not only by genetic influences, but by his lifetime experiences. How you raise your foal can have an enormous impact on these experiences, hence the emphasis on giving a young horse the best possible start.

Naturally, this begins immediately after birth. A young animal's very first experiences are among the most important in his life; recognition of this explains why so many horse owners have turned to a method of training which begins in the very first hour after birth. This method has been called 'imprint training' although, as we shall, see that term is not entirely accurate.

Foals are irresistible: Tariel at six weeks old.

Imprinting and imprint training

Imprinting is how animals learn their species identity. It is nature's way of ensuring that a duck knows he is a duck, a goat that he is a goat, and a horse that he is a horse. The image of the mother is 'imprinted' on the baby's brain to aid recognition so that the baby will not try to follow either another individual of the same species, or an animal of a different species, which in some cases could be fatal. In his delightful book *King Solomon's Ring* one of the founders of ethology, Konrad Lorenz, gives some hilarious descriptions of birds who, having imprinted on him, proceeded to treat him as another bird and would try to feed him worms and other choice morsels. At one time ethologists thought that the imprinting process was irreversible but, although this may be true of some species of birds, it is not so with many other birds and mammals. However, there is a period during which the imprinting must take place or else it will not happen at all: this is often referred to as the 'sensitive period';[1] in horses it appears to start during the second hour following birth[i] and may last for up to twenty-four hours, although the length of time involved is not known precisely.

In the 1990s an American veterinary surgeon, Dr Robert Miller, devised a technique which he believed mirrored the imprinting process. According to Miller, if a foal is handled intensively during the first few hours after birth this will make later handling easy and render the horse more trainable.

This training starts immediately after the foal is born. The foal's navel stump is treated with disinfectant and the foal is rubbed dry. The mare is allowed to lick and smell the foal; the idea is that the foal will bond with both the mare and the handler. Then a process of desensitization takes place. The handler rubs the foal all over until he relaxes; Miller recommends that clippers are run over the foal's body, including the head and ears. Finally, the entire body is rubbed with a piece of crackling plastic.

This initial 'imprint' session is said to take about an hour. On the following day all the 'desensitized' areas are tested, and if the foal does not remain relaxed, the process is repeated on any problem areas. Then the handler puts their arms around the girth area and rhythmically squeezes the chest until the foal is habituated to the sensation. The foal can be desensitized to all manner of scary objects, such as flapping bags, garden hoses, dogs, running water, etc. Having been desensitized to potentially alarming sensations, the foal can then be sensitized to respond to touch (e.g. by moving away from the handler's touch) and to being led around in a halter.

Miller claims that imprint training can make handling easier and enhance later training. He maintains that it works because:

- The foal bonds with the imprint trainer as well as his dam.
- This means that the foal sees humans not as predators but as fellow horses.
- Submission is obtained without fear. Because the foal cannot escape the exposure to frightening stimuli, he becomes dependent and submissive.

1 In some older ethological literature this is referred to as the 'critical period'.

- This is because the foal sees the human trainer as a dominant horse or herd leader.

Unfortunately, there are a number of problems with Miller's theory. First, the term 'imprint training' is misleading. True imprinting occurs because the newborn animal has an inborn tendency to follow anything that moves; in normal situations this will be the mother. In true imprinting the foal can only bond with one animal – usually his dam. If the foal did become imprinted on the human handler, he would establish a social preference for humans, which could be disastrous. Such a foal might be rejected by his dam, and would be likely to try to play with humans as he would with another horse; this could cause problems even with foals, given their strength, and with a fully grown horse it could result in serious injury to the human. A sexually mature colt could well see humans as potential mates; it does not require too much imagination to see how dangerous that could be! Second, Miller assumes that imprinting is irreversible, which many studies have shown is not necessarily the case. Furthermore, although a sensitive period has been established for true imprinting, this does not apply to the kind of training which takes place during 'imprint training' sessions. The kinds of things the foal learns during such sessions can all be taught at any stage in a horse's life, although it could be argued that such training is best started reasonably early in life rather than later, when the habits of a lifetime have already affected the horse's responses.

Even if we do not quibble too much about what label is attached to the method, there are still serious problems with the thinking behind it. Miller seems to have based his ideas on a number of faulty assumptions. These are:

- The foal's ability to imprint simultaneously on his dam and on the human trainer. The foal may well develop a bond with the latter, but unless he truly imprints on the human instead of on his dam, he is highly unlikely to see the human as another horse.

- That submission is obtained without fear. This is highly debatable. By Miller's own admission, his method makes use of flooding, as described in Chapter 7. As we saw there, flooding can actually increase fear. Foals subjected to 'imprint training' may well appear submissive, but – as with horses trained by overuse of -R – this submission may actually be a form of learned helplessness.

- That the foal sees the human as a dominant horse or herd leader. Miller states that psychologically this is the ideal relationship between horse and human. However, this brings up all the objections raised in Chapter 3, namely that horses move away from dominant conspecifics (and if they really thought humans were rather odd-shaped horses, they would surely move away from a dominant human!), and that dominance does *not* equate to leadership.

- That squeezing the foal around the girth area will, by habituating him to the sensation, prevent him from becoming 'cold-backed' in later years. This overlooks the fact that, with some sensitive horses, a reaction to the feeling of the girth is physical as well as psychological. Such horses react to a sudden or too forceful tightening of the girth by sagging at the knees or, in some cases, actually fainting.[2] The reason for this may be that the sudden tightening of the girth produces a shock to the system akin to a fear response, which results in dilation of the blood vessels in the muscles (in preparation for a flight response); in some horses the heart rate does not rise sufficiently to balance this dilation and the resulting imbalance causes a drop in blood pressure and subsequent fainting. Sometimes the reaction is more dramatic; the horse may back up or actually rear in panic. I have seen both reactions in horses who are physically sensitive, and with such horses it is necessary to be extremely careful and tactful when fastening the girth. Squeezing a foal who is sensitive in this way could well provoke a panic attack.

Some people who have tried this 'imprinting' process have claimed that it gives excellent results. However, many others report the opposite. There have been cases where foals have struggled so hard to escape the intensive handling procedures that they have been severely injured, or even died. Devotees of this method might point out that this was the fault of the trainers, not of the method. However, the problem is that Dr Miller is very specific that each desensitization procedure must be repeated until the foal is thoroughly habituated to it. If the procedure is stopped because the foal is struggling, he will learn that all he has to do to avoid the procedure is struggle. Although there has never been any suggestion that Dr Miller himself would persist until a foal was injured, his message is loud and clear: don't stop until the foal submits! Moreover, he states specifically that a stimulus can be underdone, but not overdone. This being so, it is hardly surprising that some trainers have gone too far and persisted until the foal is injured or completely exhausted.

One of the greatest dangers of this kind of training is that it interferes with the development of the foal's relationship with his mother. A human trainer carrying out desensitizing procedures on a foal very soon after birth may not only be delaying the bonding of the foal with his dam, but also preventing the foal from suckling and thus obtaining the essential vitamins and antibodies present in the colostrum (the liquid which is secreted from the mammary glands before and just after giving birth).

2 Two of our own horses, both Arabians (Zareeba and Roxzella) react in this manner if the utmost care is not taken in girthing them up.

Does imprint training actually work?

Even with all these potential problems, some people may feel that the benefits of imprint training outweigh the risks. So what evidence is there – other than a few enthusiastic testimonies from horse owners – that 'imprint training' actually works? A group of researchers from the Department of Animal Science at Texas A & M University carried out a study on 131 foals to determine the effects of imprint training. They concluded that neither the number nor the timing of imprint sessions influenced the foals' behaviour at six months of age, and they concluded that imprint training did not result in better behaved, less reactive foals.[ii] Similarly, Dr Marthe Kiley-Worthington cites examples from her own domestic herd, where she found no difference in long-term response to humans between foals handled all over (but non-invasively) immediately after birth, and those left untouched until two weeks after birth.[iii]

So the best practice would appear to be: if all is going well and the foal is suckling normally, leave him and his mother to form and consolidate their relationship for a couple of days to a week before handling the foal. Some early handling is unavoidable but this should be kept to a minimum unless real problems arise.

Building a foundation of trust

When the foal has bonded with his mother, gentle handling will build a foundation of trust in humans. Using the conditioning principles described in Chapters 7 and 8, foals can be haltered, taught to lead calmly, have their feet picked up (and if necessary trimmed), to accept being wormed, vaccinated, etc. To begin with, we do nothing more than spend a little time with the foal. Contrary to what we are often taught, foals do not 'naturally' think of humans as The Enemy. They are what is called *naïve*; in other words *everything* in this new world is potentially a little scary, just as it can be for human infants, until they learn who and what they can feel safe with. It is up to us to ensure that we do nothing to cause the foal to distrust us. This can be difficult if we have to carry out unpleasant procedures, such as getting kaolin-based liquids into a scouring foal. However, if we have ensured that the foal's very first experience of us is as pleasant as possible, most of them will quickly get over any feelings of resentment!

Handling the foal

Once they recognize us as beings whom they can trust, most foals like to be rubbed, scratched, stroked, etc. This helps to establish us as people it is good to be with; as far as our mare Imzadi was concerned it was so successful that she wanted to be with us all the time, even though she had developed normal

Brian makes himself smaller so as not to intimidate the foal. Here, he makes friends with Nivalis's daughter, Foxton Velvet. (L. Skipper)

below Now that Velvet has accepted him, Brian stands up. The foal is quite happy to stay with him. (L. Skipper)

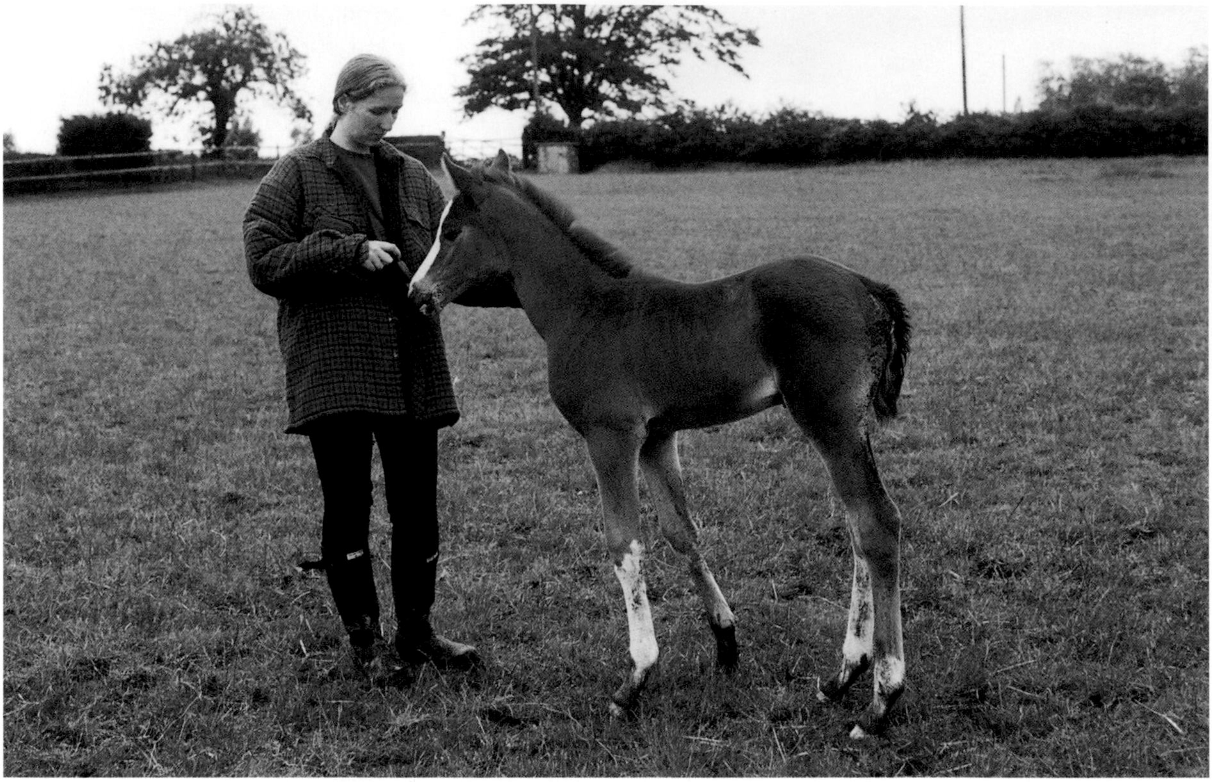

Imzadi used to follow us everywhere, even though she had normal relationships with other horses. (L. Skipper)

relationships with other horses. She would follow us around the field, often stopping to watch what we were doing as we went about our routine maintenance tasks such as mending fences, filling the water container, etc. If we stopped to examine something, we would quickly end up with an inquisitive foal peering over our shoulders!

Picking up the feet

When trust has been established and the foal is used to being handled, we can begin to teach him to have his feet picked up calmly and without fuss. First, make sure that the foal will come to you and stay with you for a stroke or a scratch, and that (based on your general observations) he has developed sufficient sense of balance to allow him to stand briefly on three feet. He should also have been introduced to the idea that a marker (whether a clicker or something such as a vocal marker, e.g. 'Good!') signals that he has done the right thing. Choose a time when there are no distractions and the foal is calm and attentive. Run your hand lightly down the back of one of his fore cannons. He may respond by lifting that foot slightly; if not, squeeze the foot behind the pastern *gently* (this is an example of mild -R). Most foals will lift the foot at this point; if your foal does not do so, repeat the action until he does, but do *not* persist to a point where he gets

Steps in teaching foals to pick up their feet

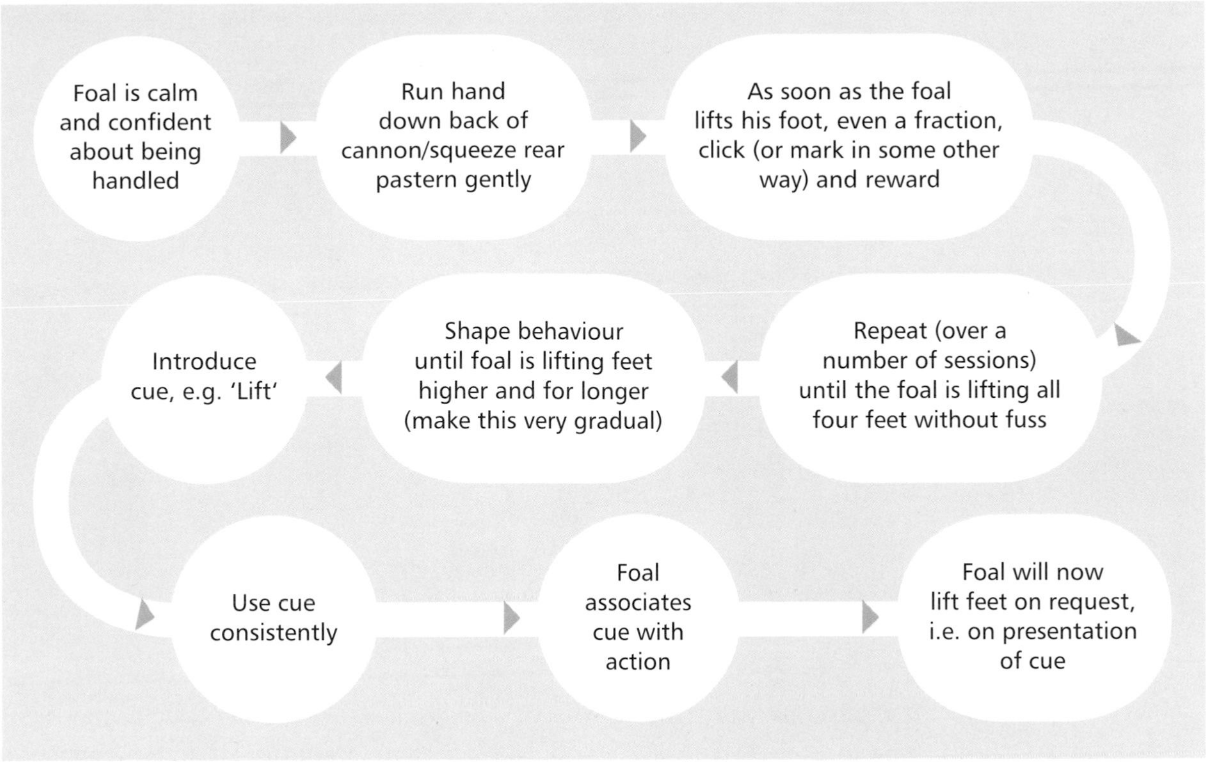

Remember to make all training sessions short and never stress the foal by asking too much, too soon. If you encounter problems, stop and go back a step. This is training, not a competition!

Figure 9: Teaching foals to pick up their feet.

annoyed or distressed. Leave the training for another time; eventually he will respond. When this happens, even if the foot is lifted only for a second or two, release it immediately and reward the foal with fuss and a scratch or, if he is already on a creep feed, a small amount of food.

Build on this by shaping as described in Chapter 7 until you can hold the foot for longer and a little bit higher. Never hang onto the foot; the last thing we want is to provoke a battle of wills. This is a training session, not a competition! If the foal pulls away, ignore it and go back a step. Try to anticipate any pulling away by feeling when tension is developing, and release the foot gently before this happens. Never try to hold the foot too high; this can cause the foal pain and may result in a loss of the trust you have so carefully built up. Once the foal will pick all four feet up sequentially while remaining relaxed, you can introduce a cue (such as 'Lift!') as described in Chapter 7.

Brian with Foxton Velvet: this filly learned to trust humans at an early age and having her feet picked up was, for her, just a normal part of her routine. (L. Skipper)

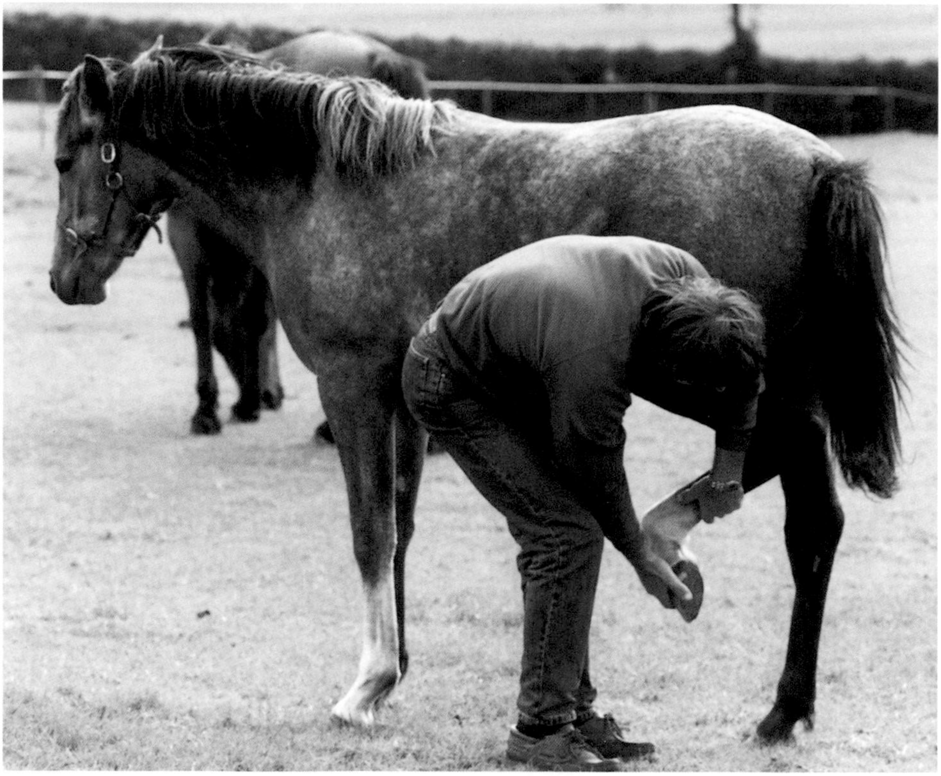

Velvet is quite happy to stand unrestrained while Brian picks up her hind foot. Too often people (especially farriers) pick the hind feet up too high, which causes the horse discomfort and leads to resistance. (L. Skipper)

Haltering and leading

There is no need to try to halter the foal too early; he may find it rather frightening as it can feel restrictive to him. Body language is usually quite adequate to guide small foals where you want them to go. I have found that as long as foals have not been allowed to become frightened or over-excited it is quite unnecessary to do more than use one's body in the way I described in Chapter 6.

Having got the foal gradually accustomed to being handled (that is, over a period of days or even weeks, with handling sessions kept very short) and, equally gradually, to having his feet picked up, even if only for a few seconds, we can then progress to haltering.

The halter should be put on very gently and carefully; the foal can be distracted by a scratch or a rub or whatever he likes best. Once he has accepted it without fuss, it should be taken off again and the foal made much of. If it takes more than one session for him to accept the halter, then that is fine; we gain absolutely nothing by rushing at this stage. When we have reached the point where we can put the halter on and take it off without any objections being raised, we can move on to teaching the foal to lead. This is an instance where the clicker or a vocal marker is invaluable, as in the later stages we will not be standing next to the foal, so be sure to teach him to associate the marker with a reward, as described in Chapter 7. If he has already learned to like being rubbed or scratched we can pair this with a cue such as his name: with our filly, Imzadi, it was of course, 'Imzadi, come!' Before long she was responding to her name and coming to us for a scratch or a rub.

When a foal is responding reliably in this way we can move on to something else. By employing the selective schedule of reinforcement described in Chapter 7 we can teach a new behaviour, that of walking on. When the foal comes to us we do not reward him; instead we move away. He may stand there, puzzled, but if his initial training has been good enough the chances are that he will take a few steps forward. As he does this we say, 'Walk on!' and reinforce the behaviour using whatever marker we have chosen (a click or a vocal marker, for example). As long as we do not expect too much all at once, the foal will soon be walking on when we ask him to. We can then reintroduce the halter and, taking hold of it very gently (we do not want to provoke any resistance), ask the foal to walk on. Before long the foal will be quite happy to be led; foals trained like this seldom pull away, and if they do they quickly learn that once they move forward again the pressure of the halter – which they have created themselves (because you are being entirely passive and *not* pulling back) – will cease.[3]

It is important that all these processes are carried out as calmly as possible,

3 This is another example of mild -R.

and it is essential to remember that foals are babies with a very limited attention span. Any lessons must be kept short and, as with older horses, do not keep on repeating a lesson once the foal has shown signs of understanding what you want. Treat even a little progress as success, with lots of fuss and rewards.

Weaning: necessary evil or unnecessary trauma?

A great deal has been written in the last couple of decades about the desirability or otherwise of weaning foals, with equestrian experts such as Dr Marthe Kiley-Worthington and Andy Beck pointing out the adverse effects the trauma of sudden or early weaning can have on a horse's psychological development. In spite of this, many books and magazine articles on breeding scarcely touch on this subject, and even where the potential problems are recognized, many such publications focus on how and when to wean foals, rather than asking whether it is necessary in the first place.

Regrettably, early and/or sudden weaning is very widespread nowadays, especially on large studs. This has not always been the case; I once asked the former stud manager of what was for many years one of Britain's leading Arabian studs whether and at what stage they weaned their foals. 'Never,' he replied, 'unless it was absolutely necessary' – for example, if the mare was ill or unable to carry on feeding the foal.

Several scientific studies have been carried out on the effects of weaning; these have concentrated largely on the short-term effects, but even here the amount of distress so obviously suffered by the foals in question suggests that longer-term effects may persist into adulthood.

Our own foals are either weaned very gradually or not at all. Our stallion Nivalis was gradually separated from his dam at the age of nine months, over a period of several weeks. To begin with they were turned out in adjoining fields so that they could still see and touch each other, for longer and longer periods each day; then at night they were stabled together. Eventually they spent less and less time together, until finally they were turned out in separate fields and housed at night in separate stables. Even then they could still see each other and, as described in Chapter 5, they have retained their mutual affection.

Kiri's son Toska lived with his dam until he was over a year old; he socialized with the other horses, and was gradually separated from his dam in the manner described above. We saw in Chapter 5 that Imzadi, Kiri's offspring by Nivalis, stayed with her dam until she was five years old; although she spent a considerable amount of time away from Kiri and with the other horses, she still shared a large stable with her mother until they were finally housed separately in the summer of 2002. Of our other horses, we know nothing of Kiri's early history and very little of Roxzella's; we do know however that Roxzella was never forcibly

Nivalis and his dam Roxzella were separated from each other gradually when Nivalis was about nine months old. When turned out in different fields they could still see and touch each other. Here they greet each other over the fence. (L. Skipper)

separated from her dam. Tiff, Zareeba and Kruger were never weaned; their separation from their dams was, as with our home-bred horses, gradual and non-stressful.

Comfort-seeking behaviour

It is interesting that, before Imzadi's eventual separation from her mother, whenever she found herself in a mildly stressful situation she would rush over to Kiri and start suckling. This is comfort-seeking behaviour and if a mare rising five still found it important, how much more important must it be for a foal? In fact, foals have been seen seeking comfort in this fashion by a number of observers; Stephanie Tyler saw several foals sucking on the teats of older fillies, and one sucking on the sheath of a gelding. Two of our foals have done this to our geldings Zareeba and Toska, who have both been very tolerant of this behaviour.

Of course many horses survive weaning without permanent scars but the more sensitive and reactive the horse, the greater the chances of him suffering severe trauma. I hope that any breeders (of whatever breed of horse) reading this who do routinely practise weaning, will pause to consider whether this practice is, in fact, really necessary.

Why wean at all?

So why wean at all? One can see the arguments in favour of weaning from the point of view of large-scale breeders; they need to sell on the stock that they

Tariel attempts to suckle from Toska – even though the latter is a gelding!

breed, and the longer they keep a foal, the more this is costing them and eating into what may very well be their livelihood. Therefore it is in their interest (if not the horse's) to wean foals in order to sell them on. But for those of us who breed horses not for gain but for the pleasure of raising our own youngsters, there would seem to be few reasons why weaning should be necessary. The exceptions have been mentioned above: if the foal is taking too much out of the mare, if she is ill, or even dies – these are valid reasons for weaning. Where the mare and foal are both healthy, though, it is surely better to let nature take its course and for weaning to take place gradually at around nine months to one year, as it would in the wild.

Methods of weaning

If weaning does prove to be necessary, what is the best method? I have already described the gradual weaning process we used with Nivalis; at no time was it abrupt, he and his dam could still see each other at all times and neither of them seemed at all upset by the process. If such a gradual method should prove to be impossible (for example because the foal's dam has died), it may be possible to persuade an older horse to 'adopt' the foal. In earlier chapters I mentioned that bachelor stallions seem ready to take care of lost or orphaned foals and we have used a good-natured gelding in the same way. When Zareeba was two, Brian and his niece acquired a Connemara foal, who was promptly 'adopted' by Zareeba. Zareeba has also performed a 'baby-sitting' role for other foals, notably Nivalis and, later on, Nivalis's daughter Imzadi. When the latter was very small and it was necessary, for safety reasons, for her to be separated from her dam for a short time (for example when the mare's feet were being trimmed), rather than leave her in the stable on her own we would simply put her in with Zareeba. He tolerated the presence of a foal in his stable with great good nature, and she in turn learned to endure short separations from her dam without stress. At a later date she was occasionally turned out for brief spells with Zareeba and Roxzella (her grandmother); they behaved towards her with as much solicitous care as if she had been their own foal and, in fact, a number of people mistook them for a real family group!

One study showed that foals weaned in pairs did better than foals weaned singly. However the problem with this is that unless such foals are integrated with a mixed-age, mixed-sex group, they will only learn from others of the same or similar age. Lacking the social skills that older horses have acquired through experience, they will be unable to learn these skills from each other, and so will be ill-equipped to deal with mixed groups of older horses. They are also likely to be slower to learn; horses do learn from each other, and part of this learning process involves building on new skills and perceptions. As Dr Kiley-Worthington points out, 'The practice of raising peer groups without adults appears often to be at the root of later behavioural problems.'[iv]

Regardless of the method used, the age at which foals are weaned is important. Katherine Houpt and Harold Hintz suggest that the best age for weaning should be determined by measuring the foal's response to a brief separation each week for the first twelve to twenty weeks of the foal's life. They conclude that 'Foals should probably not be weaned at the time of maximal response to separation because they would be most stressed at that time.'[v] I would certainly never recommend weaning before around nine months of age unless it is absolutely necessary (i.e. for other than commercial reasons). In the wild, youngsters normally continue to take milk from their mother until her next foal is born, which means in practice for anything up to a year; or, if she is not in foal, for considerably longer. As I previously recounted, Imzadi was still suckling until she was almost five!

Facilities for foals

Bringing up your own foal can be tremendous fun; but what does it involve? Can you provide enough space for a growing foal to run around and exercise his limbs in safety? Foals need to be able to run, jump about and play, so that their bones, muscles and ligaments can develop properly.

Companionship

Are there other horses, apart from the foal's dam, who will make suitable companions and playmates? They need to be able to socialize with adult horses, but will do best if there is also at least one other young horse to play with. Failing that, older horses who are not too aggressive with inquisitive babies may be quite adequate. You do not need to be over-protective, but it is best to ensure that any potential playmates are good-natured and tolerant.

Breeder's experience

What about your own abilities? Do you have enough time and experience to handle a foal? Do you know – or are you prepared to learn – enough to take on the training of a horse right from birth? This is a tremendous responsibility, given that a good deal of a horse's character can be shaped, for better or worse, by the way in which he is managed as a youngster. Knowledge and good management in these early stages can help to minimize problems in later life, and hopefully eliminate many of the commoner ones altogether.

To sum up: if you really want to breed a foal, ask yourself some searching questions:

- Is my mare sound and without too many or too obvious conformational faults?
- Am I prepared to do my homework in choosing a suitable stallion?
- Can I afford the necessary stud fees and all the extra costs associated with sending a mare away to stud?
- Can I afford the veterinary costs that may arise once the foal is born?
- Do I have – or can I provide – suitable facilities for the mare to give birth?
- Am I prepared for some sleepless nights until she does give birth?
- Can I provide facilities – a safe environment with enough space for the foal to run around in, plus suitable companions – for a young foal to grow up in?
- Do I have the necessary time (at least a couple of hours a day), knowledge and experience to give a foal a good start in life through correct handling and training?
- Can I provide, or guarantee, a good, permanent home for the foal?

If you are not breeding a foal but intend to acquire one after separation from his dam, you should ask yourself the same questions as you would if you were breeding a foal yourself, omitting those relating specifically to breeding and adding the following:

- Is the foal to be separated from his dam by the gradual process described in this chapter and at a suitable age?
- If you feel the answers to the above questions to be unsatisfactory, can you persuade the breeder to change anything so as to minimize stress to the foal?

If you can honestly answer 'Yes' to all these questions, then you have the foundations for providing a foal with an excellent start to life. However, before making that final decision to breed a foal, you need to ask what may be the most important question of all: Why do I want a foal?

This is a vital question to ask yourself, because there is too much indiscriminate breeding carried out by people who are unable or unwilling to accept responsibility for the end result. Nevertheless, if you *are* prepared to accept that responsibility, and can guarantee your foal a loving, caring home, then you will find that breeding and/or bringing up your own youngster can be one of the most rewarding experiences any horse lover can have. Certainly, you will make mistakes along the way – everyone does, no matter how knowledgeable or experienced they may be. But at least you will know *what* mistakes have been made, and how they were made, and that means you are more than halfway to being able to put them right. You will know your horse's whole history, right from birth – and that can be a tremendous bonus. By careful choice of companions, and thought and care in early handling, you can give your youngster the best possible start in life. What is more, you can direct his education right from the start, helping to develop his mind and body in the right directions. And that is a truly humbling yet exciting prospect.

i George Waring, *Horse Behavior*, Noyes 1983, p.221.
ii J.L. Williams, T.H. Friend, M.N. Collins, M.J. Toscano, A. Sisto-Burt and C.H. Nevill, 'Effects of imprint training procedure at birth on the reactions of foals at age six months', *Equine Veterinary Journal* (no.35 (2)) 2003, pp.127–132.
iii Kiley-Worthington, *Horse Watch –What it is to be Equine*, pp.136–137.
iv Kiley-Worthington, *Horse Watch – What it is to be Equine*, p.257.
v K.A. Houpt and H.F. Hintz, 'Some effects of maternal deprivation in maintenance behaviour, spatial relationships and responses to environmental novelty in foals' *Applied Animal Ethology*, (no.8) 1982–83, pp.221–230.

CHAPTER 10

Man about the House

> A contented stallion, gentle in his strength and brilliant in his pride, is a joy both to watch and to be with.
>
> LUCY REES, *The Horse's Mind*

In many parts of the world, stallions are still far more common than geldings and it is now commonplace everywhere for entires to take part in a variety of equestrian disciplines. Traditionally, however, in the English-speaking countries, stallion-keeping has been the preserve of stud farms and specialist establishments. For several hundred years, the main equestrian sporting occupations of the British were racing and hunting; although stallions did of course race, they were relatively uncommon in the hunting field. Cavalry officers and generals did sometimes ride stallions (the Duke of Wellington's Copenhagen being one example) but for those who could afford to ride for leisure, mares and geldings were the general rule.

Nowadays, however, the prestige attached to ownership of a successful competition stallion, and the breeding potential of such a horse, means that more and more horse owners are thinking of owning stallions, or are keeping male youngstock entire. In a culture that is not geared to stallion ownership, or where cultural prejudices about stallions abound, this can create all kinds of problems. Not least of these is the fact that many of the people who like the idea of keeping an entire have no previous experience of handling stallions and/or hold all kinds of preconceived ideas about stallions which may not be correct.

Negative perceptions

These notions include the perception that stallions are aggressive and difficult to manage, a situation not helped by writers obsessed with aggressive interactions

A proud, gentle stallion is a joy to behold. Sylvia Loch's Lusitano stallion Prazer, here ridden by Elaine Herbert. (L. Skipper)

between animals. Regrettably, many of these negative ideas are reinforced, rather than diminished, by the teachings of some of those purporting to offer a more enlightened approach to horse training. Some of these trainers dwell on the worst aspects of stallion behaviour, telling horror stories about people being savaged and even killed by stallions. By stressing the extreme negative side of stallion behaviour they reinforce the idea of stallions as innately aggressive and difficult. This idea is further reinforced by distorting beliefs regarding a stallion's supposed role in equine society. For instance, Pat Parelli states that 'A stallion's job is to procreate and to fight for dominance. He lets nothing stand in his way. Stallions will even fight to the death for dominance.'[i]

This is very misleading. First of all, although procreation is certainly one of the most powerful factors in the lives of animals, it can often take second place to other important factors, such as defence. Second, if stallions really let nothing stand in their way, bachelors attempting to steal mares or take over established bands would have a much higher success rate than is generally the case. As it is, they are usually driven off by the band stallion, normally without any physical contact. Third, 'dominance' on its own is, as we have seen, a meaningless concept. The stallion's main role is to protect his family group, and he will indeed fight in order to do this if necessary. However, this does not happen nearly as often as many people like to believe. Most stallions will avoid physical conflict if at all possible, relying instead on ritual posturing to warn off intruders; actual combat is a last resort. Even when stallions do fight and inflict injuries on each other, these injuries are seldom immediately fatal. For example, of all the stallion fights observed during Joel Berger's five-year study of the Granite Range horses, only 3 per cent resulted in the death of one of the combatants, and in each case the stallion did not die until some time afterwards. The idea of stallions fighting to the death is therefore largely a figment of fiction; the few reliably documented cases have almost always taken place in highly unnatural conditions, for example where the stallions have been in a confined area and are thus unable to escape from each other.

These and similar beliefs can mislead people into thinking about stallions in terms of aggression and dominance, whereas in fact they should be recognizing the stallion's immense potential for co-operation.

Potential for aggression

This is not to say that we can overlook the stallion's potential for aggression: it is certainly true that an enraged stallion is an immensely powerful, dangerous creature. Even when only mildly aroused, a stallion who is not handled correctly can cause injuries to his handler, other horses, and anyone who is foolish or unfortunate enough to get in the way. No matter how experienced the handler, accidents can still happen.

We must never underestimate a stallion's potential for aggression: here Nivalis expresses his annoyance at the presence of a possible rival. (B. Skipper)

Experience with stallions

This is why novices should never be allowed to handle stallions, although there is no harm in their getting to know a good-natured, well-behaved stallion under close supervision – after all, we all have to start somewhere! My first experience of an entire was when I was about six years old, when I fell desperately in love with a Thoroughbred colt called Sportsman, who lived in the field behind my parents' country pub. Sportsman used to hang over the wall of the pub's back yard, waiting for me to come home from school (and no doubt thinking of the carrots I purloined from my long-suffering mother to give to him!). Great was my grief when Sportsman was eventually sold on, but my time as his best (human) buddy did teach me a great deal about colts, and especially about equine social behaviour, as Sportsman ran out with his dam and several other mares and their offspring until he was two years old.

Nowadays increasing numbers of people come to horse owning without this kind of childhood experience; many owners, even very experienced ones, may never even come into contact with stallions at any point during their equestrian career. Advice about handling stallions is often contradictory and frequently based on the kind of 'received wisdom' which sees stallions as dangerous wild animals, to be handled like nitro-glycerine (if at all); even more moderate views tend to stress the negative side of dealing with them. This being so, it is hardly surprising that the people who seem to get the best out of their stallions are those who have a natural empathy with them – the kind of empathy which seems to transcend experience and conventional wisdom.

Mismanagement

Too often, stallions are condemned to lead a life of misery, their temperaments warped by mismanagement. The practice of isolating colts at weaning is greatly to blame for this sad state of affairs. Colts isolated in this way will never have learned appropriate behaviour with adult male horses, whether entire or gelded. In addition, they will never learn how to approach a mare without being rebuffed, as their mothers will normally reject any sexual advances and after weaning – which will very often be both abrupt and too early – they are prevented from coming into contact with any other horses until it is time for them to cover mares. Having no idea how to approach a mare, they will usually be far too excited and may become aggressive to both the mare and the handlers. They are then subjected to all kinds of restraint, including severe bits and/or chains pulled tight over their noses or round their gums. This tends to worsen their behaviour, not improve it. Writing about the behaviour of stallions presented to a mare who is restrained, twitched and perhaps hobbled as well, Pat Parelli says (and I, like many others who study the behaviour of horses, fully agree with him) 'In my opinion, this is controlled rape. Stallions treated like this are taught to be rapists.' [ii]

Natural courtship

The truth of this is brought home to us when we see the difference between the behaviour of stallions allowed to run with their mares and those who only ever cover mares in-hand. Under natural or nearly natural conditions courtship is quite a lengthy process. The experienced stallion will be able to tell from a mare's body language, as well as her scent, whether she is receptive and will make advances to her accordingly. This is not a one-sided affair; mares who are accustomed to the company of a stallion will frequently initiate mating rituals. These rituals, which can be rather noisy and energetic, with lots of squealing, grunting and running about, can be rather alarming if one is not familiar with them, but they also include a great deal of tenderness. The stallion will spend a considerable amount of time licking and nibbling the mare's neck, withers and flanks; the

Equine courtship is a lengthy, sometimes noisy, but often tender affair. Here, Nivalis is courting Tiff. She seems unsure, but five minutes after this was taken, she accepted him without fuss. (Racheal Jones)

Nivalis and a visiting mare, Rosie. (L. Skipper)

Rosie has accepted Nivalis and is happy to stand for him. There is no restraint or coercion whatsoever involved here. (L. Skipper)

pair may also indulge in mutual grooming and nuzzling before finally proceeding to the mating act itself, which may be repeated numerous times in a day if they run out together.

Isolation and deprivation

Unfortunately all too many stallions are deprived not only of the ability to socialize – being kept isolated from contact with any other horses – but also of any kind of emotional comfort or mental stimulus. A good example of how this can affect them is the case of a stallion whom I knew quite well. When I first met this horse he was friendly and easy to handle. The last time I saw him, however, he was so wild that I would not have approached his stable too closely, let alone gone in the box with him. What had gone wrong?

The answer was simple, and very sad: he was being driven demented by lack of exercise, company and mental stimulus. Kept in a stable isolated from other equines, he did not even have the consolation of a close human relationship, or a companion of another species. He was not ridden, or otherwise worked in any way. Indeed, he was seldom handled; the only time his owner visited him was to give him fresh straw, feed and water. On the odd occasions when he was let out, he understandably became extremely excited and difficult to handle, so he was let out less and less often.

The owner of this horse was not intentionally cruel; on the contrary, he was basically a kind-hearted person who would never have done anything deliberately to harm horses. His crime was one of ignorance and a refusal to admit that, if he was not prepared to give the horse the personal attention, exercise, companionship and mental stimulus he needed, he should not have kept a stallion – or indeed, any horse – in the first place.

Stallions need companionship and exercise: as well as riding Nivalis, Brian sometimes takes him for a walk in-hand, allowing him to look around and exercise his natural curiosity. (L. Skipper)

The family group

By far the most natural way of keeping stallions, which will result in contented, manageable horses, is in a family group. This enables them to fulfil their role as protector of the family while enjoying the company of their mares and progeny – without, of course, any sexually mature colts to upset things! Sexually mature fillies are not necessarily a problem. As we saw in Chapter 3, in most social mammals there appear to be strong inhibitions against mating between those

An extremely muddy Nivalis (right) in the field with his family: the mare Tiff (centre) and their foal Tariel. This photograph was taken in December 2004 when Tariel was six weeks old. (L. Skipper)

who have grown up together, which has the effect, in most cases, of preventing incest. (This does not appear to apply when the two related individuals do not know each other.) In Chapter 5 I mentioned the rather touching relationship that Marthe Kiley-Worthington's Arabian stallion Oberlix has with his daughter Shemal. My Arabian gelding Zareeba was still being turned out with his full sister Zarello when he was sexually mature. He was stabled next to Zarello, close enough to touch noses, but even when she was in season he showed no sign of being aroused, although he reacted normally to in-season mares whom he did not know.

This being so, it is unlikely that a stallion kept with his own daughters would attempt to mate with them, as long as they had grown up with him. Even so, exceptions do occur, so in such a situation it would be wise to look out for signs of sexual attraction, and take steps to separate the fillies from their father if necessary.

Running out with mares

It may not always be possible to keep stallions in family groups, but an effective compromise is to ensure that they have at least one mare living with them permanently. The use of synthetic hormones to suppress ovulation in the mare is an option if you have a mare and a stallion whom you would like to run together but do not want the complication of too many foals; these are mentioned further in Chapter 11. The alternative is to let them run together but simply remove the mare when she shows signs of coming into season. If the stallion has been properly managed he should not object to being separated from her for a few days, especially if he knows she will eventually be returned to him.

If an inexperienced stallion is to run with mares, it is best if he is first turned out with an older, experienced mare who can teach him manners and the proper way to approach and court mares; the same applies to a stallion who has previously only covered mares in-hand. One of the main reasons why stallion owners insist on in-hand service is the risk of injury to the stallion if the mare kicks him. This caution is understandable, yet provided mares are unshod (as they should be, on the hind feet at least) serious injuries are not common. Most stallions quickly learn to keep out of range of a full kick, while a kick at close range is unlikely to cause real damage as there is insufficient power behind it. Only two days before writing this I watched a mare lash out at a stallion; she caught him several times but the only injuries were very minor scrapes and bruises. It is surely a risk worth taking for the sake of giving both mare and stallion a chance to perform the mating behaviours that are so important to them.

Suitable companions

If the stallion is not to be bred from, a barren mare (i.e. one who is unable to conceive, as opposed to one who is simply not in foal) can make a very good companion for him; failing that, and always provided that he has been properly brought up and allowed to socialize with other horses from an early age, it might be possible (if no mares are nearby) to turn him out with one or more geldings. Obviously this requires a very careful choice of companions (and not too many of them), and an equally careful introduction process; one way is to allow them to meet initially over a fence, while being controlled on a lunge-line. However numerous people have managed to keep stallions and geldings together like this successfully, without too many problems. One stud in the north-west of Britain even turns serving stallions out together!

If no suitable equine companionship can be found, an animal companion of another species is often welcomed. Some stallions like sheep and goats; however others may attack them, so be careful if you are trying this! Even where stallions get on well with their non-specific companions, accidents can happen, so care needs to be taken in the selection of a companion, and the pair needs to be monitored for any changes in behaviour towards each other. This is true whether the horse is a stallion, a gelding or a mare, but obviously special care needs to be taken in the case of a stallion.

Good behaviour

In countries where it is the general rule to ride a stallion, good stallion behaviour is taken for granted. In Spain and Portugal, for instance, no one thinks anything of riding stallions in company, stabling them side by side or tethering them next to each other. Because these entires are not segregated from other horses, they do not regard them as threats in the same way that stallions kept apart may well do. The same applies to the stallions of, say, the Spanish Riding School; they are continually in each other's company, and while jealousies and rivalries do of course arise, so do lasting friendships and attachments.

Do stallions get frustrated?

Many people feel it is unfair to keep a stallion entire if he is not intended for breeding. However, many feral horses never breed, even when they belong to a two-stallion band. The same applies to any number of stallions kept as school horses in establishments such as the Spanish Riding School (although a number of the stallions do retire to stud once their school career has ended), yet there is no real evidence that such horses suffer psychologically; in the absence of in-season mares, the libido of most stallions seems to become naturally dormant.

Stallion owners often express concern because they have seen their stallion masturbating, which they do by swinging the erect penis until it strikes their belly. This is nothing to be concerned about. It is not a sign of frustration; almost all stallions masturbate, even when they are covering several mares a day. Contrary to popular belief, it does not affect fertility either, as no sperm is ejaculated. So it is pointless to try to stop a stallion masturbating; it is perfectly normal stallion behaviour!

The positive aspects of entires

So what are the positive aspects of keeping entires? When my husband's niece first acquired her Belgian Warmblood stallion, she was fortunate enough to have the guidance of a wise old horseman. He told her: 'With stallions, you have to get them on your side. Then they'll do anything for you.' This reflects the natural desire of most stallions to co-operate. Our farrier has often stated that he would infinitely prefer to work with well-mannered stallions, because he says that once they know what is expected of them, they are much easier to handle than most mares or geldings. This 'trainability' factor, together with their extra presence, is why many circus trainers, academic institutions such as the Spanish Riding School, and some stunt riders and trainers, such as Gerard Naprous, prefer to use stallions.

Obviously, every horse is very much an individual, but in general stallions are potentially much more sensitive and responsive than a gelding or even a mare might be. They will have more presence, and may well have enhanced athletic ability, owing at least in part to the action of their hormones and greater muscular development. Once mutual trust and respect are established and the stallion accepts you as a friend and partner, he will be more trainable, and more obedient, than the average gelding.

Careful consideration

This is not to say that the decision to keep a colt entire – or to take on a mature stallion – should ever be taken lightly. If you intend to keep a colt entire for breeding purposes, he must not only be physically sound but must also have good conformation; remember too that genetic defects can be recessive, which means that they can skip generations, so find out all you can about your potential stallion's parents and grandparents – and if at all possible look at some of his full siblings, if there are any.

Practical difficulties

Apart from the points already raised, there are all kinds of management issues to consider with stallions and there may be a number of practical difficulties involved. Many livery yards will not have an entire on their premises, because of concerns about the safety, not only of the other horses being kept there, but also of those members of staff who might have to deal with the horse. This is understandable, as the equestrian culture referred to earlier means that comparatively few people, apart from those working on stud farms or with competition stallions, have experience of handling them.

In addition, such livery yards may not have a suitable enclosure where stallions can be turned out safely. Even with the best-mannered entires, there is always a danger (especially if they have served mares in the past) that their hormones will get the better of them and they will break out in search of a mare if there are any nearby. One should not underestimate the possible consequences: a stallion intent on having his way with a mare can wreak havoc and may injure other horses or any humans foolish or unfortunate enough to get in the way.

The same warnings apply to the stallion owner fortunate enough to have their own land. Our own land adjoins that of a local riding stables and livery yard. The photograph on page 159 shows our own stallion, Nivalis, confronting another entire belonging to the previous owners of the riding stables. The fence is quite inadequate to separate them safely, and we would never have put Nivalis in that field had we known that the owners of the other colt were going to turn

Nivalis, here aged three, is confronted by another entire male. If he had been a mature stallion who fully understood what he was, this fence would have been quite inadequate to separate them. (B. Skipper)

him out in the adjoining field. Fortunately no harm was done, because Nivalis at the age of three was only just beginning to realize what he was and, as the photograph shows, his reaction to the other colt's aggressive stance suggests that he was rather taken aback by the challenge.

High quality modern electric fencing, in conjunction with good old post-and-rail, will deter most stallions from going walkabout. Siting the turnout paddock away from mares will also lessen the temptation to roam. In addition, stallions who are kept mentally occupied, with suitable companionship and lots of human contact, will usually be content enough to want to stay put.

Now that Nivalis is a mature stallion and the land adjoining ours has changed hands, our turnout strategy has been revised several times to take account of changing circumstances. As Nivalis now lives with Tiff, they are normally turned out either in the grassed-over *manège* or in the stallion paddock, which has triple strands of electrical tape. Sometimes, after consultation with the owners of the riding stables to make sure that they are not intending to turn any horses out in the fields next to ours, we are able to let Nivalis and Tiff have the run of three adjoining fields, which makes a nice change for them. We have to balance Nivalis's need for adequate turnout with safety and our responsibilities to our neighbours. It seems to work, as both Nivalis and Tiff are relaxed and appear content with their situation.

Training and handling

General management issues apart, what about training and handling? Provided one gives them the respect they deserve, stallions who have been properly brought up can be relatively easy to manage. This is true of serving stallions as well as those who have never been used for breeding. While the former do tend to become distracted more easily than the latter, managing them just means that one has to be extra vigilant and aware of how they might react to the presence of mares or geldings, or – especially – other entires.

Managing a stallion does, of course, mean that one has to be continually mindful of his heightened awareness, and the fact that he is *potentially* more aggressive, and certainly more reactive, than most geldings would be. This means anticipating his reactions in a variety of situations, and knowing how to deal with possible problems before they arise. It involves a few elementary precautions such as making sure you have control over your stallion when leading him out or riding him; ensuring that he cannot escape and run amok among other horses, as well as not putting yourself in a situation where you could get hurt. This ability to anticipate and avoid situations really only comes with experience of stallion behaviour. Stallions also demand more attention than geldings or even mares; most stallions thrive best when handled on a one-to-one basis, and some – especially Arabians, Andalusians and Lusitanos – can become extremely attached to their human riders and handlers.

If you train your stallion in accordance with the +R principles laid down in Chapters 7 and 8, you will find him very much easier to manage. There are occasions when even the best-behaved stallion will become upset or distracted – usually just when you are trying to do something with him! If you have trained him to respond instantly to your request for attention, you will be able to gain control of the situation before it gets out of hand. In Chapter 7 I described how we taught Nivalis to stand still in his stable: once standing in this manner, he will continue to do so even if we go away leaving the stable door ajar. This has become so much a part of his behavioural repertoire that sometimes, if he has been told off for something (e.g. nipping at my jacket through excitement), he will go and stand to attention in the middle of his stable, as if saying, 'Look! I'm being *good* now!' If he is being boisterous or impatient (as he is sometimes when waiting to go out), I just say, 'Nivalis – stand!' and instantly he forgets all idea of nipping, nudging or head-butting. Because he has been taught this with the use of +R, he associates it with something good for him, which increases his willingness to do as we ask.

Could you keep an entire?

If you are thinking of keeping a stallion, ask yourself the following questions:

- Do I have the knowledge and experience to deal with a character who may be rather more complex than the average gelding?

- Do I have (or can I arrange) suitable facilities for turning him out and providing the necessary companionship?
- Do I have the time to build a relationship with him, and establish mutual respect and understanding?

If you can honestly answer *yes* to all three questions, then you may have what it takes to manage a stallion successfully. Owning a stallion entails a great deal of responsibility, but once you have established mutual liking, respect and understanding it can be one of the most rewarding relationships a human could possibly have with another living creature.

i Pat Parelli, 'Stallions Demand Savvy', www.parelli.com, article 15.
ii Pat Parelli, 'Stallions Demand Savvy', www.parelli.com, article 15.

CHAPTER 11

Mares – Awkward or Misunderstood?

> I have always felt that no rider's education can be completed without riding many mares. As a rule, a mare will not tolerate rude and sustained leg aids, and must be ridden with good balance.
>
> PAUL BELASIK, *Dressage for the 21st Century*

If stallions are still the favoured sex in many parts of the world, the same cannot be said about mares. In many equestrian cultures there is a strong vein of prejudice against mares, who are often regarded as being fit only for breeding from. This sometimes goes hand-in-hand with the mistaken belief that it is the stallion who is principally responsible for passing on any desirable qualities – a belief which has resulted in all too many unsuitable mares being bred from.

Courageous mares

Yet some cultures have celebrated the qualities of mares as enthusiastically as others have extolled those of stallions. The *bedu* of Arabia proper and the neighbouring Arabic-speaking countries have traditionally preferred mares for warfare; Islam forbids the gelding of horses, and the *bedu* considered stallions too noisy and easily distracted for their raiding, hit-and-run style of warfare. So perforce they rode mares, and came to appreciate the sterling qualities of a noble mare, which are celebrated in countless *bedu* tales and poems. My own Arabian gelding, Zareeba, descends in the tail-female line from Rodania, a famous war-mare bred by Ibn Rodan of the Ruwala tribe and later acquired by Lady Anne and Wilfrid Blunt for their Arabian stud at Crabbet Park.

Although stallions dominate Spain's equestrian culture, especially in the *rejoneo* or bullfight on horseback, some exceptional mares can break with

Arab war mares: a sham fight between warriors of Ibn Rashid. (From a watercolour by Lady Anne Blunt)

tradition and win renown. Such a mare was the great Espléndida, the bullfighting mare of the celebrated *rejoneador* Alvaro Domecq Senior. The *rejoneo* horse must have exceptional courage, which was the quality Domecq most valued in Espléndida: 'She was a mare of pure gold. Valiant, which is more than not being afraid; it is overcoming fear...'[i]

Sensitivity

So mares, then, can be every bit as courageous as stallions, and just as athletic and effective in warfare. That being so, why are so many people prejudiced against them? This seems to have a lot to do with the fact that mares are undeniably more 'temperamental' than geldings, and just as sensitive as stallions. The comments of American classical dressage trainer Paul Belasik in the epigraph to this chapter are borne out by our experiences with our own mares, especially the pure-bred Arabian Roxzella and her part-bred granddaughter Imzadi. Both need tactful riding, especially Roxzella, who is so sensitive that the rider must sit as still and as centrally as possible; any twist to the right or left will cause Roxzella to fall in or out, while riding a straight line – never easy with any horse – is a real challenge with this mare. Yet she is wonderfully responsive, and will repay the rider's tact and politeness many times over. I think that many people who dismiss mares

Mares can teach riders a great deal about feel and sensitivity in the saddle. Here, Arabian mare Roxzella gives a friend a riding lesson. (L. Skipper)

do so simply because they do not want to have to deal with these issues of sensitivity and tact. This is a pity, because if one can learn to develop such tact in riding it serves one in great stead when dealing with any horse.

Outstanding mares

Certainly, there have been any number of mares who have proved outstanding in competition; if prejudice against mares had not been so strong in some quarters, who knows how many more there might have been? In the 1930s Alois Podhajsky, later Director of the Spanish Riding School, trained a very ordinary-looking mare, Nora, to Grand Prix level in dressage, competing successfully with her at international level. Nora was generally considered ugly but Podhajsky wrote of her, 'To me she had never been ugly because I knew her wonderfully straight and decent character, her tenderness and her loyalty, and because I loved her.'[ii] One of the most notable competition mares was Halla, the famous showjumping mare ridden by Hans-Gunter Winkler to victory in the 1956 Olympic Games. Halla had been dismissed as crazy and unrideable, but Winkler thought otherwise; Halla more than justified his faith in her and together they went on to win the team gold medal for Germany, as well as the individual gold medal. My own equestrian heroine of the 1950s was showjumper Pat Smythe with her outstanding mare Tosca. Closer to the present day, there have been other remarkable mares such as Heureka Z, one of the most successful international jumpers in the

Ratina Z, one of the most successful showjumping horses of the 1990s. (Elizabeth Furth)

period 1969–71. Her daughter Ratina Z has had an equally illustrious career. With Piet Raymakers she won both the team European Championship title in 1991 and the team Olympic gold medal in Barcelona (1992), where she also won the individual silver medal. In a later partnership with Ludger Beerbaum, Ratina Z won many championships, including the 1993 World Cup and the team championship at the 1994 World Championships, and in 1997 they were the European team and individual champions.

A firm favourite at Classical Riding Club demonstrations was internationally renowned teacher and trainer Sylvia Loch's Alter Real (Lusitano) mare Andorinha, who sadly died just after I had completed this book. Andorinha competed successfully in dressage to Advanced Medium level, but her main role was as a demonstration horse and, perhaps more importantly, as a schoolmistress for Sylvia Loch's pupils. Andorinha's even temper, responsiveness and sweet nature helped countless riders to understand the horse-rider interaction – an understanding which is infinitely more important than merely being able to get the horse to perform 'movements'.

Closer to home, my husband's niece Vicki Rowe trained her Hanoverian x TB mare Coral (BSJA registered name Red House Murphy's Law) herself, and Coral's sensitivity made her something of a 'one rider' horse. Nevertheless, this very sensitivity gave Coral an edge rarely matched by geldings, and she and Vicki enjoyed a very successful amateur showjumping career during the 1990s.

Andorinha, Sylvia Loch's Lusitano mare, proved her worth both as a schoolmistress and as a demonstration horse. (L. Skipper)

Andorinha, having given a pupil a lesson, was given lots of fuss and attention – not to mention Polo mints! (L. Skipper)

Hanoverian x Thoroughbred mare Coral Crown (Red House Murphy's Law) and Vicki Rowe winning the Toggi Discovery Championship in 1993. (Harry McMillan, Peak Photography)

The effects of the reproductive cycle

So, given that mares are capable of performing just as well as stallions and geldings, what lies behind their temperamental behaviour, and how can we deal with such behaviour in an understanding manner?

The behaviour of mares, like that of stallions, is affected by hormones to a much greater extent than that of geldings. A mare's reproductive cycle usually spans twenty-one or twenty-two days; for five or six of these days (sometimes as many as ten) she is in season (oestrus), and for the remaining fifteen to seventeen days she is out of season (dioestrus).

In the wild, mares would normally start cycling in spring and stop in late autumn, although in some populations the mares appear to cycle all year round. Where seasonal cycling applies, it ensures that foals are not born when the weather is cold or excessively wet. However, mares kept in a domestic setting may be stabled for much if not all of the winter and artificial lighting in the stables may trick the body into producing the hormones that affect a mare's oestrus cycle. Some mares may therefore come into season all the year round. As in some feral populations, certain mares keep cycling throughout the winter with or without the aid of artificial lighting or hormone therapy. This is more common than many people suppose; when mares run with stallions it is not unusual for foals to be born throughout the year. Our colt foal Tariel was born in October, while Dr Kiley-Worthington reports that one of the foals at her stud was born two days after Christmas, having been conceived without any of the usual intervention employed by studs to achieve conception early in the year.[iii]

The oestrus cycle is much longer in mares than it is in most mammals. Some observers[iv] have speculated that this may have been an evolutionary advantage for because the resulting prolonged courtship helps to strengthen the bond of affection between the mare and the stallion. This would make sense, as such bonds help to maintain the stability of the family group. It may also explain why some mares are receptive to the stallion even when they are not actually in oestrus. Dr Kiley-Worthington carried out an experiment of running a vasectomized stallion with a group of mares. She reported that all the mares had intercourse with the stallion regularly throughout the year; in a number of cases this occurred even when the mares in question were not due to come into season.

This underlines the fact that mares do not simply await the attentions of the stallion passively, but actively seek him out whether they are in season or not. I have certainly found that mares living with male horses (whether gelded or not) are generally happier and better-tempered than mares living in all-female groups.

Many mares show no behavioural changes during oestrus; others can become quite moody and temperamental. During oestrus the ovaries produce egg-bearing follicles (usually one, occasionally two). These follicles enlarge as they mature, eventually rupturing to release the egg. This enlargement of the follicles may sometimes cause the mare discomfort, which could help to explain why some of them become extremely touchy, flinching or even becoming aggressive when being saddled, girthed up, etc.; in some very sensitive mares this may extend to showing signs of annoyance when being ridden, such as resistance to leg aids, tail-swishing, laying the ears back, etc.

When in season, some mares may cause disruption to other horses, especially geldings; they may call to the geldings or walk up and down the fence if they are in separate fields, or they may 'show' to the geldings, i.e. by straddling the hind legs, 'winking' (everting the clitoris) and often squirting thick yellow urine. Whether this is considered a nuisance or not may depend on the situation; as with stallions, a mare used for competition may expend too much energy trying to attract a possible mate, or she may upset other horses with her calling and fence-walking. If a mare is competing in disciplines where stallions also participate (for example showjumping and some races) her being in season could also upset the stallions. Some geldings who have retained stallion-like qualities (see Chapter 12) may also be affected.

Dealing with problems

What can you do about these problems? You could simply avoid competing when your mare is in season, or you could remove her to a separate paddock away from geldings. However, this is not usually necessary these days. Rather than curtail

Mares may flirt with geldings: Imzadi 'shows' to the talent next door. (L. Skipper)

your mare's activities, you could consider the use of a synthetic hormone such as Regumate. As well as regulating a mare's cycle, this can also be used to suppress ovulation altogether: this is rather like an equine equivalent of the contraceptive pill. Until comparatively recently the use of Regumate was forbidden in certain types of competition, but under FEI regulations its use is now approved under certain conditions. If you have a mare with whom you would like to compete, but who is likely to make a nuisance of herself when in season, check the rules of the organization regulating your particular discipline to see if Regumate is approved at your level of competition and in your specific circumstances. You can then decide (of course in consultation with your vet, who will need to prescribe it) whether you want to use it to suppress your mare's breeding cycle. This option is not cheap, so it may only be worth pursuing if you want to compete at a relatively high level. Otherwise you could try one of the herb-based feed supplements that are supposed to help mares with hormonal problems. I do not know whether any clinical trials have been carried out on these products and have no personal experience of them, but many people report that they do appear to help.

When in season, the majority of mares do not behave in the extreme manner described above – although people tend to think of it as a major problem simply because they hear more about the problem cases! We have four mares at present, and we have never had any problems with any of them when they are in oestrus, although all are sensitive and require tactful handling and riding. The worst that normally happens is that Roxzella and her granddaughter Imzadi will hang around the fence that divides our land from that of the riding stables next door, flirting with the geldings in the next field. This tends to annoy Zareeba, who (as described in Chapter 4) appears to act as a surrogate stallion; however, apart from occasionally driving the mares away from the fence and pulling faces at the geldings, he usually just keeps an eye on them to make sure things do not get out of hand.

Segregation

A number of livery establishments and private yards segregate mares and geldings and at such places there are unlikely to be any problems with mares pestering geldings when in oestrus. I do not necessarily believe that it is a good idea to separate mares from geldings in this manner – a matter dealt with in Chapter 12. In natural family groups mares would tend to form close relationships with each other and this may also be the case in all-mare groups in a domestic situation. However, my observations of groups of mares kept together without any male presence – even that of a gelding – suggest that there is likely to be more aggression between members of the group than would be the case in a mixed-sex group. This is especially true if the group is large and its members are unrelated, which is not like an all-mare band in the wild (which does occur occasionally where the band stallion has died), where the mares would know each other well and would still have some of their offspring with them; those are, above all, family groups. If a mare is turned out in a mixed-sex group, then unless flirting with geldings becomes a real problem causing major disruption, I would advise leaving well alone.

Breeding from your mare

As we saw in Chapter 9, increasing numbers of ordinary horse owners are considering breeding from their mares. Many people put their mare in foal simply because she is no longer sound and cannot be ridden. This is fine – if she is a good mare and her unsoundness was caused by an accident rather than some inherent disease or fault. However, every owner needs to be realistic about their mare. It should go without saying that no horse with grossly defective conformation should be bred from. This does not mean that minor conformational defects cannot be overlooked; no horse is perfect, just as no human is! As mentioned, deformities resulting from injury may also be ignored, unless there is a strong possibility that a conformational defect was a contributory factor.[1]

Temperament is always a factor to consider when breeding but, given that people vary in what they consider to be a 'good temperament', it can be a very tricky factor to determine. In any case, how do we decide how much of a horse's temperament is inherited and how much is a product of environmental influences? That said, if a mare has a nasty temperament it is probably best not to breed from her. She may not pass her temperament on genetically but a foal is likely to learn behavioural habits from her.

Breeding problems

Problems often arise when mares are sent to stud. It is not unusual for mares to become extremely difficult to handle even when they are, biologically at least, receptive to the stallion. Stud grooms naturally have to consider their own safety as well as that of the stallion so, as we saw in Chapter 10, mares are often twitched and may be hobbled as well; in addition they are sometimes given a mild tranquillizer. The effect all this has on the mares can only be imagined; small wonder so many of them lose weight while away at stud.

Modern breeding and management practices are actually responsible for

1 For more about conformation features which predispose to injury, see my earlier book *Realize Your Horse's True Potential.*

many, if not most, of the problems which arise. Very few mares are raised in anything like a natural family group, so many will never have seen stallions in their lives, let alone had the chance to observe their behaviour and learn how to interact with them, until they go to stud. It must be a very frightening experience for a maiden mare to be suddenly taken away from her normal surroundings, whisked off to a strange place where she knows no one, either equine or human, then subjected to all kinds of invasive procedures prior to being suddenly introduced to the stallion who is to cover her. Even a quiet, well-mannered stallion can be a daunting sight as he rears up to mount a mare; a noisy, rough-mannered stallion must be absolutely terrifying to a mare completely unused to such behaviour. No wonder some mares have to be twitched or hobbled before they will stand to accept the stallion. Forced copulations do occasionally occur in natural environments, but these are exceptional and in such a situation the mare often has at least some chance of getting away. The mare restrained by twitches, hobbles or severe bridles has little such chance – although some mares do break away, a situation which is both frightening and dangerous for the handler. It is scarcely surprising that many mares fail to get in foal; in many cases they are not yet ready to be mated, but are compelled to submit anyway. Of in-hand matings only 68–70 per cent actually result in conception, as opposed to a 95 per cent conception rate among mares running out with a stallion.[v]

Similar problems may arise when a maiden mare gives birth for the first time. Unless she has been kept in a natural family group, it is unlikely that she will ever have seen another mare give birth; on most stud farms, especially if the mares are valuable broodmares, they will have been brought into a stable to foal. The maiden mare therefore has no idea what is happening; this could well be the reason why a significant number of mares reject their foals. It is true that, in the wild, certain mares go some way away from the family group to give birth. However, many do not and most young mares living in natural family groups will not only have seen mares give birth, they will also have witnessed the mating process. There are therefore no unpleasant surprises in store for them when the time comes for them to mate and subsequently give birth; it is all simply a normal part of life.

Far from just being awkward and 'mare-ish', those mares who do create difficulties when away at stud are more often than not simply reacting to a frightening and frequently unpleasant situation. Those who have been through it a number of times may accept the situation but some are understandably grumpy and sullen about the whole process. This is hardly surprising, yet such mares are often cited as evidence of the generally disobliging nature of mares. Naturally, not all mares find the process of being sent to stud unpleasant; much depends on the individual mare and how she is treated, both before and during the breeding process. Even so, the fact that for many mares this process is often painful and distressing must surely raise serious questions about the ethics of so much of what is usually considered standard stud management practice.

Running out with the stallion

The alternative – running mares out with stallions – is often not even considered, although it is common in some countries. It is true that it involves watching the mare and stallion to see if mating has taken place; if the stallion is smaller than the mare he may also need some assistance (although some stallions are adroit at positioning the mare on a slope or in a slight hollow to make mounting easier). However, mares and stallions have been getting on with the business of sex for millions of years; they really do not need us to show them how it is done! Mare owners may worry about the mare being injured by the stallion; however, unless the stallion has been made vicious by bad management (in which case it would be inadvisable to run him out with mares, at least until his behavioural problems have been ironed out), he is most unlikely to attack a mare. She, on the other hand, might reject his advances forcibly, in spite of his attempts to court her. In such cases it is best to give them time; if the stallion knows his job he will usually be able to persuade the mare to accept him.

Just recently we had a visiting mare who was very obviously in season. She was turned out with Nivalis but rejected his attempts at courtship and foreplay. Nevertheless, they mated numerous times, each time without any preamble; when the mare was ready, she just presented her rump and squatted for Nivalis, sending him about his business once it was all over. I found this somewhat amusing – 'Wham, bam, thank you sir – now clear off!' – yet at the same time rather sad. This mare clearly wanted the stallion and was all too ready to stand for him, yet – perhaps because of her previous experiences at stud (although that is only conjecture) – had become so inhibited in her behaviour that she was no longer capable of responding to natural courtship rituals. Perhaps she would have learned to respond in time; sadly she was not with us long enough for us to see if that was the case.

Misunderstood, not awkward

Mares, then, are not necessarily awkward; they may simply be misunderstood. In spite of this, many people feel unable to cope with the extra sensitivity and responsiveness shown by so many mares; if this is the case, they will probably get along better with a gelding. As described earlier in this chapter, the *bedu* had no such qualms; they rode their war-mares into battle regardless of whether they were in season and being 'mare-ish' or not! It might even have been that they found the increased aggression of some mares an advantage at such times, although nearly all their stories and poetry extolling the virtues of their war-mares concentrate on the mares' courage, swiftness and agility. People who make the effort to treat their mares with consideration and who are prepared to work around any quirks associated with oestrus generally find that they develop a relationship with them that is much deeper than they would have had with a gelding.

Points to remember are:

- Mares require tactful riding, with subtle use of the aids.
- They are generally more sensitive than geldings.
- This sensitivity may make them touchy, especially when they are in season.
- Often this touchiness is caused by discomfort.

We can avoid or minimize problems by:

- Improving our riding skills.
- Using the power of +R in training and being very subtle with any -R we may use.
- Being tactful in our handling of mares. This does not mean fussing about, which may simply annoy them – it means being polite in grooming, tacking up, general handling; not pushing the mare around or being abrupt and impatient.

(Naturally, all of the points above should apply to all horses. It is with mares, though, that the 'softly, softly' approach really pays dividends.)

Mares can be a good test of our horsemanship. They demand rather more of us than geldings do, in terms of management skills and riding ability. Yet, if we are prepared to meet the challenge and make just that little extra effort to be tactful and considerate, a good mare can give us the best of both worlds: more responsiveness than we might get from many geldings, without as many management difficulties as we could have with a stallion. Real horsemen and women do ride mares!

i Alvaro Domecq Snr, in *El Caballo en España*, Madrid 1975 (quoted by Sylvia Loch in *The Royal Horse of Europe*, J.A. Allen 1986, p.148.

ii Alois Podhajsky, *My Horses, My Teachers*, J.A. Allen 1997, p.76.

iii Kiley-Worthington, *Horse Watch – What it is to be Equine*, p.265.

iv e.g. Kiley-Worthington, *Horse Watch – What it is to be Equine*, p.214.

v Kiley-Worthington, *Horse Watch – What it is to be Equine*, p.182.

Chapter 12

Geldings: The Odd Ones Out

> I've always reckoned a good horse has to put a proper value on hisself, or no one else will.
>
> Richard Adams, *Traveller*

In many equestrian societies geldings have been devalued and regarded as second-class citizens. However, one of the greatest equestrian peoples of all time, the Mongols, rode mainly geldings into battle, finding them easier to manage than either mares or stallions in the large numbers required for the Mongols' massive battle formations. For many people – especially the average rider as opposed to those competing in top-level competitive disciplines – geldings are the most sensible choice when acquiring a horse. They are generally easier to manage than mares or stallions, and tend to be much more forgiving of less-than-perfect riding than entires of either sex.

From a biological point of view, geldings are certainly the odd ones out. They are the products of an artificial process – castration – so there is not really a direct equivalent of a gelding living within, and participating in, natural equine society. That being so, how do they fit in with equine life and society, and in what ways does their behaviour differ from that of mares and stallions?

Stallion-like behaviour

Geldings are not complete neuters, whatever many people might think. It is sometimes suggested that a gelded horse takes on the voice and demeanour of a mare, but this is both inaccurate and misleading. Most geldings retain at least some masculine characteristics, while some behave in a very stallion-like manner. Contrary to what many people believe, such stallion-like geldings are unlikely to be rigs. A true rig, or cryptorchid, is a male horse whose testicles have not descended into the scrotum. Such a horse may be a bilateral cryptorchid (both testicles fail to descend) or a monorchid (only one testicle fails to descend). Sperm produced by the retained testicle(s) is not fertile, but testosterone is produced, which is why such horses still behave like stallions. The causes of cryptorchidism are not fully understood, but they involve genetic and hormonal effects which combine with other physical factors to create a defect in development. Whatever the causes, cryptorchidism is not common, and modern castration techniques generally ensure that stallion-like behaviour in geldings is unlikely to be caused by the retention of testicular material.

Is separating geldings from mares necessary?

Because of this residual stallion-like behaviour, many people believe that it is unsafe to turn geldings out with mares, and insist on keeping them separated. Sometimes this belief is so strong that dire warnings are given about the possible disastrous consequences of mixing mares with geldings, such as otherwise placid geldings going mad when they see mares, attacking them and inflicting severe injuries. Some commentators state that the probability of this happening is so great that mares and geldings should *never* be turned out together.

Having kept geldings together with mares for many years without serious problems, both at our own yard and at various livery establishments, I am at a loss to understand this rather extreme view. In the spring and summer I spend a great deal of time observing the behaviour of the horses belonging to the riding stables next door, where mares and geldings have been turned out together for years, and I have never seen, or heard of, anything resembling the kinds of problems described above. There have been minor incidents, certainly, but in my experience most mares are very well able to take care of themselves; in fact, my observations suggest that it is much more likely to be the mares who act aggressively towards geldings than the other way round. I do know of establishments where mares and geldings are rigidly segregated and I wonder whether this in itself may be at least part of the cause of geldings 'going mad' when they see mares in the field. This is a very abnormal reaction in such a social species. As far as these apparent actions on the part of geldings are concerned, they may very well be – in some cases at least – the *result* of segregation, especially if this occurs at an early age and even more so if the horse in question has been weaned forcibly or too early, as happens all too frequently. As with stallions, such segregation practices commonly result in horses who have no idea how to behave with members of another sex; in such cases it is hardly surprising if they behave inappropriately and/or aggressively.

All-gelding groups

As we saw in Chapter 3, single-sex groups are not the norm in natural horse society, in spite of the existence of the so-called bachelor groups described in Chapters 1 and 3; in any case these tend to be short-lived, having none of the stability of the mixed-sex family group. In fact there is some evidence to suggest that geldings do not necessarily form well-integrated groups when kept as the equivalent of a bachelor group. Andy Beck of the White Horse Ethology Project made some systematic observations of groups of varying compositions; he found that the least well-integrated group was that composed of seven geldings. This group displayed a high level of aggression and lack of co-operation; splitting the group into three smaller units appeared to solve the management problems created by aggression within the group. Andy concludes that:

> More studies on other groups of geldings would be required before it could be reliably stated that, as unnatural animals, they do not respond well to being kept in the equivalent of a naturally occurring bachelor group. For this reason it may be more appropriate to keep geldings in small groups of not more than three, in order to lower social stress.[i]

Problems can, of course, arise with mixed groups, but this is true of any mixed group of horses who have not been brought up together or spent many years in the same group. Regular observation of such groups will help to identify the

Geldings can indulge in the same kind of rough play as they did when they were colts. Too many geldings in a single-sex group could result in disruption, so it may be wise to keep such groups small. (L.Skipper)

potential for problems before they get out of hand. If geldings are brought up in mixed age/mixed sex groups, as all of ours have been, and are generally well-integrated socially, there should be absolutely no reason why they cannot be turned out safely with mares.

Over-attachment to mares

One situation which does seem to occur sometimes is that in which geldings become very attached to certain mares and become extremely distressed when separated from them, even for a short time. Some equine behaviour experts have suggested that, in extreme cases of this type, complete, permanent separation from the mare may not be sufficient to prevent the gelding in question from becoming distressed; it may also be necessary to keep him away from all other horses. I would advise this only as a very last resort, because social isolation of this kind can be most detrimental to horses, as we will see in Chapter 13. I would rather try habituation to separation, as described in Chapter 5, before taking the extreme step of complete separation.

The attachments of geldings to mares can be every bit as strong as those of mares to other mares and, in some instances, may be even stronger. This is important in view of the idea, described in Chapter 5, of emotional bonding as mainly occurring between horses of similar age and the same sex. The attachments that geldings and mares form for each other do however – in some cases at least – appear to differ in some respects from those that mares form with others of their sex. There may be a sexual element to the relationship, which causes the gelding in question to show some elements of stallion behaviour.

Sexual behaviour

This may come as a surprise to people who believe that the only geldings to retain any sexual feelings are rigs or so-called 'false rigs'. This is far from being the case. The results of surveys suggest that at least 30 per cent of geldings may retain some stallion-like behaviour; the actual number may be even higher. Certainly, of the geldings I have observed over the years, more than 50 per cent have exhibited some form of stallion-like behaviour.

As we saw in Chapter 10, virtually all stallions masturbate and this is part of the normal repertoire of stallion behaviour. It is normal for geldings, too; I have seen all our geldings do it. Again, it is nothing to be at all concerned about, as it is not in any way harmful (although some people may find it embarrassing!).

Geldings may also mount mares, and in some cases actually have intercourse with them; I have observed this myself on numerous occasions, some of which I described in my earlier book, *Inside Your Horse's Mind*. Apart from this, the most obvious stallion behaviour in geldings is herding. Many people will have seen geldings who herd mares away from other horses; in some cases there may be just one mare involved, or there may be several. As with masturbation, herding is a normal aspect of equine behaviour; it is perfectly natural for a stallion to herd his mares away from perceived danger, and hardly surprising that some geldings perform this aspect of stallion behaviour. Unless it is causing obvious distress to the mares in question – in which case separation might be advisable – the best policy is probably to do nothing about it. Attempts to prevent geldings from doing what male horses do are unlikely to be successful!

There are many other, more subtle ways in which geldings can demonstrate stallion-like behaviour. Zareeba, put in a stable recently vacated by a mare whom he likes and socializes with (such as Roxzella) will sniff the straw and paw at it, just as Nivalis does, although I have only occasionally seen him perform flehmen. When ridden, he can sometimes be extremely inattentive; this caused me some concern until I looked at the contexts in which it was occurring, and realized that he was acting like a stallion, i.e. exercising vigilance on behalf of the group. He is therefore much more aware of his surroundings than many geldings might be, which means that his rider must also be aware of the surroundings, just as if one were riding a stallion!

Some geldings – such as Zareeba – may readily accept the baby-sitting role described in Chapter 4; such geldings may adopt the same kind of protective attitude towards youngstock as a stallion in a natural family group.

Although geldings do not occur naturally (except as rare pseudo-geldings, i.e. males with very low levels of testosterone), they do retain sufficient male characteristics to be able to take on at least some of the stallion's roles. In Chapter 9 I mentioned the way in which Zareeba and his girlfriend Roxzella behaved towards the foal Imzadi, acting like a real family group. Although the other geldings have not taken on a similar role to Zareeba, Toska at least has shown a considerable degree of protectiveness towards Tiff in the days before she and Nivalis started living together. In summer we have often arrived at the stables to find Tiff and Roxzella lying down in the field, with Toska and Zareeba respectively standing guard over them.

Effects of early gelding

Many people hold beliefs about geldings which are either not supported, or are actually contradicted, by scientific evidence. For example, one common belief is that gelding horses when they are very young stunts their growth. In fact the opposite is true. Testosterone affects both the growth of the long bones and the closure of the growth plates. In horses who have been gelded at an early age, the

Zareeba has often assumed a baby-sitting role, as he did here with Connemara foal Dandy. (L. Skipper)

below Zareeba keeps an eye on the geldings next door. (L. Skipper)

long bones will continue to grow for longer than would be the case in a horse left entire, and the growth plates in the legs will close at a later date. It is possible to estimate the eventual height a foal will make by measuring his height at the withers at several stages. At the age of six months he could be expected to attain approximately 83 per cent of his mature height at the withers, 91 per cent at twelve months and 95 per cent at eighteen months.[ii]

This is not an exact science, of course; it is merely a predication based on probabilities; furthermore growth can be affected by all kinds of factors such as nutrition, exercise, etc. Apart from this, height at the withers is not an absolute; the shoulder blades have a purely muscular attachment to the trunk, which means that the withers can be higher or lower depending on the horse's posture. Nevertheless, it does generally provide a reasonably accurate way of gauging how tall a horse is likely to grow. Using this method, and also looking at his sire and dam and their ancestors, I estimated that my Arabian gelding Zareeba was unlikely to grow much beyond 14.1 to 14.2 hh (145 to 147 cm). He was gelded at the age of two and subsequently, rather to my surprise, grew to 14.3 hh (149.8 cm). His half-brother Kruger, also gelded at the age of two, likewise exceeded the height predicted when he was two years old. Of course there could be other factors such as nutrition involved; however, the effects of reduced testosterone on the growth of the long bones is indisputable, having been studied in a number of species, including humans. (There is a human genetic condition known as Klinefelter's syndrome, in which males have an extra female chromosome; low testosterone levels can result in excessive growth of the long bones of the arms and legs.)

The benefits and drawbacks of geldings

The benefits of keeping a gelding rather than a mare or stallion are clear: they are less likely to be affected by hormonal changes, less temperamental, and less likely to become aggressive towards other horses. So what, if any, are the negative aspects of geldings? As with horses of any sex, it all depends on the individual gelding. Those who have not retained many masculine traits may be very easy to manage, but they may not be as responsive as a mare or a stallion. In the higher levels of competition they may lack the extra presence which stallions generally possess; this may not matter so much in disciplines such as showjumping or eventing but in dressage, where an element of 'show' is required these days, it could mean the difference between a good performance and a great one. However, some geldings do have the kind of charisma that makes them sparkle every bit as much as a stallion might; a fine example of this is Sylvia Loch's demonstration horse, the Lusitano x TB gelding Espada, who loves to show off in front of a crowd.

Geldings may not have the extra presence of stallions but they can still be outstanding performers. This unremarkable looking grey is none other than the great Milton, one of the most successful showjumpers of all time. (L. Skipper)

Sylvia Loch's Lusitano x Thoroughbred gelding Espada sparkles at demonstrations; Espada has as much presence as a stallion. (L. Skipper)

Getting the best out of a gelding

How can we manage geldings sympathetically and get the best out of them? In managing them we need to bear in mind that:

- Although they have been neutered and will not display the more extreme characteristics of stallions, many geldings do retain some stallion behaviour.
- This stallion behaviour may include masturbation; this is nothing to be concerned about, so it is unnecessary to interfere and possibly make your horse's life a misery.
- Most geldings can be safely turned out with mares, but some may become over-attached to certain mares.
- If a gelding shows herding behaviour, unless it is causing obvious distress and/or difficulties in catching and removing either gelding or mare(s) from the field, it may be best not to interfere; again this is perfectly normal behaviour.
- Occasionally geldings may become aggressive towards mares. In my experience this does not happen often but it pays to know as much as you can about how your gelding has been kept and how he responds to other horses, especially mares.
- If you have to keep your gelding in an all-gelding group, try if possible to ensure that this group is not too large; no more than three or four would be ideal. As with all groups, whether mixed or not, it helps if this group is kept as stable as possible.
- Geldings may be easier to ride and be much more tolerant of poor or clumsy riding than either a mare or a stallion might be. However, they can still be sensitive and deserve to be treated with as much consideration as a mare or a stallion.

If you bear these few points in mind and do not expect your gelding to be a pushover just because he has been neutered, you will be able to build a partnership based on respect for him and his unique position in the horse world.

i Andy Beck, White Horse Ethology Project website www.equine-behavior.com.
ii Captain M. Horace Hayes FRCVS, *Veterinary Notes for Horse Owners*, rev. ed (ed. Peter D. Rossdale), Stanley Paul 1987, p.599.

CHAPTER 13

Home Alone

> Now horses – horses need friends. Who's going to keep the flies off your face and out of your ears? Who's going to get your tangles out and clean you up? And you gotta do the same for him, o'course.
>
> RICHARD ADAMS, *Traveller*

We have already seen how important social interaction is for our horses. Yet countless horses, in Britain and elsewhere, are kept on their own, often with minimal contact even with humans. Why should this be, and what effect does it have on the horses concerned?

Why keep a horse on his own?

There are many reasons why people keep horses on their own. They may only be able to afford to keep one horse, or they may have very limited stabling and/or grazing facilities. They may move around a lot, and so resort to tethering their horse wherever there is a plot of waste land where few objections may be met with from councils or the local inhabitants. They may never have thought about the matter, and simply assumed that the horse, being (as they believe) a creature of very simple needs, can manage quite nicely on his own. The horse in question may have behaved aggressively to other horses in the past, and so his owner believes he can only be kept on his own. These are perhaps the commonest reasons but, whatever the circumstances, all of these horses have something in common: they are being deprived of one of their species' most basic needs.

Some people might object to this statement, pointing out, quite rightly, that humans are social animals, and yet some people become hermits, virtually cutting themselves off from all contact with other humans. This is perfectly correct, but if we look at those people we will almost invariably find that they have exercised a choice in the matter: they have deliberately chosen to isolate themselves in this way. Furthermore, they will usually be found to have some deeply engrossing interest which makes social contact almost an irrelevance to them. And, finally, there are very few such people (apart from some religious fanatics) who do not have at least some kind of sporadic, if brief, contact with fellow humans.

The effects of solitary confinement

The people cited above are exceptions, and rare ones at that. That social contact is essential to humans is borne out by the reaction of prisoners to solitary confinement. The latter have reported vivid hallucinations involving all the senses: agitation and excitement sometimes leading to aimless violence; hyperreactions to external stimuli, especially noise; loss of the ability to concentrate, and acute depression, leading in some cases to actual physical self-harm. Charles Darwin observed inmates in solitary confinement 'dead to everything but torturing anxieties and horrible despair.'[i] 'Solitary' is therefore regarded as an extreme form of punishment or social ostracism, in most civilized countries reserved for the worst type of criminal, or those in danger of being attacked by fellow prisoners. Yet humans regularly condemn other social animals to the equivalent of 'solitary', apparently without giving the matter much thought.

Prisoners kept in solitary confinement have been able to report their feelings directly to other humans. Non-human animals cannot, so what evidence do we have that solitary confinement affects other social mammals adversely? In the 1960s Harry Harlow carried out some experiments on infant rhesus monkeys.[1] As part of these experiments Harlow raised baby monkeys in total isolation for up to two years, in stainless steel boxes with no contact, either physical or visual, with another living creature. It is hardly surprising that, as a result, the monkeys had very few social skills, were timid and fearful and females who were subsequently impregnated frequently killed their offspring.

Experimental animals kept in isolation may develop a wide variety of behavioural problems, including self-mutilation. The latter is also common in dogs who are kept chained up, without contact with other dogs; in such dogs (and possibly in other species), self-mutilation often appears to start off as an exaggerated form of self-grooming, which then progresses to actual physical harm. Examples of this need for social contact among social mammals abound, from

1 H. F. Harlow and M. K. Harlow, 'The Development of Affectional Patterns in Infant Monkeys' in *Determinants of Infant Behaviour*, Vol. 1, ed. M. B. Foss, Methuen 1961.

macaques to rats, from chimpanzees to cats and many other social species. It is now recognized that much stereotypical behaviour in zoo animals is the result of inadequate or non-existent social interaction. As primatologist Robert Yerkes pointed out, 'one chimpanzee is no chimpanzee'.

The need for social interaction

We have established that one of the basic welfare requirements for horses is that they should be kept in a manner which allows them to perform as many of their natural behaviours as possible. When we deprive horses of companionship we deny them the ability to perform one of the most necessary of those behaviours: social interaction.

No doubt there are many horses who do manage to adapt well to a solitary life, especially if they live in an enriched environment where there is plenty to interest them and they have a very good, one-to-one relationship with whoever looks after them. However, this raises the question of whether the limited amount of time most humans can spend with their equines can ever really compensate for the lack of equine companionship.

Can humans make adequate companions?

Apart from the time spent eating, and the minimal time horses spend sleeping, social interaction forms the greater part of a feral or free-ranging horse's daily routine. Furthermore, this interaction does not simply take place during a limited number of daylight hours, but is spread out over the entire twenty-four hours of a day. Horses are not, strictly speaking, nocturnal animals; even so, anyone who has ever observed them at night in a field will have seen how much activity there is during the hours of darkness. They do not simply spend this time eating; their night involves a considerable amount of socializing. This may take the form of mutual grooming, play, the odd squabble, sexual activity, or simply loafing in the company of an equine friend or two. Even if their human caretakers were to camp out in a solitary horse's field every night (a course of action which is impractical for most people) or, alternatively, sleep in his stable (which I have done, on occasion), they would still be unable to compensate fully for that horse's lack of social interaction for much of the rest of the time. Horses generally sleep or doze for short periods at a time but humans have different requirements regarding sleep. Most of us need relatively uninterrupted sleep during the night in order to function well during the day. We would therefore make poor companions during the night, as we tend to spend most of it asleep! Then, during the day, most of us have to earn a living, which means that only a very few of us will be able to spend the greater part of every day with our horses.

Even where horses are looked after by grooms or stable hands who do spend most of their day in the stable yard, the humans concerned will be unable to spend a great deal of time with individual horses, as they usually have many jobs to do throughout the day. Finally, even those people who are really gifted at communicating with horses cannot match the rich and subtle body language with which horses 'talk' to each other; humans simply do not have the right kind of physical equipment! With the best will in the world, therefore, humans are a poor substitute for equine companions.

Distress caused by isolation

Unfortunately for them, stallions tend to suffer most from isolation, because of the unnatural conditions in which so many of them are kept. In some management regimes stallions are not only kept isolated as described in Chapter 10, but shut up in loose boxes, often tied up, and sometimes without light. The idea is that this makes them subdued and easier to handle and some stallions do appear to respond in this manner. However, these horses are almost certainly in a state of depression similar to that experienced by many prisoners in solitary confinement. The mental distress caused by such confinement can become redirected internally in an attempt to cope with the resulting stress. This can lead to a passive state of acceptance in which the individual's personality and emotions

All too many stallions are kept isolated, behind bars. At least this stallion was turned out every day, albeit alone; many are not so fortunate. (L. Skipper)

are severely repressed; the long-term stress experienced can have the effect of suppressing the immune system, making the body susceptible to infections. It should go without saying that this is an unethical and totally unacceptable way of keeping any horse, let alone a stallion; in such cases the end can never justify the means.

Apart from stallions, other horses who are confined to a stable for long periods may develop a similar passive acceptance; at first they may be grumpy and difficult to handle, then after a while (which may vary from several days to several weeks) they become listless and apathetic, at which stage to the inexperienced, insensitive or merely unobservant eye they may simply appear to be very quiet. However, with some horses this behaviour may change abruptly when they are removed to a different environment; they may become extremely excitable, explosive and even violent.

Horses kept in isolation may become very dependent on their handlers. This is particularly noticeable among stallions kept segregated from other horses; if they have a good relationship with their handlers, they may become ultra-dependent on them to the extent that, if that person is absent, they can be very difficult to manage. This often gives rise to the belief (sometimes, but not always, justified) that such stallions are 'one-person' horses.

It is not only stallions, however, who can pose problems in this respect: geldings and mares can also become over-dependent on their handlers if they are denied the company of other horses. Sometimes, too, mares and geldings may be kept isolated because they are so anti-social that they cannot be turned out with other horses. This anti-social behaviour may have been caused by earlier experiences with other horses, for example if the horse in question has been badly bullied. In some other cases it is the result of inadequate socialization when they were younger. Foals weaned in isolation frequently have very poor social skills and may be fearful, timid horses or else they may become bullies – bullying is very often the result of fear and a sense of inadequacy and/or insecurity. The answer is not to isolate them still further, but to try to resolve their problems in such a way that they can be re-integrated with a group of other horses. See Appendix II for some suggestions about how this can be achieved.

Alleviating the situation

Having recognized the potential problem, what can the one-horse owner do? If you keep your horse on your own property and you have sufficient space, there are a number of options open to you. You can:

- *Acquire another horse as a companion for your own.* This is a common solution; there are many people desperately seeking a good home for an old or unsound horse or pony, or who simply can no longer afford to keep a horse. Such people often advertise in equestrian magazines; you could put your own advert in the 'Wanted' columns of such magazines. You would need to be very careful about accepting animals with behavioural problems, as unless you have experience of dealing with such problems you could find yourself with a difficult and even dangerous horse on your hands and the well-being and safety of your own horse could be compromised as a result. You would also have to be aware of the potential problems associated with accepting unsound and/or old horses, such as health problems, the need for extra feeding and veterinary care, for example.[2] If you are accepting a horse or pony on loan, you will need to draw up an agreement setting out precisely what responsibilities you are accepting with regard to the companion horse; it is always advisable to take legal advice on such matters. However, as long as the pros and cons are weighed up carefully and the horse's suitability as a companion ascertained, this option could turn out to be the best of all. If the companion is sound and rideable, you might even end up with a good second horse to ride!

- *Take another horse at livery*. If space permits and you have sufficient grazing and or/stabling, you could accept another horse at livery. You would need to check on the legalities surrounding horses at livery in your particular area, especially if you intended to charge livery fees, but as long as the practicalities are thought through properly and any agreement properly drawn up and witnessed, this could also be a very attractive option.

- *Adopt an animal of another species as a companion*. This is the option most commonly chosen where the single horse is a stallion, as most people believe that stallions can only be kept singly. As we have seen, this is not necessarily the case, but a companion animal of another species is certainly preferable to no companion at all. Many horses share their stable with cats, a species which seems to get on well with horses. However, cats spend a great deal of their time asleep, and when they are awake they tend to like to wander, so although, in general, horses seem to like to have them around, cats do not make ideal companions if theirs is the only company a horse is likely to get.

A mare who lives next door to our stables shares her field with a small herd of beef cattle and seems to get on with them very well, so this is another possibility if you have sufficient grazing – I have known of a number of horses who have settled down quite happily among cattle. You would, however, need to discuss this very carefully with someone who is knowledgeable about the care and

2 For people taking on an older horse as a companion, I can thoroughly recommend *Care and Management of the Older Horse*, by Heather Scott Parsons, J.A. Allen 2001.

behaviour of cattle. If the cattle have not been de-horned you would also need to watch out for any signs of aggression on their part. Having said that, I know of several horses who live quite happily with a herd of Highland cattle whose rather ferocious-looking horns have been left intact. Sheep and goats are other favourites as companions for horses, although some horses can be too boisterous for them, and if yours is that type of horse then sheep especially might not be suitable, as they are easily stressed. Another point to consider regarding mixed

Most horses seem to like cats; Zareeba is quite happy to let them sit or lie on his back. (L. Skipper)

below This mare, named Anna, has lived among beef cattle for a number of years. She gets on well with them but is often, as here, somewhat apart from them. (L. Skipper)

Anna with one of her bovine companions: he is friendly but her body language says that she is just a little wary. (L. Skipper)

grazing is that any supplementary fodder given in the field should be of suitable quality for horses, as sheep and cattle are often fed (without apparent harm) fodder of a quality not acceptable for horses.

Livery and stabling

Keeping a horse with animals of other species is, of course, a compromise; the horse will be unable to communicate with them as fully as he would with another horse. However, it is certainly preferable to keeping him alone, and where space and/or finances are limited, it may well be the only real option.

But what happens if you keep your horse at livery? In theory there should be few problems here, as (except for quarantine purposes) horses will seldom be expected to remain isolated from other horses on a livery yard. However, such isolation can occur, for example where a horse cannot be turned out with other horses because he is too aggressive. As I mentioned earlier, this need not be an insurmountable problem. Nevertheless, there may be occasions when it is a question of which is the lesser of two evils: isolation or some other unacceptable situation.

A more common situation in which owners of horses at livery might find themselves is that turnout is restricted in winter. This can lead to long spells during which horses are not turned out at all, in some cases spending the entire winter cooped up in a stable, apart from periods when they are taken out to be ridden or lunged.

As well as compromising the horse's physical well-being (a point to which we shall return in the next chapter), this can result in social isolation for the horses concerned. Of course, much depends on the type of stabling used, and how it is arranged. In some systems the horses can still touch each other, and although such limited social contact is no real substitute for free association of the kind they would experience at liberty, it is at least better than the types of stabling where the horse is totally enclosed.

The best types of stabling I have seen are those which combine a barn-type system with external doors. In this kind of stabling the horses can see and, in the best designs of this type, touch their neighbours; they can also see what is going on outside their stables. People who have moved to this type of stabling from the conventional separate loose-box style have reported that their horses seemed much happier and more relaxed as a result of the change.

A study carried out at the University of Lincoln[ii] showed that horses who were previously confirmed weavers reduced their stereotypical behaviour considerably within a week when shatterproof acrylic mirrors were fitted to the interior walls of their stables. It is not clear whether the horses thought the mirrored reflections were other horses and so gained release from a sense of social isolation. (We don't know for certain whether horses recognize that the image in a mirror is their own, or whether they think it is another horse.) However, the study does suggest that the presence of what they may perceive to be another horse considerably reduces the distress caused by social isolation.

Even so, such stratagems can only reduce the sense of isolation; they cannot remove it entirely. They should only be used when there is really no possible alternative. In any case mirrors placed in stables must be shatterproof; ordinary glass mirrors should never be used.

Reducing stress

If, like perhaps the majority of horse owners, you keep your horse at livery and have no choice but to stable him during the winter, there are ways of reducing the amount of stress felt by horses cooped up in this way. My Arabian gelding Zareeba has lived for a number of years in a stable with a window in the back wall. When not turned out, he can look out onto the fields belonging to the riding school next door and watch their horses. In 1998 Tiff came to us and, being mildly claustrophobic, she lived in a former hay barn forming a large lean-to, enclosed on three sides, at the back of the stable block. Tiff had her own little yard which opened onto the *manège*; when stabled, she could communicate with Zareeba through his back window, or with our stallion Nivalis via the top half of his back door (see the photographs on page 192). All three horses liked this arrangement; it meant that even when they were stabled they could still interact with each other, albeit not as fully as they would have done in the field.

If you keep your horse at livery, and the yard owner would agree (and provided your horse and the horse stabled next to him get on well), you could

Tiff and Zareeba could communicate through Zareeba's back window.

Even when stabled apart, Tiff and Nivalis could still touch each other. (L. Skipper)

arrange for part of the dividing wall between the two stables to be removed so that the two horses can see and touch each other, as in the situation described above. With a small opening there is always the risk of the horses bumping their heads if they move suddenly (for example, if one of them nips the other, as even the best of friends will do on occasion!), although I am not aware of this happening to Zareeba or Tiff in their particular set-up. You could make the opening tall enough to prevent this; you would, in any case, need to ensure that the lower part of the opening was high enough to prevent the horses attempting to climb through and possibly injuring themselves in the process.

A slightly less satisfactory alternative is to construct barred partitions above a certain height, with kicking-boards below. The bars need to be constructed so that a horse cannot get his feet trapped in them in the event of kicking out, yet wide enough to allow him to touch noses with his companion. A similar arrangement was used in the University of Lincoln experiment referred to earlier; some of the horses taking part were housed in stables modified with barred partitions, separating the weaver from a non-weaver stabled in the next box. Such partitions were just as effective in reducing weaving as the mirrors were.

I once visited a very well-run stud farm where the stallions were housed in stables with a similar arrangement: they could see and touch each other but could not bite or kick each other. All four of the stallions housed like this seemed very content, and there appeared to be no squabbling between them. It should go without saying that all stables should have adequate kicking-boards.

With the same careful choice of neighbours as one would make with turnout companions, this can be a very effective way of ensuring that stabled horses can maintain contact with their own kind. Such an arrangement would cost money, of course, and many livery yard owners would understandably be reluctant to foot the bill for what they might consider to be an unnecessary refinement. However, if you offered to pay for the alteration, and could persuade other livery clients to share the cost, it need not be prohibitively expensive; a competent do-it-yourself enthusiast could easily manage such a job.

Perhaps the best solution to the problem of winter turnout or limited grazing is to have a large barn where the horses can be turned out together. If it is big enough to allow them all sufficient personal space and hay piles are spaced well apart they will not generally squabble, and it does mean that they can maintain their social contacts. I know of some establishments where the indoor school is used for this purpose; clearly this could pose some problems if the school is also used for lessons or is hired out, but there could be some portion of the day set aside for horses to be turned loose in there to socialize and enjoy some freedom.

Of course not all establishments, especially in the UK where space is at a premium, are fortunate enough to have an indoor school or a barn big enough for the purpose; even if one has the means to construct such a building, planning permission may be denied. In these cases it may be necessary to set aside a 'sacrifice' paddock, where it does not matter if the ground is cut up and poached. At least horses turned out in such a paddock will be able to get fresh air and exercise as well as being with their friends and companions. If there is a large number of horses space might be a problem; we have already seen, in Chapter 3, the kind of problems that can arise with overcrowding. However, with a little organization this need not be insurmountable: the horses can be turned out in smaller, compatible groups, with one group being brought in after being out for a specified length of time, and another being turned out in its place. This is a compromise, as the horses are still spending a lot of their time indoors, and it is less convenient for owners, but it is certainly better than either extreme: horses standing around looking miserable in cold, windy, muddy fields with little or no grass for the entire winter, or alternatively trapped in small stables with insufficient exercise, freedom or social contacts.

This brings us to another question arising from the topics discussed in this chapter. In Chapter 14 we will go on to consider whether horses should live in or out, or a combination of the two, and what can happen if we insist too rigidly on one approach or another.

i P. Liederman, 'Man alone:sensory deprivation and behavior change', *Correctional Psychiatry and Journal of Social Therapy* no. 8, 1962, pp.64–74.

ii D.S. Mills and K. Davenport, 'The effect of a neighbouring conspecific versus the use of a mirror for the control of stereotypic weaving behaviour in the stabled horse', *Animal Science* no. 74, 2002.

Chapter 14

In or Out?

> I had a stable by then, you see, and I often used to feel bored in there: lack of company. One time I even got to biting my crib for something to do...
>
> ...you can't settle down to grazing if it keeps raining and blowing on and off all the time. You want to get out of the wind; and if you let yourself get wet through you start shivering...
>
> Richard Adams, *Traveller*

From the late 1990s onwards there has been a movement in some equestrian quarters towards more natural systems of keeping horses, including working them without shoes, and keeping them outdoors at all times. There is much to be said for this way of thinking; it considers what is good for the horse rather than simply what is convenient for humans. However, as so often happens, it has in many cases been turned into a kind of dogma, which insists that what is 'natural' is right at all times, regardless of whether it is what horses would actually choose for themselves if the choice were freely offered to them. It also ignores the question whether what is natural is invariably the best. If we were to keep our horses in completely natural conditions, we would not worm them or vaccinate them; indeed some people do not do so, maintaining that their horses remain healthy without such interventions. This is debatable, and I would not advise anyone to abandon vaccination or worming programmes without some very detailed research and a lot of careful thought. A completely natural lifestyle would also preclude any veterinary intervention if the horse was injured or ill; quite apart from the legal implications of allowing animals to suffer through lack of proper attention, I imagine few of us would want to stand by and watch our horses endure pain and discomfort without doing anything to alleviate it.

A selective natural lifestyle

Of course the proponents of a more natural lifestyle could point out that this is not what they are proposing, and that I am distorting their ideas. They would be quite right; I am merely pointing out that if we extol the undoubted virtues of a more natural lifestyle for our horses, we should (unless we are fanatics, and to my mind fanaticism and horsemanship do not mix) be aware that we are being selective in what we propose, and be prepared to compromise accordingly. For example, I am a great believer in working horses barefoot if at all possible, since shoes affect the foot's natural shock-absorbing qualities. However, one of our previously barefoot horses now needs the support of shoes; if this is what is required in order to keep him sound (and careful research has convinced me that it is), then so be it. Horses care about comfort, not principles!

Out all the time?

The question which particularly interests us here is whether horses should live out at all times. There is no doubt that being cooped up in small areas such as the average sized (12 ft x 12 ft, or 3.66 m x 3.66 m) loose box is not healthy for horses. Such a small space is barely adequate for the horse to turn around in; ventilation is likely to be inadequate and the lack of space means that the horse must defecate very close to where he sleeps, eats and drinks – a situation few humans, given the choice, would endure. But even so, having taken all these factors into account, can we truthfully say that it is possible or even desirable for all horses to live out at all times?

Because of their location, horses such as the stallions of the Spanish Riding School in Vienna may have to be stabled for much of the time. However, in this and similar instances there are many aspects of the horses' lives which compensate to some extent for their lack of freedom: exercise (by no means all of it school work) and the constant close company of their own kind, together with the special relationships they frequently form with their grooms and riders, all help to provide them with a far richer environment than is enjoyed by some horses who live out permanently. This is not to say that such a restricted lifestyle is preferable, simply that in some situations there are compensations!

Some of the proponents of natural management regimes make much of the fact that their horses live out all the year round, and are much healthier for it. That may be fine if you have fifty acres or more in an area of mild climate and low rainfall, but what happens in winter if all you have is a few acres of heavy clay in an exposed area with high rainfall? The answer is that, even where you have efficient land drains, you end up with poached fields and no grass; your horses (even though rugged up) stand around wet and miserable and wanting to come

In some areas, fields may turn to mud in the winter. This was a 'sacrifice' paddock which did at least enable the horses to get some exercise, although it was not very entertaining for them once they had eaten all the haylage. (L. Skipper)

in; you have endless problems with mud fever, frozen water troughs, icy winds from which the horses can find no shelter (because there are no trees or other natural shelter and an unsympathetic council will not allow you to put up a field shelter) and a host of other winter woes. In such a scenario horses, given the choice, will usually vote with their feet; they like to be out, but not at any price: there has to be some incentive to stay out, and cold, muddy fields with no grass to speak of do not come into that category. In winter our horses are usually banging on the gate to be let back in after being out for an hour or so; of course we can provide all the forage they need out in the field, but even that does not tempt them to stay there.

Necessary compromise

In some parts of the world it is simply not possible to turn horses out all the year round. Severe North and Eastern European winters, for example, mean that all but the very toughest of native breeds must spend a good part of the winter inside; the same applies to some parts of Canada and the USA. In such situations compromise is necessary, possibly of the kind suggested at the end of Chapter 13.

But, you may ask, how do we *know* that horses are miserable in cold, muddy conditions? Might we not simply be projecting own emotions onto them because we would be miserable in such conditions? Well, that is certainly possible, and may indeed sometimes be the case. However, it is my experience that if horses are standing around looking miserable then it is usually because they *are* miserable. The one sure way to find out what horses want is to give them choices, and see what they end up with. In winter, if we open the stable doors and the gate leading from the yard into the field, most of the horses will trot out into the field and be quite happy to be out – for a short while. Then they come back in again; they might come and go like this several times but invariably they end up coming back in after a comparatively short time.

Giving horses a choice

The ideal would therefore seem to be a situation in which horses can come and go as they please, and in fact we have been able to adopt such a system for our stallion, Nivalis, and his companion mare Tiff. As previously mentioned, they live together; this used to be in a former hay barn. Since then we have built them another, larger barn; this consists of Yorkshire boarding, that is boards of 6 inches (15.24 cm) in width and 1 inch (2.54 cm) in thickness; gaps are left between the boarding for ventilation and the front of the barn is open, facing away from the prevailing wind. This accommodation, which resembles a glorified field shelter, is roomy enough for the two of them and the gaps between the boards provide good ventilation without being draughty. Even when it is cold and windy outside, the Yorkshire boarding acts as a wind-brake, ensuring that their barn stays cosy. In winter, when Tiff and Nivalis are not out in the stallion paddock, they live together in the barn; the gate into their little grass yard is always open, and they can either stay in the barn or wander freely about the grassed-over *manège*. The grass is supplemented with haylage, so there is always something

Tiff and Nivalis in their new barn. Straw bedding was later put down in here to encourage the horses to lie down. (L. Skipper)

for them to eat outside, yet they do choose to spend a considerable amount of time inside.

The important thing here is the element of choice. It is all too easy for us to decide what is best for our horses based on our own ideals and perceptions, while ignoring what they would actually choose for themselves if allowed to do so. For example, I have often read (and heard) assertions to the effect that we should not provide our horses with soft bedding because they would have to lie down on

Horses will seek out a soft surface to lie on; here a group of them have bedded down on haylage put out in the field. (L. Skipper)

Horses may prefer a soft bed; Tiff has come in to lie down, while inside the barn, to the left, Nivalis stands guard over her. (L. Skipper)

hard ground in the wild. There is indeed a case to be made against certain types of stable bedding, especially where horses are expected to stand for a good part of the day on soiled bedding, their feet soaking up stale urine and becoming embedded with dung. The answer to this is not to deprive them of soft bedding, but to change the management system so that they do not have to stand for prolonged periods on soiled bedding. The fact is that free-ranging horses will lie down on a soft surface if they can find one and I have seen our own, with an entire field to lie down in, bed themselves down on a mound of soft sand left over from a building project. I have also seen horses seek out a temporary riding surface of tan and wood bark and use it as a bed. In fact, many horses will not lie down on a hard, uncomfortable surface and, although the stay apparatus in their limbs enables them to sleep standing up, they do need to lie down in order to relax fully. It also appears that they will only dream when lying flat. The purpose of dreaming (if, indeed, there is one) is still far from being understood but it does seem to be essential for many mammals, including horses. So if we insist on providing a 'natural' (i.e. hard) surface for our horses and they refuse to lie down as a result, might we possibly be depriving them of something essential to them?

Health Risks

Risk of laminitis

One important consideration for many horse owners, especially in temperate climates such as the UK, is the risk of laminitis. Even where pasture has been sown with grass mixes specifically for horses, in mild climates such grasses may still tend to be far too rich in soluble carbohydrates, which have been identified as being among the principle culprits in triggering off feed-induced laminitis. Unless grazing is restricted, certain horses will always be at risk. I know one can use grazing muzzles to prevent too large an intake of grass, but not every horse will accept these. In such cases the only option is to restrict grazing, possibly by confining the horse to a paddock where the grass is poor and sparse.

Grass sickness

A more sinister problem facing horse owners is the risk of grass sickness. This dreaded disease has occurred throughout Europe for over a hundred years, and has been known in North America, but the UK has by far the greatest incidence of the disease. The cause of this terrible disease is still not known for certain but, as the name suggests, it is associated with horses who are out to grass. It appears to be most prevalent in areas experiencing spells of cool, dry weather, with temperatures ranging from around 7–11 °C and lasting ten days or more; it is also more common during spring and early summer, although cases have been recorded in autumn. Stabling horses for at least part of the day during those times of year would make good sense, especially in areas commonly affected by the disease. In fact, in such areas it is advisable to stable horses when the above-mentioned weather conditions occur.

These are not hard-and-fast rules, simply recommendations based on current research.[1] I certainly do not wish to alarm people whose horses live out full time, simply to point out that in certain areas the ideal of year-round turnout for horses may simply not be practical, and that it might be a good idea to keep them in a system where stabling for part of the day (or at night) is combined with turnout for as many hours as possible. The latter is, in any case, the only practical system to adopt as far as many people are concerned, especially where grazing is limited.

Considering individual needs and preferences

So yes, we should try to keep our horses as naturally as possible, but we should be aware of the possible pitfalls of a so-called 'natural lifestyle'. We should certainly not allow ourselves to be bullied into accepting dogmatic assertions about how we should keep our horses, but should consider the circumstances together with the needs and preferences of the individual horse, and weigh these carefully in deciding what is really the best option to adopt on their behalf.

In doing this we must take into consideration what kinds of things matter to horses and are essential for their health and happiness:

- Horses turned out full time must have free access to water and any supplementary feed that may be necessary without being bullied or driven away by other horses.
- Horses turned out for long periods or full time must have adequate personal space (see Chapters 2 and 3), access to shelter and a place to lie down free from harassment by other horses.
- Horses who are turned out full time should be given adequate companionship as described in Chapter 13; care must be taken to ensure that the horses in a group are compatible with each other.
- Stabled horses must have sufficient space to turn round and lie down comfortably; there must be sufficient bedding to encourage them to lie down and

1 For more information, contact the Equine Grass Sickness Fund, The Moredun Foundation, Pentlands Science Park, Penicuik, Midlothian EH26 0PZ, Scotland, or visit their website on www.grasssickness.org.uk.

they should not be expected to stand for any length of time on heavily soiled bedding.

- Stabled horses should be given the opportunity to socialize with others of their own kind, or at least be provided with a suitable companion animal of another species (see Chapter 13).
- Stabled horses should be given opportunities for mental stimulation as well as sufficient forage to enable them to perform their most basic behaviour: eating. Feral or free-ranging horses spend up to 60 per cent of their time eating; stabled horses fed *ad libitum* hay and straw and able to see and touch each other may spend considerably less time than this eating (around 47 per cent) as opposed to stabled horses unable to touch each other and fed restricted forage (only 15 per cent of the time spent eating).[i]

Even for horses spending 47 per cent of their time eating, there is still a lot of time spent standing around, so horses stabled for any length of time should be given the kind of stable toys that contain feed which is only released when the horse performs a certain action; other stable toys such as Likits (see photograph on page 203) are a great favourite in our stables for occasions when the horses cannot go out because of severe weather conditions. Hay or haylage given in nets with small holes will also help to increase the amount of time spent eating.

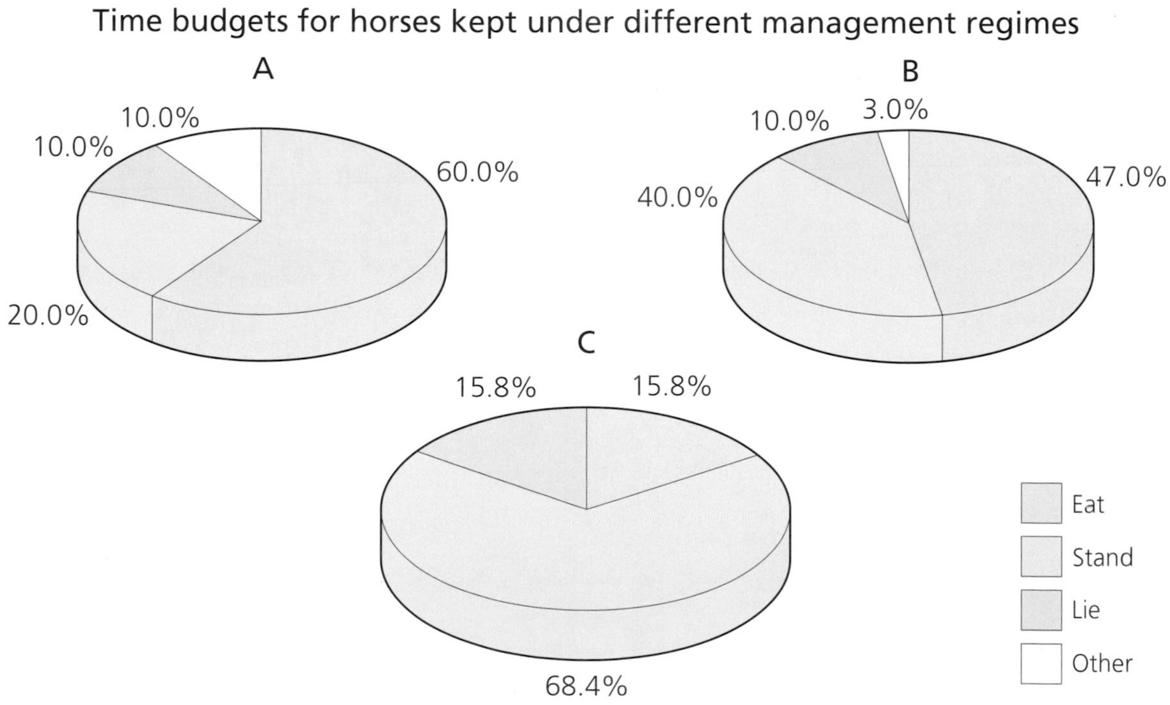

Figure 10: Time budgets for horses: A, feral and free-ranging horses; B, horses in individual stables able to see and touch each other and fed ad-lib forage; C, horses in individual stables unable to touch each other and fed restricted forage. (Adapted from *The Behaviour of Horses in Relation to Management and Training* by Dr Marthe Kiley-Worthington, J.A. Allen, 1987)

Likits and similar toys are an excellent way of giving horses something to occupy themselves with and 'forage' for food at the same time. Inset into two sides of this particular ball are carrot and mint-flavoured mineral blocks, with an apple-flavoured cylindrical block on top of the ball. This provides horses with a considerable amount of entertainment. (L. Skipper)

Making changes

Setting out these most basic requirements like this brings home to us what an enormous responsibility we take on when we decide to keep horses. As I said in Chapter 1, few of us are able to keep horses in conditions which are optimal for either them or us and most of our management practices involve compromise of one kind or another. If our management falls very far short of the ideal we may have to consider making major changes, which many of us find difficult, especially if we have always been taught to do things in a particular way with little if any deviation being allowed. We may feel as if such changes are really too big for us to contemplate. However, if we really have our horses' welfare at heart we must be prepared to make that effort. There are always ways around problems if we think hard enough about possible alternatives.

If you keep your horse on your own property you may be able to arrange for him to have a suitable lifestyle without making too many changes, if any. However, if you keep your horse at livery, things may be rather different. It can be very difficult for owners of horses at livery to change the way in which a yard is run, especially when the yard in question is a large, professionally-run establishment where everything is done 'by the book', and the proprietors may not take kindly to suggestions involving considerable changes to their stable management. They may resist the idea that established stable management practices may be rather less than desirable from the horse's point of view (indeed, some may be reluctant to accept that the horse *has* a point of view). However, as always, where an unacceptable situation arises as a result of the ignorance of others, or their unwillingness to change the way they do things, there are a number of things you can do to combat this resistance; I have listed these in the Conclusion.

For the time being, in deciding what you can do to improve your horse's lifestyle, consider:

- Which of the aspects that need attention can be changed, and which cannot. In deciding the latter, make sure change really is impossible and not just inconvenient!
- Where change is desirable but not possible, look at ways in which you can alleviate the current situation. These might be, for example, providing adequate forage and toys and a degree of social contact for a horse who must spend a good deal of his time stabled.
- Where change is possible but difficult, look at all the alternatives and, if you keep your horse at livery, enlist the assistance of other livery clients in implementing changes. This might involve something like persuading the yard owner to allow you to put up a field shelter (sharing the expense with other clients, and always assuming permission can be obtained from local authorities) or setting aside part of the land for winter turnout.
- Where change is desirable and easy – go for it!

i Figures taken from *The Behaviour of Horses in Relation to Training and Management* by Dr Marthe Kiley-Worthington, J.A. Allen 1987, p.158.

Chapter 15

The Ethics of Training and Competition

> We should ride to do something good for the horse's sake so that he can be beautiful and display himself by his own will to his own advantage. We should not manipulate horses to make them our competitive vehicles for winning ribbons.
>
> Charles de Kunffy, *The Ethics and Passions of Dressage*

In our enthusiasm for achieving success with our horses, we frequently overlook the fact that equestrian sports differ from other sports in one very important respect. Human athletes plan their training regimes with a view to attaining maximum fitness for their chosen discipline while attempting to avoid injury and undue stress. In spite of this, injuries and stress are still common, especially at higher levels where athletes push themselves to the limit. They know the risks and choose to take them because they are doing what they want to do and can make informed decisions about how far to push themselves.

In equestrian activities, however, riders do not only have themselves to consider. They have a living partner – one who, moreover, has no direct way of telling them that he has had enough, that he is fatigued, stressed or in pain, and cannot continue. While consideration for one's equine partner should lie at the very heart of equestrian training and sport, it can be all too easy for us to override or ignore any signals of distress coming from the horse, which raises the question of whether or not it is ethical to involve horses in activities which may cause them injury or an unacceptable degree of stress.

How much stress is acceptable?

This is not an easy question to answer, not least because we have no reliable means of gauging what levels of stress are acceptable to our horses. What is

Preparation is the key: Racheal lunges Toska to build up his muscles and, through systematic work, improve his balance and way of going. (L. Skipper)

acceptable to one individual may not be so for another; so much depends on an individual horse's degree of motivation and general attitude to training and competing. In any case, how do we recognize stress – in itself an ill-defined concept? One definition of 'stress' in animals is '…the effect on organisms of environmental demands beyond the normal range'.[i] This raises yet another question: what do we define as 'normal'? In the present context I think 'normal' describes the range of environmental conditions in which horses can thrive, and activities that are within their mental and physical capabilities, for which they have been adequately prepared and which are not carried on to the point where the horse can no longer cope comfortably with what is expected of him.

Spotting early signs of stress

If we know what to look for, we can easily learn to spot signs of stress when they start to appear in the course of training and either stop or change to something less stressful before the horse becomes *dis*tressed. However, some horses will not give off any obvious warning signals, and these can be very tricky to deal with when working out a training plan. Usually one only becomes aware that the horse is stressed when he behaves out of character in some way, often following a training session. This is yet another good argument in favour of getting to know as much as you can about a horse before planning his training. This is especially the case with young, green horses; at least with older and/or more experienced horses you either know the horse's response to training quite well, or you may be able to get information from a previous owner. In any case, I would recommend drawing up a profile as suggested in Chapter 1 before you start to plan what to do with a horse.

CASE STUDY

When we first started to work our home-bred mare Imzadi on the lunge at the age of four, she proved willing and co-operative, if rather high-spirited. The latter we expected, as she takes after her sire Nivalis, who is also high-spirited. Imzadi's early training sessions went well, and she proved a quick and apt pupil. However, at that time she was still sharing a stable with her dam Kiri, and I noticed that when she returned to the stable after a training session she immediately took refuge in the comfort-seeking behaviour described in Chapter 9: in other words she would go to her mother and start to suckle. After this had occurred a couple of times I realized that Imzadi was actually finding the training sessions quite stressful, even though she had given no obvious indication of this during the sessions themselves. I watched her carefully during the next couple of sessions, and noticed that at a certain stage in the session she would start to glance periodically in the direction of the stable she shared with her mother. By noting the point at which this started to happen, I was able to determine at what stage she had had enough; we would then stop the training sessions at this point. Once we started to do this, Imzadi no longer felt it necessary to rush to the 'milk-bar' after every session; she would enter the stable calmly and, after greeting her mother, settle down to eat hay until they were turned out. Alternatively, depending on the weather, she would be turned out with the other horses, including her mother, immediately following a training session; again, she no longer displayed her earlier comfort-seeking behaviour.

Perhaps some people will express doubt about our course of action, maintaining that by stopping the training sessions as soon as Imzadi indicated she had had enough, we were actually 'giving in' to her, and teaching her that she only had to show signs of distress and we would stop the training sessions. It can certainly happen that, if we respond to certain situations in training by stopping work, we are indeed teaching the horse that if he takes a specific course of action then work will cease, and if that course of action is either unsafe or detrimental to his training, then we certainly do not want to encourage it. However, in Imzadi's case, the training sessions were stopped *before* she started to show any signs of distress, so it is highly unlikely that she would connect the cessation of training with something that had not happened yet. In fact, because she was no longer finding the training sessions stressful we found that we were able to extend the length of the sessions gradually and to start asking a little more of her than she was naturally inclined to give us. Because she did not feel pressurized, she responded beautifully, and by the time she came to be ridden away she was able to accept this next step without any problems.

So, when planning your horse's training, make sure you find out, by means of close observation, what your horse's natural limits are.

Quick-start techniques

One rather worrying trend that has emerged from the 'natural horsemanship' movement is the fashion for taking an unhandled horse and getting him saddled and ridden away in a matter of minutes. This is not so apparent in Europe (although its popularity is growing), but in some parts of the USA so-called 'horse-whisperers' hold contests to see who can get horses ridden away in the shortest time. Some people, rightly concerned about this practice, have tended to blame Monty Roberts, as he was one of the first to demonstrate a 'quick-start' technique. However this is unfair: Monty Roberts does not say that one should necessarily use such a technique; he and his pupils, such as Kelly Marks, have tended to use it as an example of what *can* be done, rather than what *should* be done. The problem with such 'quick-start' techniques is that, while they certainly get a horse ridden away much more quickly than more standard practices, they do nothing to prepare the horse either physically or mentally for ridden work. The virtue of classical starting techniques is that nothing takes the horse by surprise; he is introduced to work gradually from the ground, with exercises designed to supple and strengthen him before a rider comes anywhere near him. Commencing ridden work without such preparation may work with some horses, but with others it could be very damaging both physically and mentally.

This is not to say that such techniques should never be used. For example I have watched Kelly Marks and her team 'start' a number of green horses, and there is nothing in their method that would cause me any anxiety if it were one of my own horses being tacked up and ridden for the first time. One could easily combine such a quick-start technique with the classical techniques referred to above: once the horse is accustomed to the saddle and the weight of a rider, further ridden work could then be deferred until his muscles have built up and he is stronger in the back and the limbs. Indeed, we did something similar many years ago with one of our own youngsters, and he has proved one of our most willing and reliable riding horses. What I object to is the idea of 'quick-start' methods being used without regard to the individual horse and his current state of physical development.

Can horses enjoy their work?

Regardless of how their ridden work is started, can horses actually enjoy their work? In Chapter 4 I suggested that if we take the trouble to build up a good relationship with them, they will want to work with us and for us. This relationship is essential if we are to get the best out of them because, initially at least, they have to take a great deal on trust.

In my earlier book, *Inside Your Horse's Mind*, I cited the case of the ghetto student in an English Literature class, who exclaims indignantly, 'Whaffo I wanna read no *Tale of Two Cities?*' I compared it with the horse who, on being introduced to schooling, says through his resistances something like, 'Whaffo I wanna trot in no circles?'[ii] We cannot explain to the horse that if he does as we ask he will, through correct training and riding, become better balanced and even more athletic than he is already, and will stay sounder and healthier as a result. Even if we could, the horse might well think that he is well-balanced and athletic enough, thank you very much; and so he is, if we leave him alone in the field. However, most of us want to ride our horses; if we want to do this and keep our horse sound and healthy, then schooling is a must, as an unbalanced, unfit horse is much more likely to break down under the strain of being ridden.

Since we cannot say all this to the horse, we have to persuade him that schooling is good for him in terms he can understand. Many people try to do this by force ('do this, or I'll hurt you'), but force is unlikely to result in any kind of understanding. What, then, can we do? Well, we have seen the immense power of +R. Those of us who have had the good fortune to work for someone for whom we feel great trust, liking and respect, will know that even if that person asks us ('ask' being the operative word) to perform a difficult and possibly unpleasant task that is nevertheless within our capabilities, we will most probably – because of that trust, liking and respect – do our utmost to oblige them. If the task is difficult but brings a reward in spite of that, we may try even harder.

This works with horses, too. If they like, trust and respect us, their natural tendency will be to co-operate with us, rather than resist (provided, that is, our horsemanship is up to scratch). If we use the power of +R to enhance that willingness to co-operate, we have laid the foundations for the horse not only to accept being schooled and ridden, but actually to enjoy it.

This all sounds fine, but what evidence is there that horses do enjoy being schooled and ridden? Animal behaviour scientists are understandably cautious about committing themselves here, because horses cannot tell us directly what they are thinking and feeling. However, by watching their demeanour and general behaviour, we can get a pretty good idea of how they are feeling. If they seem apathetic and unwilling to work, then that is probably exactly how they are feeling; it is up to us, using our knowledge of them, to try to decide why they may be feeling like that. They could be tired, ill, depressed or simply bored; or the work may be too difficult and taxing for them. If, on the other hand, they seem jaunty and enthusiastic about their work, that probably means they enjoy it, and may even look forward to it. There is no doubt that many horses who regularly take part in public equestrian displays do respond positively to the enthusiasm of the audience and some horses take their work seriously enough to practise even in the absence of a rider or trainer. In *Inside Your Horse's Mind* I described seeing two of our horses – Zareeba and Nivalis, one leading, the other following – trotting in circles, figures of eight, etc. with as much concentration as if they were working with a trainer. Only recently I have seen something similar among the riding stables' horses turned out in the field next door. Stunt trainer Gerard Naprous has described how one of his horses, trained as a 'faller' (a horse who falls on cue), used to practice his falls alone in the field. One could argue that this is conditioned behaviour, but why would a horse perform such behaviour in the absence of a specific stimulus or cue? Some horses seem to derive some kind of internal satisfaction from such behaviour and it seems entirely possible that many horses can derive satisfaction from performing well, especially if their work is kept within their capabilities and is carried out in the company of someone with whom they have a good relationship. Equine Behaviour Forum member Dr Sharon Cregier reports the enthusiasm of her horse for training:

> When training for a 100 mile endurance ride, the relationship with my horse grew deeper. He not only looked forward to the daily sessions, but came to the fence or front of his box and whinnied when he saw the saddle coming...I think he looked forward to our training rides because while I worked to exert him, I avoided exhausting him.[iii]

This suggests that horses can indeed enjoy their work; certainly many of them seem to look forward to it, if their demeanour is anything to go by. Zareeba always pricks up his ears when he sees tack being brought out, and pulls faces to indicate his displeasure on those occasions when it becomes obvious that it is intended for someone else!

How much does competition matter?

Now that most of us ride horses for leisure rather than necessity, it is difficult to imagine a time when the only equestrian competitions were generally those which had a practical value, such as enhancing the abilities of horse and rider in war – even racing was originally linked to training for combat. Racing apart, it was really only in the nineteenth century that equestrian competitions for their own sake started to become popular. Since then, competitions of all kinds have come to dominate the horse world, so it is hardly surprising that so many people feel as if success in competition is the only yardstick by which their horsemanship can be judged, or by which the value of their horse can be assessed. Indeed, some riders are so competitive that they ride simply in order to compete. How does this competitive mindset affect horses?

All too many riders behave as if their horses should share their competitive spirit. They seem to think that their horses should try harder for them simply because the competition is important, and I know of all too many horses who have been severely beaten because their performance failed to measure up to the rider's and/or trainer's expectations. Most competition horses do not, of course, receive such extreme punishment for failure in competition, yet in all too many cases disappointment results in riders treating their horse roughly and without consideration. The fact that this is both unjust and illogical scarcely seems to occur to such people; they feel that their horses *should* have gone better, *should* have tried harder.

Of course, not all riders behave in this way and people like to compete for a variety of reasons.

- They may do so in order to have something to aim for.
- To give themselves a standard against which to measure their and their horse's progress.
- To have rosettes and cups to display.
- Because they enjoy the whole process, the atmosphere and the cameraderie (and sometimes the rivalry) of competition.
- Because they feel they should, i.e. pressure from other people.

This last situation is actually very common, and may be one in which you have found yourself at some time or another. If you keep your horse at livery, the chances are that most, if not all, of the activities of other riders on the yard will be geared to competition. All too often this means that riders are pressurized into competing by their peers. They are made to feel that if they do not compete, they are somehow wasting their horse's potential. Even people like us, who have their own land and a private yard, are often made to feel that they must compete or else they are not doing their horses justice; this may then lead to feelings of guilt because you start believing that your horse is being deprived in some way.

None of this is true. What is really happening is that other people are projecting their own ambitions onto you. It may even be, in some cases, that they are not really sure whether what they are doing with their horse is in fact to the horse's advantage, and they are subconsciously trying to eliminate their own vague feelings of guilt by making *you* feel guilty for not doing the same as they are. If you have a mutually satisfying relationship with your horse, if you enjoy each other's company and have fun together at home, why on earth should you feel guilty about not competing? You may be sure that your horse won't!

It is true that some horses are so gifted athletically that it seems a shame not to show them off and display their talents. There is a parallel here with certain humans – people who are exceptionally gifted in some way yet who choose not to make use of their gifts. Does anyone have the right to try to compel them to do so, or to make them feel guilty for not making more of their abilities? The answer is 'No': their lives are their own, and it is not for anyone else to tell them how they should live. The important thing is to put competition into some kind of perspective and, regardless of how you feel about it, to put the interests of the horse before your own ambitions.

CASE HISTORY

In 2003 we took Kruger and Zareeba to their first show in a number of years. At that time my friend Racheal had only been riding Kruger for a few months but she had already built up a terrific relationship with him. She put a great deal into their preparations for the show, as it was the first time she had ever had the chance to compete at such a show, most of her previous experience having been with racehorses, point-to-pointers and hunters. Prior to the show, Kruger was going beautifully, and we had high hopes that he and Racheal would distinguish themselves.

As luck would have it, the show was held on one of the hottest days of the year and in spite of all our efforts to keep him cool, Kruger started to show signs of distress. This was extremely disappointing for Racheal, who had put so much effort into preparing him for the show, not only with regard to his schooling but also his general turnout. However, as soon as Kruger's distress started to become apparent, she withdrew from her class. For Racheal there was never any question of putting her ambition before the horse's welfare; to her a rosette is only a rosette, but Kruger is her friend and companion, and she knew that there would be plenty of other opportunities for them to shine.

Evaluating your goals

Whatever your reasons for training and/or competing, make your goals realistic. Ask yourself, as objectively as possible, 'What am I trying to achieve?' Competing can be a great way of giving yourself something to aim for, but be careful not to set your sights too high to begin with. The stresses of competition will create tensions in both yourself and your horse which might not otherwise be present.

Racheal and Kruger: their relationship, and Kruger's well-being, is far more important to Racheal than winning rosettes. (L. Skipper)

For many riders, the 'buzz' they get from competing is one of the reasons why they do it but it is all too easy for them to forget that their horse may not be feeling the same! Regardless of the level you are working at in your horse's home environment, aim to compete at least one or two levels below that for his first few outings. That way, you are working within limits that are comfortable for yourself and for your horse.

Preparation

Preparation is the key to making competition enjoyable for you and for your horse. The atmosphere at most showgrounds, especially at bigger shows, is quite electrifying; there is usually a great deal of activity, all kinds of scary objects, including other animals (remember that some horses may never have seen sheep or cows before and some may feel threatened by the close presence of strange horses). Veterans of many shows will probably accept all these things quite well (although some never do), but for novice horses it can be a mind-blowing experience until they grow accustomed to it all.

Preparation for competition: Brian is riding Toska in before a dressage test, encouraging him to stretch forward and down. (L. Skipper)

Even show veterans can get a bit 'wound up' at their first show of the season so, whether your horse is a novice, or is returning to competition after a break, introduce him to the show scene gradually. Long before your first competition, try to re-create some of the atmosphere, so that your horse is not too shocked by it all when he eventually gets to the real thing. If you can introduce your horse to as many as possible of the unfamiliar sights and sounds generally found at shows and competitions, he is more likely to settle quickly when he arrives at the venue.

One way in which you can prepare your horse is by staging 'mini-competitions' at home, in familiar surroundings. All that is needed is to get together as many equestrian friends and acquaintances, with their own horses, as you can; rope in some others without horses to act as the 'crowd' of spectators. Set up some of the kinds of spooky objects you could expect to find on a showground, such as brightly-coloured poles, flapping tape, waste bins, flags, etc. and make use of the habituation process outlined in Chapter 7. You can emulate just about any kind of competition which does not involve complex equipment: we have done this with showjumping, dressage and showing classes among others.

Before you actually take part in a big competition with your horse, take him to some small local shows. The first time you take him anywhere, simply walk him round to soak up the atmosphere. In this way you can accustom him to the sights and sounds without any of the pressures of competition. Let him know that all this is no big deal; you are there to have fun!

If your chosen discipline is showjumping, before the day of the competition try to find out as much as you can about the type of jumps likely to be present. Show organizers are usually helpful people, and most will be happy to answer your queries. Then see if you can set up some similar jumps to practise over. However, this should never be overdone; two or three times should be sufficient. All too many riders over-jump their horses; they do not seem to realize that, although they may find jumping exciting and enjoyable, it can also be a frightening experience for a horse, especially if he is over-faced and ill-prepared. Many horses develop the habit of rushing at jumps out of fear and the desire to get the whole process over with as soon as possible; some people mistake this for enthusiasm, which compounds the problem. Nothing makes a horse sour quicker than asking him to jump continually!

You can prepare for cross-country events by hiring a cross-country course. Your local riding school may have one, or there may be farmers in the area who allow hunter trials on their land, and have some permanent jumps set up for that purpose. Ask around, or look at adverts in tack shops; there are cross-country courses available for hire in many areas. Most of these charge reasonable prices; in many cases you may be able to find other riders to share the cost with you. As with showjumping, never over-face your horse. If you push him beyond his capabilities he may become frightened, resulting in loss of confidence. He might then develop all kinds of behavioural problems, such as rearing or bolting; these are often responses to fear or pain on the part of a horse pushed too hard, too soon.

Dressage is another discipline where horses are often put under enormous pressure to perform. The thing to remember here is that dressage is really nothing other than the education of the horse under saddle, by means of

Well-prepared both mentally and physically: Kelly Marks's gelding American Pie, ridden by Daisy O'Halloran, is shown here winning the Working Hunter class at Kent County Show and qualifying for the Horse Of the Year Show. (Eventer Equestrian Photographer)

suppling and strengthening exercises, to carry himself and the rider with the greatest efficiency and the minimum effort, regardless of the use to which the horse is put.[1] Too often this is forgotten by trainers (and some judges!) in the quest for accuracy in performing tests and in executing the movements required in those tests. I would suggest that riders first tackle some of the Classical Riding Club Dressage Training Tests, devised by Sylvia Loch together with other experts specifically to encourage good riding and training practices and to help riders to improve themselves and their horses. These tests are becoming more and more popular; if you want to know more about them, contact the Classical Riding Club (see Useful Organizations, p. 237) for further information.

Whatever discipline you intend to compete in, make sure you know as much about your horse and his capabilities as possible before you ever go near a competition arena.

Do competitions matter to horses?

If success in competition is important to huge numbers of riders, what about their horses? Does competitive success have any meaning for them at all? And if it does not, what implications does that have?

It may be that some horses do sense that what is happening is important to their riders; it is even possible that, having learned that if certain things happen in a given sequence (such as jumping a series of fences without knocking any down), they recognize that this pleases their rider, who in turn makes a big fuss of them. That being so, it is conceivable that such horses might make an extra effort to please a rider with whom they have a good relationship. However, it is extremely unlikely that it means any more to them than that!

What about racehorses, though? Surely, when they make a supreme effort, they do so in order to get or to stay ahead of the others. Or do they? In Chapter 4 we looked at the powerful influence of social facilitation. This influence appears to be principally what causes racehorses to run. It may well be that some horses do want to be in front; there could be many reasons for that (a dislike of being crowded is one that springs immediately to mind). There is also the fact that galloping fast in company may be satisfying an internal drive which is rewarding in itself. Some people insist that dominant horses make the best racehorses, but I have found no evidence that this is actually the case. This seems to be yet another example of confusing dominance with leadership!

All this is not to say that horses do not or cannot enjoy racing, or jumping, or any other of the competitive equestrian sports. It simply means that they do not – and cannot – share our ambitions with regard to those sports.

1 For a more in-depth discussion of this, see my earlier book, *Realize Your Horse's True Potential.*

The conditions for making training and competition ethical

This places an immense ethical burden on those of us who wish to take part in such competitions. It means that, unless we want to coerce our equine partners into performing, we have to ensure that certain conditions are met. These are that:

- The horse is physically capable of performing at the level required.
- The horse is fit; a horse in pain or discomfort cannot – and should not – be expected to perform well.
- The horse is adequately prepared.
- The rider is adequately prepared and competent at the required level.
- Training is carried out with maximum +R and minimum -R.
- Success is always rewarded, but failure is never punished.

If you can make training – and, by extension, competing – an enjoyable experience for both of you, your horse will look forward to his training sessions and to going to shows. Since horses are geared to co-operation, not conflict, most of them want to work with us rather than against us. If we take the trouble to gain their trust, and build a good relationship with them, they will also, in general, want to please us. If you do well, make a big fuss of your horse. If things don't go so well, does it really matter? We should regard competition not as an end in itself, but as

Shows can be fun for horses too: Zareeba (seen here with Brian) is now eligible for veteran classes but he still shows every sign of enthusiasm for going away to shows. (L. Skipper)

a way of testing our skill as trainers and riders. A rosette is only a piece of ribbon folded into a fancy shape; the greatest challenge lies in bringing out the best in our horses while keeping them healthy, both mentally and physically.

We should take note of the words of a great horseman, a classical trainer who is also an FEI judge, and who therefore understands the challenges of both training and competition:

> No serious riders ever believed the training goal was to compete. They believed that you ride a horse to unfold his natural potential until it was fulfilled and the horse could offer no more physically because he had no more genetically defined talents to display. [iv]

Finally, whatever you wish to do with your horse, and regardless of whether you compete or not, you should ensure that:

- The horse's tack fits. Is the bridle the right size? Does the bit sit correctly in his mouth? Does the saddle fit and is it placed correctly on his back?
- Your horsemanship is up to scratch. Do you understand the principles behind what you are doing with your horse? See Chapters 7 and 8, and Recommended Reading for suggestions on how to improve your knowledge.
- You understand how your posture in the saddle, together with the amount of control you have over your body, affects the way the horse can use *his* body. See Chapters 7 and 8, and Recommended Reading for suggestions on how to improve your riding.

Incorrect and/or forceful training and riding can break a horse down physically and destroy his confidence in people. If, however, we understand the correct principles of training, are prepared to work at improving our riding skills and – above all – are willing to listen to the horse when he tells us he cannot do what we are asking of him, then we can train our horses so as to enhance their beauty, their confidence and their sense of well-being. Then we can truly say we have done something good for the horse.

i Klaus Immelman and Colin Beer, *A Dictionary of Ethology*, Harvard University Press paperback edition 1992, p.297.
ii Lesley Skipper, *Inside Your Horse's Mind*, J.A. Allen 1999, p.272.
iii Dr Sharon Cregier, e-mail discussion, White Horse Ethology Project Equine Behaviour Group.
iv Charles de Kunffy, *The Ethics and Passions of Dressage*, Half Halt Press 1993, p.29.

Conclusion

> I know that I still have much to learn, and will go on learning until my dying day.
>
> NUNO OLIVEIRA, *Reflections on Equestrian Art*

Now that we have considered the kinds of things that matter to horses and looked at ways of training and management which take into account their needs and preferences, we should also be able to identify training and management methods and practices which may be harmful to them. This is not always as easy as it may seem; as we have seen, many ideas are put forward, often in good faith, as being beneficial for the horse, while in reality this may not be the case. However, by using the knowledge gained in previous chapters, you should be able to assess the claims made on behalf of a particular method and decide whether they are justified. You should also be able to see which elements of a particular method you can make use of and which you would want to discard. There is nothing that says you have to stick to every aspect of any method!

Keeping an open mind

The important thing is not to get bogged down in dogma, or so tied by loyalty to a particular trainer that you cannot see any flaws in their method. Any training method or system of management is open to critical scrutiny – or at least it should be. Many trainers refer to training as a science and indeed more and more people are looking into the science behind various training methods. Good science is supposed to be self-correcting; as new discoveries are made, or as old theories and assumptions are re-examined, hypotheses are revised and errors corrected. (At least, this is what is supposed to happen; that this is not always the case is simply a reflection of the fact that scientists are only human!.) Ethologists in particular are always having to revise their thinking as they learn more and more about the animals they study. One of the founders of ethology, Konrad Lorenz, wrote a very influential book on dogs (*Man Meets Dog*, 1954). When Ray and Lorna Coppinger met Lorenz in 1977, he greeted them by saying, 'So you are the dog biologists. Before we start our talks I just want to say, everything I've written about dogs is wrong.'[i] Lorenz was a world-renowned scientist, yet he was not afraid to make such an admission, because he knew that science is not static, that as our knowledge grows it will confirm some theories and hypotheses while compelling us – if we are honest – to reject others.

The best animal trainers have always been ready to admit their mistakes and to change their methods when something better comes along, or when it becomes apparent that what they are doing is not working. The late John Fisher, a much-loved figure renowned for his work with problem dogs, was never afraid to hold his hand up to errors of judgement, and to state what he could or should have done differently. The nineteenth-century French equestrian master François Baucher devised a system of training which was so radical that it provoked outrage in the equestrian community; several years later he revised his system completely, sometimes referring to his later method as 'riding in bedroom slippers' because it emphasized light, subtle aids. Nuno Oliveira, one of the greatest horsemen of the twentieth century and much influenced by Baucher's later system, wrote, 'I have made countless errors in the training of literally thousands of horses…I know that I still have much to learn, and will go on learning until my dying day.'[ii]

Letting go of cherished beliefs

However, for many of us it is not so easy to let go of cherished beliefs and ideas; changing one's ways involves questioning the whole basis of what one has been doing, perhaps for many years. This is especially the case if the person concerned has devoted a good part of their life to particular methods of dealing with horses. Others may suspect that their training methods and management practices could be improved, yet are reluctant to change, either because it seems too difficult to do so, or in some cases because of loyalty to people who taught them such practices in the first place. No one likes to be told that they are wrong, and the more experience they have, the more difficult it will be to persuade them that this is the case.

Changing people's ideas

For the owner of a horse kept at livery, who wants to improve their horse's quality of life, one of the biggest problems can be getting the yard owner and other people keeping their horses at the yard to go along with the changes that would lead to that improvement. So many people in the horse world are committed to one way of doing things that it can be very difficult to persuade them that there may be a better way; this is compounded by the fact that, while another way of doing things might be better for the horse, it may be less convenient for the owner!

So how can we persuade others to re-examine their ideas about the training and management of horses? Direct approaches seldom work, for the reasons set out above; if you simply tell someone that you think their practices are harming their horses, they are likely to take offence and to resent you for interfering. A far better approach is by indirect means. If you keep your horse at livery, there are several strategies you could try.

- Organize regular 'brainstorming sessions', during which you and other horse owners can discuss books, magazine articles, demonstration, etc. You could make this into a mini-social event, to put people at their ease and prevent it all getting too intense.

- Circulate equestrian magazines carrying thought-provoking articles, and ask people for their opinion on the contents. (Make it clear, though, that you are only interested in constructive debate!)

- Many well-known trainers give demonstrations in various locations. Consult the equestrian press and see who is giving such demonstrations at venues within easy travelling distance, then see if you can organize a group outing. Most trainers welcome questions at the end of the demonstration, so this gives members of the group an opportunity to question what they have seen. Never be afraid to ask searching questions, but remember that these people may be relying on their training methods to earn a living, and if you appear to be threatening them in any way they may understandably become defensive and/or evasive. Also, bear in mind what I said in Chapter 8: not all trainers know exactly how they achieve their results; in some cases they may believe their success results from something completely different from what is actually the case. By all means ask questions, but make it clear that you are seeking enlightenment, not confrontation – and be tactful!

If you keep your horse on your own premises you can of course manage and train him in any way you please, without interference from anyone else. However, if you want to try to influence other people to improve training and management practices, you can still try the approaches outlined above. You could, for example, start an informal group with meetings held at your own yard; the local tack shop is a good place to advertise such meetings.

Another good way of getting people into discussions is by means of some of the many forums now in existence on the Internet. Some of these forums are very good and well-regulated, but some of them are not so well-run and may be used as a means of spreading inflammatory gossip and/or inaccurate information. Many of the people who take part in discussions on such forums are not really interested in what others have to say, seeking only an outlet for their own prejudices. However, if you have strong nerves and do not mind being on the receiving end of comments which may vary from the harshly critical to the outright abusive, then you may feel that your contributions to such forums can make a difference. More satisfying are the kind of forums where abusive and/or inflammatory postings are strictly forbidden, and where a genuine exchange of ideas can take place. One of the best of these is the Thinking Horsemanship Forum, whose members offer intelligent, informed discussion in a very civilized manner (web address: www.network54.com/Forum/235380). Also of interest is the online forum to be found on the Intelligent Horsemanship website (www.intelligenthorsemanship.co.uk).

Flexibility is the key

However you decide to train and manage your horse, remember that each horse – like each human – is an individual, and as such will respond as an individual. This means that you will have to be flexible in order to take account of that individual's personality and preferences. The more knowledge you have to fall back on, the more flexible you can be in your approach and the easier it will be for you to change your plans if things go wrong. We should never allow ourselves to fall for the idea that there is only one possible solution which will fit all cases. Trying to shoehorn training, management and problem-solving into a single blanket system, without regard for individual cases, can either create problems where they did not previously exist, or make existing problems very much worse. Regardless of what approach you take to your horse's training and management, listen to your inner feelings. If you feel that some aspect of what you are doing – or being advised to do – is having, or could have a negative effect on your horse, reject it! If something does not work for you and your horse, there is always an alternative.

Horses are not machines

One of the negative aspects of the current flood of different training methods is the way in which people are so often given the impression that if their horse is less than perfectly behaved it is because they have not followed the prescriptions of whatever training method is being promoted. More often than not, as we have seen, problems *are* of our own making; this results more from the breakdown of communications between humans and horses than from a failure to follow any specific method. Nevertheless, there are occasions when even the best-behaved horse will have lapses; this is true no matter who the owner might be. I am sure that many people – perhaps most – will think that anyone who writes about animal behaviour and animal training must have animals who are perfectly trained and behaved. However, as the late John Fisher once remarked, that would be rather like saying that a doctor's children should never become ill.

There are times when my animals make me blush, because they always choose to act up just when we have visitors to our yard or when the vet or farrier calls. Such visitors are always impressed to see our stallion Nivalis ridden bareback in a headcollar; less impressive were the occasions when Kruger, being led out, took off down the field with Brian literally hanging on round his neck, or when our old gelding Mo, being held for the farrier, got excited by the passing hunt and broke away to try to join in…

The point is that horses are not machines, and even the best-natured, most correctly trained and handled horses can, on occasion, behave badly or contrary to all the careful training we have carried out with them. Trainers, too, are only human: we make mistakes, do things we should not do even though we know better, or fail to do things which we know we should. If anyone tells me they have a horse who is always perfectly behaved, who never puts a foot wrong, never acts up in any way – then frankly they are either telling fibs or their horse is actually a cyborg, a semi-organic robot programmed to behave perfectly all the time. What a dismal thought!

I cherish my horses because of who they are, not because of some idealized picture I have of them. I have made mistakes with them; I try to do my best for them, and sometimes, for various reasons, I fail. None of us is so perfect that our management and training practices cannot be improved on. Having read this book, you may have found that, while some of your current training and management practices are spot on, others may fall far short of what is required to keep your horse happy and healthy. If this is the case, please do not feel guilty and despondent! Guilt is a destructive emotion, while despondency robs us of the power to change things for the better. Rather than feel bad about what you could or should have been doing for your horse, think about what you can do for him *now*!

In the first decade of the twenty-first century we have an unprecedented amount of accessible knowledge at our fingertips. If we can learn to evaluate it critically and use it wisely, we will be doing horses an incalculable service, both now and in the future.

i Ray and Lorna Coppinger, *Dogs: A New Understanding of Canine Origin, Behavior, and Evolution*, University of Chicago Press 2002, p.35.

ii Nuno Oliveira, *Reflections on Equestrian Art*, J.A. Allen 1976, p.30.

APPENDIX I

Zareeba: A Brief Profile

> Be to his faults a little blind
> Be to his wirtues ever kind.
>
> R.S. Surtees, Handley Cross

Subject: Zareeba

Pure-bred Arabian gelding

Sire: Count Kasbah

Dam: Solkie

Date of birth: 15 May 1988

Colour: Chestnut

Height: 149 cm (14.3 hh)

I acquired Zareeba in June 1990, when he was two years old. He was still an entire colt; as I did not then have the facilities for keeping a stallion, I eventually had to have him gelded. He was very lively and full of himself, as colts often are, but I quickly managed to build a good relationship with him. Never having had any bad experiences with humans, he is bold and confident with them, and likes to receive visits from strangers, whom he charms by batting his long Arab eyelashes and adopting his comic pose (see Chapter 7).

Zareeba was initially backed by my husband's nephew, a very tactful rider, and ridden away by Brian and myself; since then he has mainly been ridden by the two of us, occasionally by friends whom I can trust not to pull on the reins or kick the horse in the ribs (Zareeba would soon make them regret it if they did!). When he was younger I did quite a bit of dressage and ridden showing with

Zareeba at the age of sixteen. (L. Skipper)

him. He did well, and I was told by one dressage trainer that I could aim as high as I liked with him. However, my lack of inclination to compete meant that I never followed this up; I was quite happy just to continue building my relationship with him and seeing what we could achieve together. In the event, he has never reached as advanced a stage of training as he could have done, mainly because recurring problems with old injuries have often prevented me from riding for long spells, resulting in some extended holidays for Zareeba! Nevertheless, he is very responsive and willing under saddle. He is definitely not a novice ride, but in spite of this makes a very good schoolmaster; friends who have ridden him in the *manège* under close supervision have all learned a great deal from him. He is very tolerant of inexperienced riders but, like many Arabians, does not suffer fools gladly. Unlike his half-brother Kruger, who will do what he *thinks* the rider wants, Zareeba will do *exactly* what the rider has asked for, whether or not it was what they actually thought they were asking him! This, in fact, is his value as a schoolmaster: riders have to learn to be very precise in their use of the aids.

Although traffic never bothered him and I used to hack him out on the road regularly, in recent years I have been increasingly reluctant to do so because the local roads have become extremely busy and dangerous. However, we do sometimes take him and Kruger to the riding stables next door to make use of their indoor school. There is also a short stretch of bridleway nearby for added variety.

Below is a short profile of Zareeba and an outline of his management and training regime.

In the stable

• General demeanour:	Bright and interested in what is going on.
• Appetite:	Good, will eat most normal horse foods. Also likes a number of human foods, especially chocolate biscuits and crisps.
• Behaviour towards humans in the stable:	Very friendly, easy to handle, likes physical contact.
• Reactions to anything new:	Curious, but very wary.

In the field

• Relations with other horses:	Very good; gets on well with most horses. A peacemaker (Dr Kiley-Worthington would describe him as a 'sticker'), he avoids confrontation if possible but often steps in to break up petty squabbles. Other horses tend to follow him.
• General demeanour:	Energetic and playful.
• Reactions to anything new:	As in the stable: curious but very wary.
• Easy to catch?	Very; he usually comes when called.

Foot trimming and shoeing

• Behaviour with farrier:	Well-behaved; stands patiently to have his feet trimmed. Not presently shod, but equally good when having shoes fitted.

Being tacked up

• Reaction to the sight of tack:	Responds with interest.
• Reaction to being tacked up:	Variable; usually co-operative, but because of his sensitivity great care must be taken, especially in girthing up. If girthed up too quickly may suffer vaso-vagal syncope (fainting).

Training and work

• Responsiveness:	Willing and co-operative; very responsive to aids.
• Under saddle:	Very forward going.
• Level of calmness:	Can start off tense and spooky (very aware of surroundings), especially if fresh. May

need anything from ten to fifteen minutes of riding in, but regular work will shorten this period to about five minutes or less.

- Response to fast work: Excitable, but depends on context. Once ridden in, is steady across country and at shows.
- Easy to stop? Rider must be very correct and precise with aids.
- Response to jumping: Enthusiastic, but a little nervous, so tends to jump too high. However, he does not rush jumps.

Loading and travelling

- Ease of loading: Usually very good; most times loads without hesitation.
- Travelling: Travels well on his own or with other horses.

Current management regime

- Turnout and stabling: In spring and summer, out at night and in for several hours during the day. In autumn and winter, out during the day, in at night.
- Type of stabling: Wooden loose box with (front) view of the yard, a small copse, the road gate and part of the road beyond; (back) window through which he can communicate with Tiff and also see out over the field to the riding stables beyond.
- Turnout: Several acres of meadow pasture; usual companions are his girlfriend Roxzella, his half-brother Kruger and the other gelding, Toska; sometimes Kiri and Imzadi as well.
- Feed: Spring and summer: ad-lib mature meadow hay, dampened; autumn and winter: ad-lib haylage. Supplemented in autumn and winter by alfalfa-based chaff (approved by the Laminitis Trust) and corn oil with garlic.
- Exercise and schooling: Schooling (mainly suppling exercises) in the *manège* interspersed with in-hand work, free schooling and hacking out in the fields.

Although he is generally extremely easy to manage and causes us very few problems, Zareeba has his share of quirks. He has never kicked (or even threatened to kick) a human in his life but if I do not take sufficient care girthing him up or grooming him, he will definitely give me a very painful nip (and serve me right)! He also gets grumpy if someone asks him to move over in the stable without sufficient respect; if we say to him, 'Move over, please' in a polite tone, he will comply instantly but if someone were to say 'Move over!' in a harsh tone and/or try to push him over, he might well respond with the threat of a nip.

He is rarely unco-operative but, having known him for almost all of his life, I am able to tell whether the odd lapse is caused by fatigue or discomfort or whether it is simply that he doesn't feel like doing something! If the latter should happen to be the case, it does not concern me greatly as a rule, as long as it does not put him or me in danger or risk of injury; I do not expect my horses to respond like automata. The thing is that Zareeba and I are good friends who enjoy each other's company and occasionally one has to allow friends to 'do their own thing' or the friendship is not worth anything.

Zareeba's good nature and well-adjusted personality, together with his friendly disposition, make him a great favourite with visitors to the yard. He is so at ease with humans that if he is lying down in the stable, he is quite happy to entertain visitors without getting up; on one occasion a few weeks before I wrote this he had three people all sitting next to him in the straw!

Zareeba and I may never have won any major competitions together (and not too many minor ones!) but to us that is irrelevant as we have learned so much from each other over the years. His bouncy, zestful nature and obvious enthusiasm for everything he does make him, in the words of Lady Anne Blunt, 'delightful as a companion and to ride.'[i]

i Lady Anne Blunt, writing about her Arabian mare Sobha, cited in *The Crabbet Arabian Stud, Its History & Influence*, by Rosemary Archer, Colin Pearson and Cecil Covey, rev. ed. Alexander Heriot 1994, p.248.

APPENDIX II

Some Common Problems

> Defence...can be habit-forming. It is aroused by threat. It can be activated when no threat is intended. And it sometimes continues when there's nothing left to defend.
>
> REGINALD HILL, *Deadheads*

Three of the commonest problems faced by horse owners involve a horse's aggression towards other horses, a reluctance to allow the feet to be picked up, and a refusal to load into a horsebox or trailer. There are a number of different approaches to these problems; those outlined in this appendix are not the only ways of combating them, they are simply those I have found in my own experience to be the most effective while causing as little stress to the horse as possible. The thing to remember is that these, like many other behavioural problems, have their basis in fear; however we resolve the problem we must first of all address that fear or we have solved nothing.

The anti-social horse

What makes a horse anti-social? Within this extremely social species, why do some of its members appear to dislike their fellows so much that, if turned out with other horses, they attack and injure them?

As with anti-social humans, the causes of this behaviour can be many and varied; they can be difficult enough to determine even in humans, who can (if they choose) talk about their dislike of their fellow humans. With horses, the problem can be even more difficult to solve, because we do not have direct access to their feelings. So how can we begin to find a solution?

The first step is to try to identify possible causes by looking at as much as we can discover of the horse's past history. Some of the commonest causes of anti-social behaviour are:

- Early and/or abrupt weaning; this can have devastating effects on a young horse's ability to socialize.
- Prolonged isolation, especially as a youngster; again, this can have a profound effect on the development of a horse's social skills.
- Bullying, especially during formative years. Horses who are bullied may turn into bullies themselves; no one oppresses more thoroughly than those who have themselves been oppressed.
- Overcrowding: some horses, like some people, value their personal space so much that overcrowding may cause them to react violently.

First of all we need to observe how the horse reacts with other horses (being ready to step in if things get out of hand) so that we can establish what triggers his aggression. Then we can work towards eliminating the causes. In many cases, all the anti-social horse really needs is sufficient personal space for him not to feel threatened by crowding, together with suitable companions who are well-socialized themselves and will teach him that there is nothing to fear.

Personal space

If he becomes aggressive when other horses enter his personal space – a reaction that is linked to insecurity – we can (if this is feasible) try turning him out under close supervision with one other well-socialized horse in a field or paddock large enough to enable both of them to avoid each other if they so choose. Once they accept each other, we can then try removing the other horse and introducing another of similar temperament. Once this new companion is accepted, we repeat the process of removing him and introducing another, until there are several horses he can be safely turned out with. This is the approach recommended by Dr Kiley-Worthington in her book *Horse Watch – What it is to be Equine*;[i] if we simply get him used to one companion, he may become over-attached to that one horse, which would not really tackle the basic cause of the anti-social behaviour. We should always try to get the horse used to as many different companions as possible so that he no longer sees his conspecifics as threats. I would always give horses in this situation as much space as possible so that they are never made to feel crowded or threatened in any way.

Food-related aggression

This is a comparatively easy problem to eliminate: if the horses must be given supplementary feed in the field, either remove the difficult horse and feed him on his own, or ensure that feed buckets and/or piles of hay are spaced well apart as suggested in Chapter 3.

Same-sex aggression

If a horse is aggressive with members of the same sex, try turning him or her out with a group of the opposite sex; to be on the safe side, use the same tactics as suggested earlier under Personal space.

Provided the horses concerned are given sufficient space, there are very few who cannot be reintegrated using variations on the suggestions made above. The older the horse, and the longer he has been set in his anti-social ways, the longer such reintegration will take, but as a rule such horses eventually end up accepting others as their companions and being much happier and, as a result, healthier. The key is not to expect overnight acceptance; these things take time. As with so much in the management and training of horses, patience is the key!

Reluctance to allow the feet to be picked up

From a horse's point of view, such reluctance is perfectly reasonable. The horse depends not only on his ability to escape from danger but also on being able to maintain his balance in order to make his escape more effectively. By picking his feet up we deprive him of both of these abilities, which for some horses can be very scary indeed. However much we may have bred selectively for certain traits, the flight reaction is one that is far too deeply rooted in the horse's psyche to have been bred out in the mere 6,000 years since horses were first domesticated. What is more, it is not at all certain that it would be a good thing to breed out such a trait; it may be too closely linked to many of the qualities, such as speed and quickness of reaction, that we generally value in horses.

If young horses are taught to accept having their feet picked up gradually and without any traumatic experience being involved, they will probably not develop any problems in this respect. Such problems almost always arise as a result of some bad experience.

CASE HISTORY

Our home-bred mare, Imzadi, learned to tolerate having her feet picked up at a very early age. We had no problems with her until she was almost a year old, when suddenly she developed a strong objection to having her hind feet picked up (she was fine about the front ones). She would lash out with her hind feet at any attempt to pick them up, making it very difficult for us to manage the routine care of her feet.

Was Imzadi being naughty? No. Some time before she developed this behaviour she had suffered a bad attack of mud fever, which affected her hind legs especially badly. She therefore associated any attempts to handle her hind legs and feet with the pain and discomfort of her mud fever, even though this had long since cleared up. We hit upon a suitable approach to this problem almost by accident: washing Imzadi's feet one day we noticed that when she felt the water on her hind feet she picked them up one by one. So we started by running the water lightly over one foot and, as soon as she picked that foot up, Brian gently took hold of it. If she pulled it away or lashed out, that was ignored, but if she allowed Brian to hold her foot for even a few seconds she was given a Polo mint, a scratch or a rub, depending on what kind of mood she was in at the time. Once she would allow Brian to pick up each of her hind feet for a few seconds without fuss, we progressed to asking her to let him hold each foot for longer periods; she was then given her Polo, scratch or whatever only if she would allow the time period to be extended by a few seconds. In this way we worked gradually to the point where she would let Brian pick up and hold both her hind feet for long enough to allow foot trimming to take place.

At the same time we had to work on moving her away from the water source. To begin with, all lifting of her hind feet had to be done while water was being trickled over them. After a few sessions we could progress to simply standing in a pool of water, without having the water actually running over her feet. The next step was to move out of the water altogether and, after that, away from the source of the water, until eventually we could pick Imzadi's feet up anywhere in the yard. After a few relapses (mainly caused by a painful bout of laminitis) she is now quite happy to have her feet picked up and trimmed.

What we had to do in this instance was to persuade Imzadi that nothing terrible would happen if she allowed us to pick up her hind feet. By turning it into a pleasant experience we avoided the kind of conflict that would have arisen if we had simply decided that she was being naughty and compelled her to submit. It is, in any case, difficult to do this when a horse is fighting to avoid whatever is being done to them, yet amazingly people still make the effort!

Refusal to load into a horsebox or trailer

It is hardly surprising that so many horses refuse, or are reluctant, to load. Being asked to walk into a confined, often poorly lit space, with a relatively unsteady surface underfoot, must be an extremely disturbing experience for a horse, especially as he is hemmed in and unable to escape. Some trainers refer to horses as 'born claustrophobics' and say that this is why they do not like going into horseboxes and trailers. However, this is not really an accurate description. 'Phobia' is a psychiatric term used to describe an 'abnormal intense and irrational fear of a given situation'.[ii] Horses' dislike of being shut in is neither abnormal nor irrational; it is a perfectly normal reaction for an animal who relies for his safety on being able to escape. In any case, many horses never have any problems with loading and travelling. For those who do, the reasons for those problems depend on the circumstances and the individual horse.

In all cases, we have to find ways to minimize the unpleasant aspects of the experience for our horses. How we do this depends largely on the level of our knowledge and expertise, and on the individual horse. There are numerous methods of persuading reluctant loaders to overcome their fears; the most effective of these do not depend on coercion of any kind, but on understanding the horse's point of view and working with it rather than against it.

CASE HISTORY

We acquired our Arabian stallion Nivalis, together with his dam, when he was five months old. He had been well handled, and was confident with people, albeit a bit cheeky. My husband quickly built up a great rapport with him, and Nivalis trusted Brian implicitly. He loaded without any problems until he was two, when one day he slipped going up the ramp, scraping his leg and banging his head. He suffered only very superficial injuries, but was understandably reluctant to go up the ramp again. So, we enticed him in by walking his mother up and down the ramp, and letting him follow her. This worked, and eventually he built up his confidence again to the point where he would go in without any fuss.

Then, about a year later, we were at a show, and on the point of loading Nivalis for the journey home, when it started to rain. The ramp of the horsebox became slippery, and poor Nivalis slipped again, this time banging his knee. Again the injury was not serious, and we got him home safely, but this second mishap served to convince him that horsebox ramps were a thing to be avoided at all costs.

Although we did manage to persuade him several times after that to go in the horsebox, we could sense that he was becoming more and more reluctant. He would do as many horses do: take one step onto the ramp with his front feet and then freeze, or alternatively get so far on and then pull back, sometimes violently. This upset my husband, because in every other respect Nivalis trusted him and would do whatever he asked. This loading problem made Brian feel as if he had somehow failed Nivalis, and of course Nivalis unerringly picked up on Brian's negative feelings, which inevitably made him worse.

There were numerous techniques we could have used to persuade Nivalis to go into the horsebox, but none of them would have addressed the underlying problem, which was that Nivalis's fear of the ramp caused him to switch off to virtually everything else that was going on. To persist in spite of this would not only have been cruel, but futile, so I decided we had to change tactics. I first had to be sure that I could identify definitively what was causing the fear. He had always seemed happy enough simply to *be* in the horsebox, so it seemed it was not the confined space that was bothering him. I felt sure that his attitude was entirely related to the ramp and his fear of slipping on it. I recalled that, on the occasions when he had gone in without fuss, he had done so boldly, stepping straight up without hesitation. The problems all seemed to start with hesitation; those horses who invariably load without fuss almost all step straight up the ramp with confidence. Those who dither are the ones who tend to have accidents, because they start to feel unsteady on their feet...and then of course they *are* unsteady on their feet. They start to lose their balance, slide around, lose their footing – and then their worst fears tend to be realized: this is *dangerous*!

To compound the problem, horses who are alarmed or fearful tend to put their heads up. This is a physiological reaction related to the horse's peculiar type of eyesight: raising the head enables the horse to make use of his very wide range of vision, in order to gauge the location and nature of any potentially alarming object or movement. In the loading scenario, even though the source of the alarm (the ramp) is right underneath the horse's feet, the reflex action is the same: the head is raised. This hollows the back and, while it does not make it impossible for the horse to go up the ramp, it certainly makes it very much more difficult for him, especially as he cannot see where he is going properly. Good loaders almost invariably lower their heads when going up the ramp. This is not simply to avoid banging their heads as they enter the horsebox; as well as allowing them to see where they are going, the act of lowering the head enables them to round their backs and get their hind legs underneath them – essential if a horse is to negotiate a slope efficiently.

So, with all this in mind, we set about making things easy for Nivalis. We positioned the horsebox in the *manège* with the ramp horizontal, resting against a low mound. We then turned Nivalis out in the *manège*, and left him to it. Sure enough, within minutes, after a little hesitation about putting his feet on the ramp, he was investigating the interior of the horsebox. Now that the menace of the slippery slope had been removed, he was quite happy to go in and out. After letting him spend an hour or so wandering happily in and out, we took the next step of moving the horsebox to a position where there was a slight slope on the ramp. Again, after a little hesitation, Nivalis went into the box and was soon wandering in and out. We increased the slope a bit more, until we felt we had reached the maximum degree of slope he would

The horsebox is parked so that the ramp is almost level and is secure underfoot. (L.Skipper)

below Nivalis stops to investigate the ramp, hesitates...

...but then walks in. (L. Skipper)

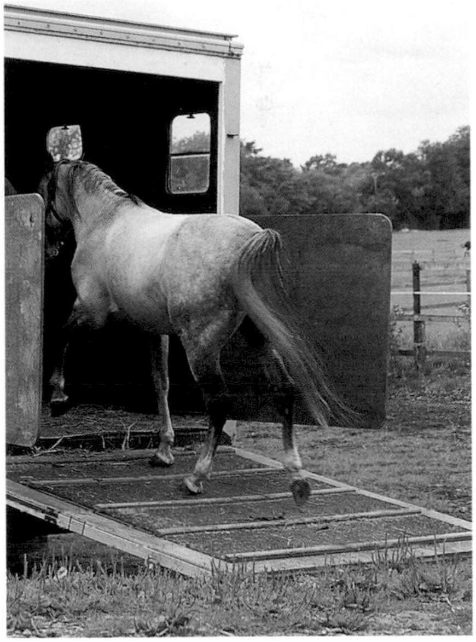

attempt. By now he was getting more and more confident, not only walking in and out by himself, but following me or my husband in and out of the horsebox.

We also had to work on our own body language so as to send Nivalis more positive messages. It is all too easy – in spite of our best intentions – to let the stress of the moment take over, and become so wound up that all the wrong signals are being sent out. We have to remember that horses do not know why it is so important to us that they go in this contraption with its worrying lack of space and its unsteady footing. If we get upset about it, they are all too likely to assume that we are angry with them, for some reason they cannot understand – and no animal, human or non-human, can respond well in that situation.

Monty Roberts and Kelly Marks both suggest a technique for understanding how to overcome problems: reverse the problem and ask, 'If I wanted to *cause* this problem, what would I do?' This can be an extremely valuable way of detecting the real nature of the problem. In Nivalis's case, knowing his sensitivity and extremely fine-tuned sense of balance, I realized that if I wanted to create a problem with loading him, the easiest way to do it would be to make the ramp unsafe (in his case, steep and slippery). Conversely, making it more secure (by making the angle less steep and the footing more stable) could help him to overcome his fear and regain his confidence.

What can you do if you have a horse who habitually gets as far as putting his front feet on the ramp and then gets 'stuck', unable (or unwilling) to move any further? Remember that you are trying to modify the horse's behaviour, and that the most effective way to do this is by using +R. Lead the horse up to the ramp; the moment he puts a foot on it, give him a tiny amount of his favourite feed. Reward any progress up the ramp, no matter how small, in this way. This may take some time and, if his hunger is satiated too soon, he may not feel like trying to earn some more, so always give him a very small amount at a time. Reinforce *only* steps taken in the right direction, i.e. up the ramp; ignore any steps backward, even if this progresses to pulling back and/or rearing! If you can persuade the horse to lower his head when you give him his reward, all the better. When he finally takes that decision to walk into the box, let him have his dinner in there (that is, if he is still hungry!) If not, make a fuss of him; give him scratches, strokes, or whatever he likes that will act as a reinforcer. Eventually, given sufficient time to learn that good things happen to them in horseboxes, most horses will go in. However, horses who have had a bad experience, like Nivalis, may take a lot longer than those who simply lack confidence. Therefore this process may take minutes, or it may take hours, days or even weeks, so make sure you only try it when you have plenty of time to spare. Do not be pressurized into rushing this process; it is not a speed competition!

In the end, the method you use to solve your loading problem (provided it is humane and does not subject the horse to unacceptable stress) is up to you; the key to choosing which method to use is to know your horse as thoroughly as possible, and to understand, as best you can, what his particular problem might be.

i Kiley-Worthington, *Horse Watch – What it is to be Equine*, pp.400.
ii *Collins Dictionary of the English Language*, p.1153, entry under *phobia*.

Useful Organizations

THE EQUINE BEHAVIOUR FORUM

Membership Secretary: Ms Gillian Cooper, 50 Marsh House Lane,
Over Darwen, Lancashire, BB3 3JB, England.
Tel: 01254-705487
Website: www.gla.ac.uk/external/EBF/

THE CLASSICAL RIDING CLUB

Eden Hall, Kelso, Roxburghshire, TD5 7QD, UK.
Fax: +44 1890 830667
e-mail crc@classicalriding.co.uk
Website: www.classicalriding.co.uk

THE INTELLIGENT HORSEMANSHIP ASSOCIATION

Lethornes, Lambourn, Hungerford, Berkshire RG17 8QS, England.
Tel: +44 (0)1488 71300
Fax: +44 (0)1488 73783
e-mail: kelly@montyroberts.co.uk
Website: www.intelligenthorsemanship.co.uk

THE COMPANY OF HORSES

Emma Kurrels, 9 Chancery Lane, Bollington, Macclesfield,
Cheshire SK10 5BJ, England.
Tel: +44 (0)1625 575344
e-mail: learn@companyofhorses.com
Website: www.companyofhorses.com

Recommended Reading and Bibliography

Although it is not my intention to portray this book as an 'academic' work, I felt that, because it challenges a number of preconceived ideas, readers should be given a comprehensive bibliography so that they can see for themselves what lines of research I have followed. Books of exceptional merit or interest are marked with an asterisk (*) after the author's name. Many of the books listed below are now out of print and may be available only through second-hand bookshops and/or university and public libraries.

Many of the journals are likewise only available through specialist libraries or by special request via public libraries; however, a number of them may be available online via the Internet. For second-hand and out-of-print books, try Amazon (www.amazon.co.uk in the UK, or www.amazon.com in the USA), Barnes & Noble in the USA (www.barnesandnoble.com) or W.H. Smith Online (www.bookshop.co.uk). These all provide an excellent service.

HORSE BEHAVIOUR, PSYCHOLOGY AND MANAGEMENT

Ainslie, T., and Ledbetter, B., *The Body Language of Horses*, Kaye & Ward 1974.

Bayley, L. and Maxwell, R., *Understanding Your Horse*, David & Charles 1996.

Berger, J.,* *Wild Horses of the Great Basin*, University of Chicago 1986.

Budiansky, S., *The Nature of Horses*, Weidenfeld & Nicholson 1997.

Fraser, A.F., *Behaviour of the Horse*, C.A.B. International 1992.

Greyling, T., *The behavioural ecology of the feral horses in the Namib Naukluft Park* (MSc Thesis), University of Pretoria 1994.

Groves, C.P., *Horses Asses and Zebras in the Wild*, David & Charles1974.

Hogg, A.,* *The Horse Behaviour Handbook*, David & Charles 2003.

Kiley-Worthington, Dr M.,* *The Behaviour of Horses in Relation to Management and Training*, J.A. Allen 1987.
—— *Cooperation and competition: a detailed study of communication and social organization in a small group of horses (Equus caballus)*, Eco Research Centre (Occasional paper no. 24) 1998.
—— * *Equine Welfare*, J.A. Allen 1997.
—— * *Horse Watch – What it is to be Equine*, J.A. Allen 2005.

McBane, S., *Behaviour Problems in Horses*, David & Charles 1994.

McDonnell, S.,* *A Practical Field Guide to Horse Behavior*, Eclipse Press 2003.

McGreevey, P., *Why Does My Horse...?*, Souvenir Press 1996.

Mills, D., and Nankervis, K.,* *Equine Behaviour: Principles & Practice*, Blackwell Publishing 1999.

Morris, D., *Horsewatching*, Jonathan Cape Ltd 1988.

Pellegrini, S., *Home range territioriality and movement patterns of wild horses in the Wassick range of western Nevada* (MS Thesis), University of Nevada, Reno 1971.

Rashid, M.,* *Horses Never Lie*, Johnson Books, Boulder, Colorado 2000.

Rees, L.,* *The Horse's Mind* (First pub. 1984; paperback ed. 1993), Stanley Paul 1993.

Roberts, M., *The Man Who Listens to Horses*, Hutchinson 1996.

Schäfer, M., *The Language of the Horse*, Kaye and Ward 1974.

Skipper, L.,* *Inside Your Horse's Mind: A Study of Equine Intelligence and Human Prejudice*, J.A. Allen 1999.

Waring, G.,* *Horse Behaviour*, Noyes 1983.

Welsh, D.A., *Population, behavioral and grazing ecology of the horses of Sable Island* (MSc Thesis), Dalhousie, USA 1973.

Williams, M., *Horse Psychology*, J.A. Allen 1976.
—— *Understanding Nervousness in Horse and Rider*, J.A. Allen 1990.

ANIMAL BEHAVIOUR GENERAL

Bekoff, M.,* *Minding Animals* Oxford University Press 2002.

Coppinger, R.,* *Dogs: A New Understanding of Canine Origin, Behavior, and Evolution*, Chicago University Press ed. 2002.

Fisher, J.,* *Diary of a 'Dotty Dog' Doctor*, Alpha Publishing 1998.

Friedrich, Heinz, *Man and Animal*, Paladin 1972.

Grzimek, B (ed.), *Grzimek's Encyclopedia of Mammals* (vol. 4), McGraw-Hill 1990.

Hafez, E.S.E (ed.), *The Behaviour of Domestic Animals*, Baillière Tindall 1962.

Masson, J. and McCarthy, S.,* *When Elephants Weep: The Emotional Lives of Animals*, Vintage 1996.

Immelmann, K., and Beer, C., *A Dictionary of Ethology* (paperback ed.), Harvard University Press 1989.

Keeling, L.J and Gonyou, H.W. (eds.), *Social Behaviour in Farm Animals*, CABI Publishing 2001.

Lorenz, K.,* *King Solomon's Ring*, Methuen 1952. (Reissued by Routledge Classics 2002.)

Syme, G.T. and L.A., *Social Structure in Farm Animals*, Elsevier 1979.

RIDING AND TRAINING

Blignault, K.,* *Successful Schooling*, J.A. Allen 1997.

Burger, Ü., *The Way to Perfect Horsemanship*, J.A. Allen 1998.

Loch, S.,* *The Classical Rider: Being at One With Your Horse*, J.A. Allen 1997.
—— * *The Classical Seat*, Horse's Mouth Publications 2003.
—— * *Dressage in Lightness*, J.A. Allen 2000.
—— * *Invisible Riding*, Horse's Mouth Publications 2003.

Podhajsky, Col. A.,* *My Horses, My Teachers*, J.A. Allen 1997.

Sivewright, M.,* *Thinking Riding* (Book 1), J.A. Allen 1984.
—— * *Thinking Riding* (Book 2), J.A. Allen 1985.

Skipper, L.,* *Realize Your Horse's True Potential*, J.A. Allen 2003.

Seunig, W., *Horsemanship*, Doubleday & Co Ltd 1976.

Wanless, M., *Ride With Your Mind*, Methuen 1987.
—— * *Ride With Your Mind Masterclass*, Methuen 1991.

Wilson, A.,* *Top Horse Training Methods Explored*, David & Charles 2004.

Wood, P., *Real Riding: How to Ride in Harmony With Horses*, Kenilworth Press 2002.

GENERAL TRAINING (INCLUDING NATURAL HORSEMANSHIP)

Hempfling, K.F., *Dancing with Horses: Communication by body language* (tr. Kristina McCormack), J.A. Allen 2001.

Hunt, R., *Think Harmony With Horses*, Pioneer, Fresno 1978.

Kurland, A., *Clicker Training For Your Horse*, Ringpress ed. 2001.

MacLeay, J.,* *Smart Horse: Understanding the Science of Natural Horsemanship*, Eclipse Press, Lexington, Kentucky 2003.

Marks, K., *Creating A Bond With Your Horse*, J.A. Allen 2000.
—— * *Perfect Manners*, Ebury Press 2002.

Mashanaglass, Marquis McSwiney of, *Training from the Ground*, J.A. Allen 1987.

Parelli, P., *Natural Horse.Man.Ship*, Western Horseman, Colorado Springs 1993.

Pryor, K.,* *Don't Shoot the Dog! The New Art of Teaching and Training* (rev. ed.) Bantam Books 1999.

Rashid, M.* *Horses Never Lie: The Heart of Passive Leadership*, Johnson Books, Boulder, Colorado 2000.

PERIODICALS

Classical Riding Club Newsletter

Equine Behaviour: The Journal of the Equine Behaviour Forum

Horse & Rider

SCIENTIFIC PAPERS

Appleby, M.C., 'The probability of linearity in hierarchies', *Animal Behaviour* (no.31) 1983.

Berger, J., 'Organizational systems and dominance in feral horses in the Grand Canyon', *Behavioral Ecology and Sociobiology* (no.2) 1977.

Berger, J., and Cunningham, C., 'Influence of familiarity on frequency of inbreeding in wild horses', *Evolution* (no.4(1)) 1987.

Clutton-Brock, T.H., Greenwood, P.J. and Powell, R.P., 'Rank and relationships in Highland ponies', *Zeitschrift für Tierpsychologie* (no.41) 1976.

Duncan, P., Feh, C., Gleize, J.C., Malkas, P. and Scott, A.M., 'Reduction of inbreeding in a natural herd of horses', *Animal Behaviour* (no.32) 1984.

Feh, C and Mazières, J. de, 'Grooming at a preferred site reduces heart rate in horses', *Animal Behaviour* (no.46) 1993.

Feist, J.D. and McCullough, D.R.,'Behavior patterns and communication in feral horses', *Zeitschrift für Tierpsychologie* (no.41) 1976.

Grassian, S., 'Psychopathological effects of solitary confinement', *American Journal of Psychiatry* (no.140) 1983.

Grzimek, B., 'Rangordnungsversuche mit Pferden', *Zeitschrift für Tierpsychologie* (no.6) 1949.

Haag, E.L., Rudman, R. and Houpt, K.A., 'Avoidance maze learning and social dominance in ponies', *Journal of Animal Science* (no.50) 1980.

Hoffmann, R., 'Social organization patterns of several feral horse and feral ass populations in Central Australia', *Zeitschrift für Säugetierkunde* (no.48) 1983.

Houpt, K.A., and Hintz, H.F., 'Some effects of maternal deprivation in maintenance behaviour, spatial relationships and responses to environmental novelty in foals', *Applied Animal Ethology* (no.8) 1982–3.

Houpt, K.A., and Keiper, R.R., 'The position of the stallion in the equine dominance hierarchy of feral and domestic ponies', *Journal of Animal Science* (no.54) 1982.

Houpt, K.A., Law, K. and Martinisi, V., 'Dominance hierarchies in domestic horses', *Applied Animal Ethology* (no.4) 1978.

Houpt, K.A., and Wolski, T.R., 'Stability of equine hierarchies and the prevention of dominance-related aggression', *Equine Veterinary Journal* (no.12) 1980.

Keiper, R. and Sambraus, H.H., 'The stability of equine dominance hierarchies and the effects of kinship proximity and foaling status on hierarchy rank', *Applied Animal Behaviour Science* (no.16) (pp.121-30) 1986.

Liederman, P., 'Man alone: sensory deprivation and behavior change', *Correctional Psychiatry and Journal of Social Therapy* (no.8) 1962.

Line, S.W., Hart, B.L. and Sanders, L.,'Effect of prepubertal versus postpubertal castration on sexual and aggressive behaviour in male horses', *Journal of the American Veterinary Medical Association* (no.186) 1985.

Mader, D.R. and Price, E.O., 'Discrimination learning in horses: effects of breed, age and social dominance', *Journal of Animal Science* (no.50) 1980.

Mal, M.E., Friend, T.H., Lay, C., Vogelsang, S.G. and Jenkins, O.C., 'Physiological responses of mares to short term confinement and social isolation', *Journal of Equine Veterinary Science* Vol.111991.

McDonnell, S.M., Henry, M. and Bristol, F., 'Spontaneous erection and masturbation in equids', *Journal of Reproduction and Fertility* (no.44 – Supplement) (pp.664–5) 1991.

Miller, R., 'Male aggression dominance and breeding behaviour in Red Desert feral horses', *Zeitschrift für Tierpsychologie* (no.57) 1981.
—— 'Interband dominance in feral horses', *Zeitschrift für Tierpsychologie* (no.51) 1979.

Mills, D.S., 'Applying learning theory to the management of the horse: the difference between getting it right and getting it wrong', *Equine Veterinary Journal* (Supplement 27) 1998.

Mills, D.S. and Davenport, K., 'The effect of a neighbouring conspecific versus the use of a mirror for the control of stereotypic weaving behaviour in the stabled horse', *Animal Science* (no.74) 2002

Rubenstein, D.I., 'Behavioral ecology of island feral horses', *Equine Veterinary Journal* (no.13) 1981.

Tyler, S.J., 'The behaviour and social organization of the New Forest ponies', *Animal Behaviour* Monograph 5 1972.

Waters, A.J., Nicol, C.J. and French, N.P., 'Factors influencing the development of stereotypic and redirected behaviours in young horses', *Equine Veterinary Journal* (no.34) 2002.

Williams, J.L., Friend, T.H., Collins, M.N., Toscano, M.J., Sisto-Burt, A. and Nevill, C.H., 'Effects of imprint training procedure at birth on the reactions of foals at age six months', *Equine Veterinary Journal* (no.35 (2)) 2003.

Zeeb, K., 'Die Unterlegenheitsgebärde des noch nicht ausgewachsenen Pferdes (Equus caballus)', *Zeitschrift für Tierpsychologie* (no.16) 1959.

Index